MW01029929

# Praise for Jaz Brisack's *Get on the Job and Organize*

"In the last few years, especially after the pandemic, one of the most inspiring things we've witnessed is the rise of the labor movement in America. All across the country, workers have been standing up and fighting back against the unprecedented levels of corporate greed that have been taking place. I appreciate Jaz's contributions in this book, which help us all better understand the aims and goals for a resurgent trade union movement and how workers all over the country can join in solidarity with it."

—Senator Bernie Sanders

"Here's the light to illuminate these dark times—an account of how workers take on corporate power and win. Even more inspiring, it's led by Gen Z. Starbucks Workers United has given new life to the American labor movement, and Jaz Brisack helped make it happen. Essential reading for anyone who cares about tackling economic inequality and saving democracy."

—Robert Reich, former US secretary of labor and author of *Aftershock* and *Saving Capitalism*

"Jaz has too much home training to rename this book, but this is not only a 'how to change the world' book, it is a percussive, necessary 'why we must change the world' book written by an activist who can write their ass off. Mandatory reading for humans in need of a literary elixir."

—Kiese Laymon, author of *Heavy*

"Jaz Brisack's *Get on the Job and Organize* is a generous offering of exactly the kind of storytelling that fuels our resistance movements. This book grounds an account of organizing by committed workers in today's service economy in the long history of militant worker resistance in the U.S., including strikes and uprisings of enslaved people before and during the Civil War. Brisack shows what intersectional, multi-issue labor organizing looks like, pulls no punches about how difficult the current conditions are for resistance, and conveys how the solidarity that arises in everyday relationships can be cultivated to buttress urgent, fierce, effective coordinated attack on corporate power."

—Dean Spade, author of *Mutual Aid* and *Lover in a F*cked Up World*

"This book is a love letter to labor organizing, at once earnest and hard-nosed. Brisack takes us inside Starbucks Workers United, offering an in-depth look at what a worker-led campaign can look like—the ups and downs, headaches and heartbreaks. Their devotion shows on every page, as do practical calculations of power and strategy. The labor movement could use a thousand more just like them."

—Sarah Jaffe, author of *Work Won't Love You Back* and *From the Ashes*

"Jaz Brisack has given us an account of the movement to organize Starbucks workers that is an education in the critical role that unions have to play in our current crisis of civilization. Part memoir and part altar call, *Get on the Job and Organize* is an invitation for all of us to be part of reconstructing an unequal economy."

—Rev. Dr. William J. Barber II, author of *White Poverty*

"Jaz Brisack may be one of the most famous union organizers in the country, but their invigorating debut, *Get on the Job and Organize*, constantly emphasizes the power of the collective. This book is an essential read for every aspiring union organizer, every fed-up worker, and anyone who dreams of a better, fairer world."

—Kim Kelly, author of *Fight Like Hell*

"By unionizing Starbucks, baristas brought the labor movement to the attention of a generation of young Americans, inspiring organizing drives at countless retail outlets across the country. *Get on the Job and Organize* continues that work. Part propulsive personal narrative, part organizing manual, Jaz Brisack's book offers indispensable answers for anyone who has wondered how Starbucks workers took on their boss, and how they might do the same."

—Alex N. Press, staff writer at *Jacobin*

"*Get on the Job and Organize* is an instant classic of American labor literature. Jaz Brisack bursts on the scene with firsthand reports of workers' struggles against corporate Goliaths of our time (think Nissan, Tesla, Starbucks) that are so fresh and direct they practically jump off the page."

—Rep. Andy Levin (ret.)

"Unionizing shop-by-shop, site-by-site is today's strategy for taking on overwhelming brands like Starbucks and Amazon. Jaz Brisack offers us a blow-by-blow of tactics chosen and considered in their campaigns in Buffalo, New York, that can inspire, inform, and engage future organizers across the country and around the world."

—Sarah Schulman, author of *The Fantasy and Necessity of Solidarity*

"A timely, well-written account from the front lines of labor organizing that grabbed me from the opening scene. *Get on the Job and Organize* offers hope in dark times and should be of interest to anyone who cares about the struggles of the low-wage workers who make the economy go."

—Gary Rivlin, author of *Broke, USA* and *Saving Main Street*

"*Get on the Job and Organize* is critical reading for anyone who wants to take on corporate power in the twenty-first century. Through stories from Jaz's historic organizing efforts and examples drawn from labor history, Jaz demonstrates how solidarity can bring the most powerful corporations on earth to the table—and that every organizing effort makes a difference for working people, win or lose."

—Sara Nelson, president of the Association of Flight Attendants-CWA

"For decades, corporate America has had organized labor on the back foot, and the whole working class has paid the price. Now a new generation of organizers and leaders are rising up to fight different, and win big. The rest of the labor movement and the whole working class need to take the lessons of the brave Starbucks workers and fight smarter and harder to take back some dignity on and off the job. This book gives some of the inspiration, playbook, and lessons we all need to build a better labor movement and a better world."

—Shawn Fain, president of the UAW

"As an organizer, Jaz Brisack has done what many would have considered impossible, helping workers fight for their rights under the most oppressive conditions. Now they've written an invaluable manual on how you can do the same. This book got me fired up to go kick some capitalist ass—read it!"

—Adam Conover, comedian and organizer

# GET ON THE JOB AND ORGANIZE

## Standing Up for a Better Workplace and a Better World

JAZ BRISACK

ONE SIGNAL PUBLISHERS

ATRIA

New York Amsterdam/Antwerp London Toronto Sydney/Melbourne New Delhi

ONE SIGNAL PUBLISHERS

ATRIA

An Imprint of Simon & Schuster, LLC
1230 Avenue of the Americas
New York, NY 10020



First One Signal Publishers/Atria Books hardcover edition April 2025

ONE SIGNAL PUBLISHERS/ATRIA BOOKS and colophon are trademarks of Simon & Schuster, LLC.



Interior design by Davina Mock-Maniscalco

Manufactured in the United States of America

1 3 5 7 9 10 8 6 4 2

Library of Congress Cataloging-in-Publication Data has been applied for.

ISBN 978-1-6680-8079-5
ISBN 978-1-6680-8081-8 (ebook)

To the courageous, dedicated, and caring salts of Project Germinal, who volunteered to get jobs at Starbucks and helped revitalize the labor movement

# CONTENTS

## INTRODUCTION

# The Right to Organize

"If you vote yes for Workers United, all you'll be able to do is bargain about your wages, hours, and working conditions," said Allyson Peck, referencing the notepad in her hand. "That's all a union can do. Wages, hours, and working conditions. That's it. Everything else, that's ours. That's Starbucks."

We were awkwardly sitting in a ring of chairs while Starbucks corporate tried to stop us from becoming the first unionized Starbucks in the United States. These gatherings, known as captive-audience meetings because companies hold them during working hours and pressure workers to attend, are a hallmark union-busting tactic. Allyson, a former McDonald's executive who had recently switched companies, had been tasked with delivering most of the anti-union lines, although Rossann Williams, Starbucks' president of North America retail, often couldn't stop herself from jumping in.[1]

The consensus among my fellow baristas was that the most important thing was to get this to stop: the "listening sessions," the overwhelming corporate presence, the managers flying in from Georgia and Boston and turning our stores upside down, the one-on-ones, the breakfasts Rossann bought each morning for one of our high-schooler coworkers in order to talk to her about why she shouldn't unionize.

My coworkers at the Elmwood Starbucks had overwhelmingly supported the union, signing cards to reach a strong majority (about 85 percent) and forming the largest organizing committee out of any of the individual stores in our city, with seven of our twenty-five employees voicing public support and adding our names to the letter launching the campaign.[2]

Corporate's mission was to instill enough fear into us to prevent us from voting yes.

They almost succeeded.

But we all knew that organizing a union wasn't simply about improving wages, hours, and working conditions. If it had been a purely financial consideration, corporate might have relented: After all, they were spending far more on their attempt to crush our organizing campaign than they would have spent on the improvements we wanted to negotiate in our first contract. They didn't want us to have a union because they didn't want to share power.

**LABOR HISTORY IS FULL** of heroic struggle, courage, care, solidarity, collective action, fortitude, hope, joy, defeat, and martyrdom. This is not to say that people always get involved in organizing efforts because of their commitment to grandiose ideological visions or their desire to transform society. Most people start organizing out of material necessity, because it offers the hope of escaping poverty, of creating a better life, of winning the right to sit across the table from the boss on an equal footing instead of submitting to the workplace hierarchy.

Organizing campaigns and strikes often force companies to make concessions. For example, to try to dissuade us from voting yes in our union elections, Starbucks granted workers seniority pay, compensating long-term workers for their tenure with the company, for the first time in the company's fifty-year history. But deciding to take on the risks of organizing—declaring current conditions untenable and rallying one's coworkers to fight for change—is no small matter. People don't start unions to extract small improvements: They start unions to fight for their rights, a voice, workplace democracy, and greater dignity and freedom. Organizing enables workers to define themselves in terms of their humanity, not in terms of their productive value to a corporation.[3]

Before Congress passed the National Labor Relations Act in 1935, establishing a legal process for unions to gain recognition, unions had to focus on forcing companies to recognize them. The fundamental demand was the simple right to *have* a union: right to organize. Throughout history, strikers have fought and died for their right to a more abundant life, not simply for ten-cent wage increases—although, after the carnage was done, companies embarrassed by their bloodlust often copped to the latter.[4]

In the 1900s, Colorado coal miners were twice as likely to die on the job than those in other parts of the country. When the miners went on strike in 1913, their demands included shorter workdays, the abolition of company towns and the scrip system that paid workers in tokens that were only valid at company-owned stores, strong health and safety protections, and union recognition. On a fundamental level, they were fighting to assert their own worth and dignity in the face of a company that treated them as disposable commodities.[5]

The mine owners, including John D. Rockefeller Jr., opposed these demands with brutal repression and mass murder. Using private security forces and the National Guard, they evicted the strikers from the company towns, forcing them into tent villages. The companies' hired detectives circled the camps and shot into their midst. To protect themselves and their families, the miners in the Ludlow camp dug pits under their tents. Then, on April 20, 1914, the National Guard raided the camp. They opened fire on the miners who tried to defend themselves and then went through the camp, dousing the tents in kerosene and setting them on fire. Some of the miners' families had been hiding from the bullets in the pits under the tents. The National Guard burned eleven children alive in one of the tents.[6]

Half a century later, in 1968, workers in the rice paddies of Tamil Nadu organized a farm workers' union, with the support of the Communist Party of India (Marxist). They were fighting for both class and caste liberation. They were Dalits, members of the lowest caste. The upper-caste landlords they worked for had formed a united front, under the name of the Paddy Producers Association. The workers' union demands combined economic asks—for a half measure more rice—with their broader struggle for dignity and against the system of untouchability. The Paddy Producers Association began to retaliate, firing workers and attacking community members who supported the strike. In response, the workers went on strike, withholding their labor during the harvest. The landlords tried to undermine them by bringing in other workers to harvest the crops and escalating their terrorism against the strikers. Their vengeance culminated in the burning of the village of Kilvenmani, where many of the strikers lived. When the raid began, many of the village's women and children took refuge in a small hut. The landlords locked them in and set it on fire. One of the mothers threw her child out of the burning building; the landlords threw him back in.[7]

Ludlow and Kilvenmani show the barbarity that oligarchs will resort to in their attempts to prevent workers from securing any measure of power or control over their working conditions and lives. While companies continue to kill workers in retaliation for union organizing around the world, most have made the calculation that they cannot continue to get away with such behavior anymore in the United States.

In fact, after Ludlow, John D. Rockefeller's reputation was so tarnished that he hired a publicist named Ivy Lee to try to restore his image. Lee advised Rockefeller to go to Colorado, arranging for him to meet with miners and send out press releases promoting the photo ops, and took over coordinating Rockefeller's "philanthropic" spending, ensuring his name got onto as many buildings as possible. This strategy formed the basis of the field of public relations.[8]

Companies will do anything they think they can get away with to preserve their power. When countries or states pass stronger labor protections, corporations often relocate in search of more exploitable employees. As recently as the early 2000s, companies like Chiquita Brands International and Coca-Cola were accused of funding death squads in Colombia that targeted and killed union organizers. While the case against Coca-Cola was dismissed, Chiquita was found liable for the deaths of eight union workers in Colombia. In 2023, Shahidul Islam, a former garment worker turned organizer with the Bangladesh Garment and Industrial Workers' Federation, was attacked outside a sweater factory and beaten to death. In the Philippines, over seventy union members have been killed—many by police—since 2016, the year that Rodrigo Duterte came to power. In South Africa, police killed thirty-four striking miners in 2012 to crush a union uprising at a platinum mine in Marikana. But, over and over, workers have shown that repression—no matter how great—cannot kill an idea, cannot silence solidarity.[9]

The right to organize is a fundamental human right. Absent a union or other means of restricting corporate power, the workplace is one of the few places in society that does not contain any system of checks and balances. The dictatorship of the bosses is absolute: They can discipline or fire at will; they can run the operation without any input from those who actually do the work and who are responsible for the success of the business; they can command absolute obedience to the most unreasonable of orders and charge workers who don't immediately comply with "insubordination." In court decisions, U.S. judges have enshrined the "master-servant relationship"—a long-standing concept rooted in nineteenth-century British laws that gave employers immense power over workers—as the basis of the employment contract.[10]

**AT SIXTEEN, I GOT** my first job working at a Panera Bread in Alcoa, Tennessee. Long days on my feet—toting ice, brewing coffee, cleaning bathrooms, and washing dishes crusted with broccoli-cheddar soup—took a physical toll. I encountered the condescension of customers toward service-industry workers and the unvarnished power dynamics of workers and management. I watched my manager tell a coworker she couldn't go home to check on her sick child. I was making $7.50 an hour, which was twenty-five cents above minimum wage. Management had promised to give me a raise and train me on other positions after I'd been there for a couple months, which they never did.

I decided to march into my manager's office and demand what they had promised me. If they didn't give me the raise and train me on register, I would quit. I expected them to agree.

To my shock, my boss' answer was a curt and immediate: "That's fine."

In under a minute, I was out of a job and into a greater understanding of the power dynamics of wage labor.

That store—like most workplaces—was probably organizable. Several of my coworkers there would have made excellent committee members.

Randy, who consistently picked up everyone else's shifts to make rent, always went out of his way to help others with their work. When I was struggling to keep up with the mountain of dishes after a lunch rush, my coworker Marcellus talked to me about Lenin as he helped me catch up: "He had some pretty good ideas."

Growing up, I barely knew what a union was. I was born in Houston, Texas, into a family riddled with contradictions and extreme dysfunction. My father, who had immigrated from India as a teenager, was half-Bengali and half-Romanian. I grew up in an atmosphere of assimilation, cut off from both cultures and family histories, not allowed to learn Hindi or Romanian. My mother was a native Houstonian, one generation away from the Nebraska farm her grandparents had tilled and a third-generation schoolteacher who quit her job and decided to homeschool my sister and me. My mother's populist political orientation led to bizarre allegiances, from Ross Perot to Al Gore, and contradictory stances on issues.

I came by my martyr complex naturally, reveling in the hatred of Democrats frequently found in conservative and homeschooling communities. At the age of seven, I became obsessed with John Kerry: The first dollar I ever spent was a contribution to his campaign. This fervor cost me the friendship of a couple of homeschool-group playmates, who explained that Democrats' main pastime was "living in the sewer and drinking sewer water." Later, in a homeschool 4-H group, one of my fellow club members told me that being a Democrat was akin to devil-worship.

At the time, these extreme takes pushed me deep into the unfortunate kinds of liberalism that the folk singer Phil Ochs sang about. To this day, one of the most tried-and-true methods of annoying Texas Republicans remains to praise Lyndon Baines Johnson to the skies. I did that and more, diving into the archive of Molly Ivins' newspaper columns, stealing Governor Ann Richards' best one-liners, and memorizing Louisiana populist Huey Long's speeches to the rich about getting back here and putting the grub that they didn't need back on the table!

We were the only interracial family in our Houston neighborhood. When my parents had considered moving to the Texas Hill Country, Realtors refused to show them houses for sale. People regularly approached my father, who was visibly Indian, to ask whether my younger sister,

Katrianna, and I—who were both white-passing—were really his children. And yet, simultaneously, my sister and I were told that the very existence of our family, as well as our lack of perception around racial differences, was evidence of society's linear, upward progression toward a peaceful and post-racial order. When Barack Obama won the 2008 presidential election, my mother believed that era had arrived.[11]

There is a saying that if you scratch a Southerner, regardless of what denomination of Christianity they may claim to profess, you will find a Southern Baptist. This was true in our household. My father had been raised Catholic; his father had grown up Hindu but no longer practiced, while the Romanian side of his family refused to discuss their heritage or possible Jewish roots. My mother's religion, which dominated the household, was a strange hybrid of Southern fundamentalism, high church aesthetics, and transcendentalist philosophy. When I would get in trouble, which was constantly, I would be assigned to write essays about Bible verses, Ralph Waldo Emerson quotes, or passages from Aristotle. Nevertheless, I was a deeply devout child, subjecting Katrianna to Sunday school lectures informed by our home's ever-growing collection of abridged Bibles, cassettes of kiddie hymns, and *VeggieTales* videos. Partly for religious reasons, our mother decided to homeschool Katrianna and me, and to move our family from place to place as part of our education. By the time I started college, we had lived in eight different states as well as in Europe.

The environment that my sister and I grew up in had many cultlike tendencies. Only, Katrianna pointed out, cults had a couple of things going for them. They were supposed to provide a built-in circle of friends, whereas we grew up in severe social isolation. Additionally, she added, cults at least brainwashed their members to believe that there was a compelling reason for belonging. "Our cult didn't even have a clear mission statement!"

I became an atheist first as an act of rebellion and then as a rational desire to live honestly. At eleven, I announced my non-belief and was forced to recant under threat of being kicked out of the house, a renunciation I immediately regretted.

Then, a few years later, my parents got divorced. This created a number of fundamental changes in my life. Blaming the failure of her marriage on "cultural differences," my mother's views grew more conservative and decidedly anti-immigrant. The cult's walls narrowed as my mother, increasingly paranoid and suspicious of everyone, cut ties with most of the outside world. With no outside distractions, she and I fought incessantly. In addition, our family's class status changed dramatically. Our father worked in technology and web consulting; money had never been an issue. After the divorce, money was tight, and I got my job at Panera Bread to start saving money for college.

In the meantime, I once again became open about my atheism, despite my mother's passive-aggressive complaints. I spent my free time reading Tom Paine, Charles Bradlaugh, and Robert Ingersoll, freethinkers who had resisted religious oppression. Ingersoll in particular resonated with me: He had spent his life attempting to erode the belief in a literal hell, which condemned so many people to a life of mental torment. I read all of his speeches and essays, admiring his flowery, poetic writing style.[12]

Growing up in an isolated environment where some of my homeschooled peers didn't "believe in" evolution, I became obsessed with the Scopes Monkey Trial, where an East Tennessee schoolteacher was charged with teaching evolution.[13] While researching Clarence Darrow, the lawyer who had represented the teacher, I learned about Eugene Victor Debs—a labor organizer who was also a fellow Ingersoll fan. Ingersoll's influence was apparent in Debs' writings, and I thrilled to his words, too. Sitting on the living room floor waiting to go to work, I read Debs' address to the jury that would sentence him to jail for urging draft resistance during World War I. I was profoundly moved by its stirring declaration of solidarity:

> Your Honor, years ago I recognized my kinship with all living beings, and I made up my mind that I was not one bit better than the meanest on earth. I said then, and I say now, that while there is a lower class, I am in it, and while there is a criminal element I am of it, and while there is a soul in prison, I am not free.[14]

Those words changed my life. Debs offered a way out of the nationalist limitations and racist undertones of the Southern populism I was already familiar with, and the labor movement provided the stories of breathtaking solidarity and heroism and the overwhelming sense of purpose I had once found in religion.

The fervor that had characterized my relationship to Christianity transferred to the labor movement. Here, too, were martyrs: Albert Parsons and Joe Hill and Frank Little. I lay awake at night thinking about how they must have felt on the gallows, in front of the firing squad, or marching resolutely into the company town of Anaconda Copper, knowing that out of their deaths—as Mother Jones said—would come the workers' lives. Here, too, were songs, conveniently set to the tunes of religious anthems. One of the first songs I'd learned as a child, and the only one I could sing on key, was "Battle Hymn of the Republic," and the labor classic "Solidarity Forever" was an effortless replacement. And here, too, was a utopian vision to fight for, knowing I might never live to see the glowing spires of the celestial workers' city but that the commonwealth of toil was inevitable, brought ever closer by the struggles of the proletariat and the linear and upward path of history. I yearned for a way to translate these feelings into action, but I thought organizing was something you read about. I didn't know it was something you *do*.

That changed when I started college at the University of Mississippi and met a labor journalism professor named Joe Atkins.

A North Carolina native who grew up working in tobacco fields and textile mills, Joe had worked as the Washington correspondent for Gannett. A former Vietnam War protester, he once told me, "Don't get burned-out—that's how I ended up in Vietnam!" As a reporter, he had interviewed everyone from union organizers and civil rights leaders to murderers and Southern demagogues. He critiqued the corporate takeover of the newspaper industry, which had eliminated small papers and centralized power—and control of the narrative—in a few hands. He was the platonic ideal of a professor: kind, understanding, charismatic, passionate, principled, defying the pressures of state legislators and a hostile higher-education board bent on stamping out the exact lessons he sought to teach.

Professor Atkins was a print journalist in a department that had mostly been hijacked by broadcasting and marketing. He was a fan of pioneering investigative journalists like Mary Heaton Vorse and Ida Tarbell; a movie buff who screened the Mine, Mill and Smelter Workers' classic film, *Salt of the Earth*, in classes designed around film and politics. In his media-history seminar, he gave a lecture on objectivity. The muckrakers who exposed corporate malfeasance at the turn of the century hadn't been "objective," not by the standards of capitalist media. The abolitionist William Lloyd Garrison was certainly not "objective" when he trumpeted out his "I will not retreat a single inch, and I WILL BE HEARD" editorials against slavery. What mattered, Joe emphasized, was *truth*, not perceived objectivity.[15]

This was a lesson that translated to his own writing.

Joe was fearless. His editorials called out politicians, exposed companies, gave voice to workers trying to organize their union, and tracked corporate donations—particularly those going to progressive causes that suddenly became mysteriously silent around the key issue of workers' right to organize. He was also incredibly supportive of student activism, agreeing to speak at my first-ever protest, a rally against the Trans-Pacific Partnership, and comforting me when I told him about the red-baiting I was encountering from fellow students in the Trent Lott Leadership Institute. "There's an old labor song called 'You Ain't Done Nothing If You Ain't Been Called a Red,'" he told me. "You're doing something right!"

**THROUGH HIS REPORTING, JOE** had become friends with one of the United Auto Workers (UAW) organizers working on the Nissan campaign, the attempt to organize the multinational company's Canton, Mississippi, factory. In March 2016, Joe arranged to bring his friend, Richard Bensinger, to campus to speak to students about the need for community support. Joe asked me to help recruit students to attend the meeting. I made some flyers to announce the event and, with shaking knees, handed them out in front of the student union. I got few takers, but began to overcome my fear of approaching strangers.

"Can you come to my office before the meeting to meet Richard?" Joe had asked me after class, earlier that day.

What I saw when I got there, standing in the office doorway, making a sweeping gesture with both arms outstretched, wearing a blue-and-gold UAW jacket, was the reincarnation of Eugene Debs. Fiercely dedicated, fun loving, and warmhearted, Richard combined a revolutionary iconoclasm with an insistence on "not being into isms" and a folksy, cowboy-boot-clad, Kentucky demeanor. When he spoke in union meetings, his blue eyes shone with solidarity.

Richard had seen the best and the worst of the labor movement and had kept the faith—or at least a joy in the fight and a commitment to the underdog that passed for faith. At age twenty-three, Richard had organized his own workplace—a sports equipment manufacturer—into the Amalgamated Clothing Workers of America. He told me about possible exposure to asbestos and fiberglass while grinding tennis rackets, about how his friends had died early of emphysema, stomach cancer, and other conditions that he believes may have been connected to exposure to these workplace toxins. "I got out in time," he said.

After the company fired him for union organizing, Richard had gotten a job at a nonunion factory to organize it, a practice known as salting. As a salt and a volunteer member organizer, he helped organize a dozen factories, which led to his election as the leader of the union's Rocky Mountain Joint Board. A decade later, at the American Federation of Labor and Congress of Industrial Organizations (AFL-CIO), the umbrella organization that presides over most of the major labor unions in the United States, Richard created the Organizing Institute, which focused on recruiting and training new organizers, providing pathways for young people—especially women and people of color—to join the labor movement. When John Sweeney became president of the AFL-CIO, he appointed Richard as his organizing director. In that role, Richard pushed hard on the AFL-CIO's member unions to expand their organizing. Perhaps too hard: After less than two years, Sweeney forced Richard out. Afterward, Richard became the organizing director of the UAW; now, he was working tirelessly to help Nissan workers organize as an adviser to the campaign.[16]

The critical thing, he emphasized, was winning the right to organize. Years before, in collaboration with his friend Dick Schubert, the former president of Bethlehem Steel, Richard had come up with a set of guidelines for companies to follow during union election campaigns. These Fair Election Principles provided a framework for holding truly democratic union elections by preventing companies from terrorizing workers into voting no. Instead of pushing for companies to recognize unions based on workers' signed union cards rather than going to elections or asking companies to stay silent and "neutral," the Fair Election Principles sought to hold elections on a level playing field. They would give the union equal time to present to workers: If a company held a paid anti-union meeting, the union would be able to follow that up with their own meeting on company time. The principles required the company not only to refrain from threatening workers, but also to disavow threats made by third parties. If the company fired a worker, the case would go to expedited arbitration rather than languishing at the Labor Board. Both sides would refrain from disparaging the other.

The Fair Election Principles sound reasonable. In fact, the first time I read them I didn't think they were radical enough. *Why would we agree not to disparage the company?* I wondered. *Isn't that almost like collaborating with our class enemies?*

I would later learn from experience just how important the Fair Election Principles are to truly empowering workers—and that my worries about class collaboration had been misguided. Where we have been able to pressure companies into signing them, workers have been able to organize in an environment largely free of fear. Companies that agree to abide by a higher standard help to put pressure on labor law violators and provide alternative and encouraging examples of straightforward unionization. Workers who organize unions and expose themselves to the risk of corporate retaliation are heroes. But, as Richard said, it shouldn't require an act of courage to organize a union.

**ON PAPER, THE U.S.** government protects workers' right to organize a union. The National Labor Relations Act of 1935 stated, "Employees shall have the right to self-organization, to form, join, or assist labor organizations, to bargain collectively through representatives of their own choosing, and to engage in concerted activities, for the purpose of collective bargaining or other mutual aid or protection." It prohibited companies from retaliating against workers because they organized unions, from refusing to bargain with unionized workers, from blacklisting workers, and from refusing to hire union members. It created the National Labor Relations Board (NLRB) as a government agency tasked with enforcing the law.[17]

From the beginning, the NLRA was flawed in many ways. To secure the votes of white, conservative Southern Democrats, the law excluded agricultural and domestic workers, which disproportionately withheld protection from Black workers. Then, in 1947, Congress passed another law, called the Taft-Hartley Act, which chipped away further at the NLRA, giving companies greater ability to try to convince workers not to unionize, taking away supervisors' right to organize, and banning "secondary boycotts" aimed at companies doing business with the primary target, among other changes. Moreover, because NLRB members are presidential appointees, decisions, rules, and enforcement of the law itself fluctuates based on who is in office.[18]

In theory, organizing a union is straightforward. Workers decide they want to organize, sign union cards declaring that they want to join an organization, and file for an election once they reach a large enough majority. The NLRB then schedules an election in which workers vote by secret ballot on whether to unionize. If 50 percent plus one of the voters vote to unionize, the union wins and the NLRB certifies the organization as the official representative of the workers for the purpose of collective bargaining. Then, the company is required to meet with the union to bargain a first contract.

In practice, the process is far more complicated. Companies try a variety of methods—some legal, others not—to prevent, dissuade, or intimidate workers from unionizing. The NLRB process is riddled with loopholes and delays. If a company fires a union leader, it can take years to win their reinstatement, and companies can appeal NLRB decisions in federal court. There are no meaningful penalties for breaking labor law: Beyond paying back wages and posting an admission, companies can get away with nearly any violation. The consequence for refusing to bargain with a union is a letter ordering the company to bargain, with no enforcement mechanism.

Despite this, workers' enthusiasm for organizing unions in their workplaces is surging. Today, there is a growing awareness of the necessity of unions. Organizing allows workers to take action against structural and societal injustices, including the soaring income inequality that has eroded many workers' prospects of career advancement along with any possibility of retirement. It is also the only means of bringing democracy to the workplace and altering power dynamics in favor of workers rather than corporations.[19]

When workers start organizing, management often wonders, *Why us? What did we do to deserve this?* In part, this reveals companies' internal reaction to union busting in the United States, which has shifted from being a literal war—with cannons and rifles—to a psychological one. Rockefeller was probably not surveying miners on what they wanted to see improved in their workplace and whether they felt their concerns were heard on the job. By the 1970s, however, many companies were utilizing these methods to create an illusion of worker voice that would, they hoped, help stave off actual union organizing. But this attitude misses the point of why workers organize. Companies aren't getting unions because they, specifically, deserve them—rather, because it should be the default. If you have a job, you should have a union.

# CHAPTER ONE

## Here's to the State of Mississippi

The mile-long factory stretched uncharacteristically silent under the Mississippi sky. The smokestacks were still, no hum emerging from the stopped lines. The Nissan water tower loomed starkly white and red against the pines and the sky.

The stillness alone made the day—March 4, 2017—remarkable. The factory was never quiet. Nissan scheduled workers to swap in for one another at the end of their ten-hour, mandatory-overtime shifts. The plant rattled through the nights and knew no weekends.

Even when Nissan worker Derrick Whiting lay dying, collapsed across the assembly line, on September 22, 2015, a worker told me that management had refused to pause production on the surrounding lines, which the company denied. Nissan workers told me later that the company had a policy forbidding workers from carrying phones on the floor and that management was reluctant to call ambulances itself. It took almost an hour for an ambulance to arrive, a coworker who had been working nearby told me later. Some workers felt Nissan should have done more to help Derrick; Nissan maintained that unsafe conditions were not a factor in Derrick's death and that they had not been negligent.[1]

On that March morning, the plant was shut down because of the March on Mississippi, a convergence of union supporters who would rally outside the plant in protest of Nissan's union-busting conduct.

I thought the silence was a victory. Nissan never closed, but their fear—of the United Auto Workers, of national figures including Senator

Bernie Sanders, who would be speaking at the march, and of the workers' power—had brought production to a halt. Now, I thought, the workers would be free to attend the march.

"Many of the workers have to drive from hours away to get to work," one of the union organizers, Rickman Jackson, pointed out. "If the plant's shut down, they won't be here, so they won't see the march or be able to join when they get off work."

Despite this, the turnout was good. The news reported five thousand attendees; drones captured footage of a long column of red-shirted marchers heading to the plant. The march brought together every segment of Mississippi progressive society: the veterans of the Civil Rights Movement groups and the churches, the abortion clinic defenders and the labor unions, the environmental activists and the students.[2]

I had been volunteering with the UAW for the past year, recruiting University of Mississippi students to support the campaign by attending meetings and demonstrations. Richard had asked me to coordinate our school's participation in the march. I spent weeks calling and texting fellow students and community residents on my underqualified flip phone to confirm attendance, going to student group meetings to talk about the union, spamming GroupMe chats, and reaching out to people on Facebook Messenger. A few days before the march, Richard asked me how many buses we would need to transport everyone traveling from Oxford, Mississippi, to Canton. I told him we needed three. He was incredulous that we had recruited so many marchers: Three buses would carry three hundred people.

On the morning of March 4, I was a few minutes late walking to the parking lot where the buses would meet us. As I came over the hill and looked down, there were hundreds there: about 250, it turned out, still enough to fill the buses. Seeing everyone assembled was wonderfully invigorating. It was a tangible representation of solidarity and community, gathered to support the Nissan workers.

**BY THE TIME I** got involved in the spring of 2016, the Nissan union campaign had already been going on for over a decade. It had started slowly: first as a probe, where the union tried to meet workers and find out whether there was interest, and then as a campaign to build an organizing committee and sign workers up on union-authorization cards. For the last couple of years, Richard had based himself mainly out of the little UAW office in Canton, Mississippi, trying to help get the campaign off the ground and force Nissan to sign the Fair Election Principles and respect the workers' right to organize.

Since the plant had opened in 2003, the state of Mississippi had given Nissan $1.3 billion in tax breaks. Nearly six thousand people worked in the giant factory; 80 percent of the workers were Black, a percentage that was higher among the large number of temporary workers.[3]

Union busting ran rampant within the plant. Nissan projected negative news stories about the UAW or unionized automakers on giant TV screens in the break rooms. They held *roundtables*—their word for captive-audience meetings—where managers told workers that unions were bad for business, showed slides of plants that had closed after workers organized, and implied that Nissan was choosing to expand production because the factory was nonunion. The managers took notes in those meetings, and supervisors often followed up with workers one-on-one afterward, asking their views on unions or telling anecdotes about plant closings and workers losing their jobs after going on strike.[4]

There were other issues, too. The workers felt that Derrick Whiting's death was a glaring example of the disregard Nissan showed for their health and safety. I learned of incidents of torn rotator cuffs, crippled necks, repetitive motion injuries, wrists injured by the force of nail guns, a worker who was hit by a car on the assembly line, falls into open pits, hernias, and workers who weren't able to insist on medically required job restrictions. The company also refused to rotate workers between jobs, sped up the production lines, and even restricted workers' bathroom breaks, forcing some to resort to wearing diapers to work.[5]

The leverage to force Nissan to stop union busting and respect workers' rights existed. The UAW had built strong relationships with many local organizations and student groups, which tried to hold the company accountable. The French government was another source of potential leverage: It owned a controlling stake in Renault, Nissan's parent company at the time. The

French parliament dragged the CEO of Renault-Nissan before a committee to ask about union busting in the U.S. South. The CEO, Carlos Ghosn, denied that the company had ever busted unions and claimed it didn't even oppose the union. After all, the company was unionized all over the world (everywhere except the U.S. South). Moreover, Ghosn promised that the company would never run an anti-union campaign.[6]

If Nissan did, Richard told me, the UAW should take the matter to the public and inform customers at dealerships of the company's behavior. He showed me designs for banners that volunteers could hold at the entrances to car lots. He explained the rules around secondary picketing and talked about building a network of activists, students, ministers, labor unions, capable of taking this nationwide. Nissan bragged that their customer base was largely young, progressive, LGBTQ, and Black. These target demographics would not continue to buy Nissan's cars, we believed, if they knew about the union busting in the plant. Under the former UAW president Bob King, the union had trained thousands of volunteer members to go to the dealerships whenever needed. Bob had hired Richard, and the two of them had put the industry on warning: If they didn't sign the Fair Election Principles and instead ran campaigns of fear and intimidation, the UAW would come for them.

**THERE'S A COMMON MISCONCEPTION** that the South doesn't have a tradition of labor organizing. Southern labor history is a long and troubled saga of massacres, intimidation, racism, brutality, courage, hope, heroism, and, every now and then, victory. In that, it is not so different from the record of labor battles elsewhere. But unlike early Northern unions, which often gained power as all-white and exclusionary organizations, the Southern experience makes evident that labor cannot win by compromising its solidarity or by participating in white supremacy. Black workers in the South organized and fought to liberate themselves from slavery, from Jim Crow, from white supremacy, and from corporate tyranny. The origins of the labor movement in the United States were not in the mostly or all-white unions of Northern industrial workers, but in revolts among enslaved people. In *Black Reconstruction in America*, W. E. B. Du Bois argued that the Civil War was actually a general strike: By organizing and demanding freedom, enslaved workers freed themselves and forced the United States to adopt abolition as central to the war. Herbert Aptheker told some of the stories of how they did it in his *American Negro Slave Revolts*, from early sit-down strikes, sabotage actions, and insurrections to general strikes during the Civil War, in which enslaved workers formed bargaining committees and literally won their emancipation and transformation into waged laborers.[7]

Over the next century, Southern labor organizing and civil rights struggles went hand in hand. In 1887, the Knights of Labor began to work with Louisiana sugarcane workers. This was an interracial union effort, although a large majority of the workers were Black. When ten thousand workers went on strike at the peak of the harvest, the plantation owners created a vigilante force and began massacring strikers in and around Thibodaux, Louisiana. The owners snarled, "God Almighty has himself drawn the color line." The owners—correctly—saw workers organizing as a fundamental threat to the existing order of white supremacy and racial terrorism they were upholding. It was no coincidence that the songs of the Civil Rights Movement, from "We Shall Overcome" to "Keep Your Eyes on the Prize" to "We Shall Not Be Moved," were first sung on union picket lines across the South. This is an ongoing struggle: The right-wing and white-supremacist power structure in the South continues to rely on racial capitalism to keep workers divided and crush unionization efforts.[8]

That power structure has mostly succeeded in systemically eliminating labor history from Southern textbooks and from our collective memory. From antebellum times to the present, they have labeled organizing in the Deep South the work of "outside agitators" come to stir up trouble among otherwise contented workers. Southern elites claimed that revolts among enslaved people—from Nat Turner's uprising to the plans of Denmark Vesey and his comrades—were attributable to pamphlets by Northern abolitionists that "infected" people who would otherwise have submitted happily to slavery. Nearly two hundred years later, the white power structure maintained the same talking points about who was responsible for organizing among Nissan workers. In 2017, I watched the governor of Mississippi give a speech at the notoriously racist Neshoba County

Fair—in the county where three civil rights workers had been murdered in 1964 and on the stage where Ronald Reagan had dog-whistled about "states' rights" during his 1980 campaign for the presidency—about how union organizers "can get back in the Bernie Sanders bus and go back to New York, and I'll pay their way."

**AS AN ANGSTY TEEN** in Louisville, Kentucky, small for his age and mesmerized by the burgeoning Civil Rights Movement, Richard Bensinger had spent days sitting on the floor by a record player, listening to Martin Luther King Jr.'s speeches and Phil Ochs' "Here's to the State of Mississippi" on repeat. As a teenager, he had gone to the Poor People's March in Washington, DC, with his older sister, capturing photos of marchers wading in the Lincoln Memorial Reflecting Pool afterward. He recognized immediately that the Nissan campaign—an undertaking of workers, 80 percent of them Black, in the heart of the state that had symbolized both white, supremacist institutions and Black resistance—was a continuation of that movement, leading him to come up with the Nissan campaign's central slogan: "Tell Nissan: Labor Rights Are Civil Rights!"[9]

Students from universities around Jackson, Mississippi, rallied to the cause. In 2014, Nissan fired an eleven-year worker, Calvin Moore, in retaliation for his leadership on the union organizing committee. It seemed unlikely that the NLRB regional office, known for its conservative holdings, would find merit in unfair labor practices around Calvin's case, but the court of public opinion had more sway. Unionized Nissan workers in Brazil leafleted their plant and nearby car dealerships in support of Calvin. Actor Danny Glover and other celebrities spoke out about his firing. Then, the students of Tougaloo and Jackson State fearlessly occupied the lobby of the plant office with a local minister, singing movement songs (including "Ain't gonna let no Nissan turn me around"), while the company threatened to have them arrested. Under pressure, Nissan caved: The next morning, Calvin walked into the union office to report that the company had called to offer him reinstatement with full back pay.[10]

Until 2014, Nissan had been mostly silent on the topic of racial justice—

even when, in 2011, a group of white youths killed a Nissan worker, James Craig Anderson, in a hate crime described as a "modern-day lynching." But when the UAW adopted the civil rights message, Nissan decided to attempt to brand itself as a movement stalwart. The company's community relations program started writing checks to churches, civil rights groups, politicians, and community groups, either to buy their support for the company or their silence about its labor practices. Some of these displays were more grotesque than others, like the time Nissan sponsored an outside workshop titled "Undoing Racism" while ignoring racism within the plant.[11]

In 2014, the UAW had sponsored the fiftieth-anniversary commemoration of Freedom Summer, and the activists who returned to Mississippi for the celebration participated in a march at the plant. A few years later, in 2016, Nissan—determined not to allow that to happen again—sponsored the fiftieth-anniversary commemoration of James Meredith's March Against Fear. In 1966, Meredith, who had integrated the University of Mississippi, decided to march from Memphis to Jackson to challenge white supremacy and encourage Black voter registration. On the second day of the march, a racist gunman ambushed and shot Meredith. Other civil rights leaders visited him in the hospital and pledged to continue the march, which turned into a defining event of the movement. Half a century later, the Veterans of the Mississippi Civil Rights Movement gathered at Tougaloo College under a giant Nissan banner, while the company's public relations person sang "We Shall Not Be Moved," omitting the pro-union verses.[12]

I protested Nissan's sponsorship of this event, distributing flyers calling attention to the company's hypocrisy. While I was standing outside the event hall, a news photographer who was covering the rally came up and told me that he used to work at Nissan himself.

"You can get fired just for saying the word *union*," he said. "I've seen it happen."

That was the climate of fear Nissan created. That was the grim reality the company sought to cover up with its donations, to preserve its reputation and image. In the century between Ludlow and Nissan's campaign of fear against the UAW, corporate public relations strategies had barely changed.

---

**THE MARCH ON MISSISSIPPI,** which shut down the Nissan plant and brought together hundreds of activists from around the state, took place in March 2017. It was the largest civil rights demonstration in Mississippi since Freedom Summer. But something seemed off. When the students, piled into our three buses, got to Canton, Joe Atkins told me that a UAW comms person had given him the runaround; Joe hadn't gotten his promised interview with Bernie Sanders, one of the rally's speakers. Despite the huge attendance, Richard was also visibly upset.

Later, I would learn that the UAW's top leadership wanted an exit strategy from the Nissan campaign. The president of the union, Dennis Williams, saw the Nissan civil rights/labor rights campaign as a vestige of his predecessor's administration and was anxious to be done with it. Under Bob King, the UAW had committed to organizing the nonunion auto companies and making companies that refused to respect the right to organize the target of dealership boycotts. Williams, who would go to prison for embezzling union funds a few years later, was a corrupt and bureaucratic leader who did not share King's vision. To lay the Nissan campaign to rest, Williams' team decided to file for an election at Nissan, knowing the union would almost certainly lose, and then quietly abandon the project. They did not force Nissan to sign the Fair Election Principles, nor did they adopt Richard's plan to send picketers to dealerships across the country to try to win the right to organize.

The March on Mississippi revealed this change in strategy. Richard had written talking points for the speakers that would have delivered a two-week ultimatum to Nissan—either sign the Fair Election Principles and respect workers' right to organize or face the consequences and the wrath of the labor movement. The UAW literally flipped the script, bringing in consultants from Hillary Clinton's failed presidential campaign and asking the speakers to simply tell Nissan workers to vote yes.

The representatives from the NAACP and the Sierra Club—organizations that both received funding from Nissan—had gotten nervous about calling for a boycott. Bernie Sanders, suffering from a cold, was supposed to have delivered the ultimatum. Instead, the UAW changed his talking points so that he merely decried the state of affairs in the country and gave a pep talk about the benefits of union membership. Nina Turner, the former Ohio state senator and head of Our Revolution, invoked Nina Simone's "Mississippi Goddam." But ultimately she talked about the importance of the workers' backbone and about how they were being "tested" to see if they could stand up to Nissan's fearmongering, instead of about the original message of how the labor movement would hold Nissan accountable and help the workers win their union. I remember thinking she was the best speaker I had ever heard, but the union had watered the message down until it was virtually meaningless. Nissan needed to pay a consequence, but the UAW—the only organization capable of making the company do so—had decided against it.[13]

**WITHOUT THE RIGHT TO** organize, the campaign had a nihilistic undercurrent. We were up against the combined odds of an anti-union company that would stop at nothing to keep the union out, allied with the most reactionary elements of Mississippi's politics, culture, and history. But we couldn't give in to the despair and the knowledge that this union drive would almost certainly end in defeat.

The Nissan campaign went to a vote in the summer of 2017. That summer, I worked full-time with the United Auto Workers, participating in every aspect of the organizing drive, from going house calling to speak with Nissan workers (or technicians, as the company called them), to drafting leaflets and designing T-shirts, to attending committee meetings, to taking workers' statements and photographs, to joining the sign team, to sorting through the health and safety records the union had compiled over the years.[14]

I loved house calling, I discovered. The first time I went out, my canvassing partner was Odessa, an autoworker from Detroit with a love of pop music and strawberry lip gloss. As she skillfully navigated the pothole-ridden streets of Jackson, singing along to Ed Sheeran and Rihanna, she walked me through the canvasser's protocols.

*Take your sunglasses off before you get to the door. Take a step back after you ring the doorbell. Watch out for dogs. Whistle loudly, several times. Fill out the sheet properly, no abbreviations or bad handwriting, but don't start writing until we pull away from their house. Race and gender go in the top right corner. Things like what shift they work and what their issues are matter.*

I didn't get bit by anything bigger than a chihuahua while out canvassing for the union—I let it nip me in order to avoid disrupting a productive conversation—but I did learn to always carry union authorization cards and pens in my pockets. Anyone wearing Nissan's red, company-issued polos caught my eye. I watched Odessa stroll up to these workers in gas stations and grocery stores, initiate a conversation, learn their names and their stories. A newly signed card was a trophy, a treasure, to be carefully tucked into the car cupholder compartment or snapped into the clipboard. But, more often, they would nervously tell us they'd signed up already—though there would be no record of their signing when we checked the union's computer system.

One day, I was house calling in Carthage, Mississippi. The town was a dusty crossroads lined with strip centers and fast-food joints. The houses were hidden down red-dirt roads carved into the piney forests and studded with Confederate flags and STAND YOUR GROUND stickers.

My house-calling partner, Handel, was a union organizer who had been forced to flee his native Haiti due to threats from the Duvalier dictatorship. He told me about his roundabout path to joining the labor movement, and we discussed world politics as we drove to the remote corners of the state.

We stopped at a KFC for lunch, eating quickly and hopping back into the car. A sign in the parking lot across the street caught my coworker's eye.

"I want to go to Dirt Cheap," said Handel. "What is that?"

"Never heard of it," I said.

"Is it really dirt cheap? C'mon, let's check it out."

For the next fifteen minutes, Handel roamed the messy, disorganized aisles of the store, shaking his head. "Not that cheap."

Then he saw the blender. It was used, and the box was battered, but all the parts were there. "Do you know how much this blender is worth? If I hadn't just bought that juicer . . ."

When we finally got back to the car, sans blender, I set the GPS to our next stop and found the corresponding sheet, with its imprecise notes:

*Works night shift, or used to; SUV door line; thinks manager is sleeping with some of the workers and giving them easier jobs, instead of rotating.*

Handel peered into the rearview mirror. "That truck is following us."

"Do you think it's because we're union?"

"No. It's because they're thinking, 'What is that n— doing with that white girl.'"

In the gritty rearview mirror, I could see the dirty white pickup behind us, with two white men in the front seat.

Handel swerved onto a different road. The truck continued past, made a U-turn in the middle of the street, and followed. We were going pretty fast, and eventually the truck disappeared, although for the rest of the day I glanced fearfully at each white truck that materialized.

"If we have time," said Handel, "I want to go back to Dirt Cheap and see if they still have that blender. You saw that couple behind us? They heard what I was saying, about how good a deal it was. I bet they picked up that blender as soon as we were gone."

We were paired together the next day as well. Because Nissan ranked among the highest-paying jobs in the state, workers commuted to the plant from eighty of Mississippi's eighty-two counties. We drove for hours, heading as far as the Alabama border. There, we had absolutely no luck in finding the Nissan workers in our call pack, finding only parents, brothers, and bad addresses. We drove through beautiful, rolling countryside, small plots of land owned by Black farmers and occupied by several generations of pro-union people who loved what we were doing and wished us luck. Still, we returned without a single card or conversation to report. It was getting late by the time we had wrapped up our call packet. The sun was low and rain clouds clustered on the horizon.[15]

On a straight and empty stretch of highway, Handel patted the dashboard of the red rental car, saying, "I want to see what kind of engine this thing has got." We had been doing seventy-five or eighty all day, but now he pushed the car past ninety, over a hundred.

"Maybe you better let me drive," I said.

"Why? Are you scared of my driving?"

"No, but after that, you can't be scared of mine."

The deluge started within minutes of my taking the wheel. As I slowed the car and strained to see through the thick wall of water, Handel queued labor songs from the Whiteville Choir, a band of mostly Black workers from a unionized North Carolina textile mill whose music blended traditional labor songs with gospel rhythms. *We're marchin', marchin' in the streets!*

As we neared the junction of the freeway to Carthage, Handel sighed: "I still wish we had time to go back to Dirt Cheap."

**ATTENDING THE NISSAN WORKERS'** committee meetings was inspiring and insightful. The meetings began early in the morning, as workers started to get off work after the night shift, with meetings for the other shifts scheduled throughout the day. The committee was an incredibly impressive group. I had met a couple of them when they came to campus to speak about the campaign before the marches and demonstrations, leaders who brought a determination, tirelessness, and strength to the fight that made me believe we could win.

Morris Mock was one of these stalwart leaders. He worked in the plant's paint department, handling vehicle hoods. He talked about the lack of personal protective equipment in his department: He believed workers needed the safest Kevlar gloves to protect against the cuts and injuries he and others had experienced, but he said Nissan did not provide them because they could scratch the paint. "Nissan cares more about the paint jobs on the cars than about my body," he said in an interview about health and safety conditions.[16]

Morris had grown up on picket lines: His parents worked at a unionized phone company and had brought their young son with them. He had studied at Jackson State and had a remarkable singing voice, although he was shy about it. He combined a deep knowledge of history with a passion for organizing and a desire to connect the Nissan fight with the broader struggle for racial and social justice. He told me that sometimes, after a grueling shift at Nissan, he would soak in a bath and listen to the speeches of the Black nationalist leader Marcus Garvey.

One of the few white workers on the committee, Travis Parks, was another dedicated union advocate. He commuted in from rural Mississippi, where he was the secretary of his deer-hunting camp. He worked the night shift in trucks and SUVs and was one of the witnesses to Derrick Whiting's death and a tireless health and safety advocate. He showed me photos of the fish he had caught on trips to his native South Carolina and told me about his adventures at the annual Chitlin Strut festival, an event celebrating that unique but controversial delicacy. He had a keen sense of strategy and messaging, frequently coming into the office before work to pull up a chair and talk through ideas for new flyers and T-shirts.

My favorite idea of his, which would have taken a better graphic designer than I was to execute, referred to the Nissan Pathway program. Pathway workers were Nissan workers who had started working at the plant as temps. About a third of the workers in the factory technically worked for agencies like Kelly, Minact, or Yates, doing equal work for unequal pay. Ginny Diamond, who was Richard's wife and a brilliant labor lawyer and organizer in her own right, coined a slogan that the ministers supporting the campaign quickly adopted: Nissan: Lead Us Not into Temp-Nation.[17]

Temp workers were disproportionately Black, and temp workers made less than direct hires. Most of the temps wanted the opportunity to become permanent, while those who had become permanent—the Pathway workers—wanted to be able to reach the top pay rates. Under the Obama-era NLRB rules, temps were eligible to vote in union elections if the union petitioned to include them in the bargaining unit. While the UAW hadn't targeted temps extensively in their house-calling program or outreach, the number of temp workers signing cards had picked up dramatically, revealing a surge of interest.[18]

Travis wanted a shirt that appealed specifically to the temps and the Pathway workers. He told the story of Robert Johnson, the Delta blues singer who supposedly made a deal with the devil at a crossroads of Highway 61, trading his soul for supernatural guitar-playing skill. Nissan workers were at such a crossroads, too, Travis explained. With the UAW, there was a pathway to victory. Without the union, there was a pathway to uncertainty. Which side are you on?

However, some within the UAW's top leadership believed that temp workers, fearing that management would retaliate against them by not hiring them full-time, would never vote for the union. There was an elitism in the UAW's position that may ultimately have cost the union the election. True, some temp workers were afraid that union activism would cost them the ability to be hired permanently. But at Nissan, they were the most mistreated, the most disposable, the most precarious. Many of the organizers on the ground had focused on recruiting temp workers; they were showing a growing interest in signing cards and getting involved. Perhaps they would have voted no, but there was a real chance they could have swung the election in the union's favor had they not been counted out.

I helped Richard photograph workers for the *Vote Yes* newsletter he was working on and collect quotes about why they were voting yes. When we interviewed workers, I checked that the camera was set up properly, fetched backup batteries, chitchatted, and tried to reassure the nervous ones. Later, Richard and I would work into the night, long after the other organizers had trickled out of the building, to assemble the footage into Facebook-friendly chunks.

I learned a great deal from Richard and tried to copy his tirelessness, joining every team: the sign team that hit the streets at four thirty in the morning to hammer signs into the sandy dirt by the plant (and step in fire-ant hills), the house-calling team, the communications committee, the plant-leafleting team, the shift-meeting team. I got angry when Rickman Jackson, worried that I wasn't sleeping enough, didn't tell me about a meeting, or when Sanchioni Butler, the lead organizer, encouraged people to make sure I wasn't working too hard.

Richard was the personification of the attitude that he described, in Antonio Gramsci's words, as "pessimism of the intellect, optimism of the will." Richard worked tirelessly, house calling, writing flyers, editing videos, attending meetings, arranging news interviews, coordinating various parts of the campaign. He had lost only one union campaign before in his entire career. He knew exactly what was coming, but worked with the same passion and energy he would have brought to the struggle despite that knowledge.[19]

Had I met any other organizer, I doubt that I would still be in the labor movement. Without Richard's example and mentorship, which helped me see past the limitations of union bureaucracy and remain focused on our goal of organizing workers, I might have burned out quickly and decided to teach or pursue other alternative careers. But at that time, Richard tried to shield me from the harshest realities of organizational ineptness and the kinds of union officials who were building expensive golf-course mansions while preventing the union from taking a real stand on organizing. He provided me with an example of a very different kind of labor leader.

We became close friends, uniting over everything from a shared love of Baskin-Robbins pit stops to the experience of being two atheists attending an all-Black evangelical church in Jackson. We went because Bishop Thomas Jenkins, the minister—an incredible leader who refused to take money from Nissan—was a strong advocate for the union, introducing us to his Nissan-worker congregants after the service. One of these workers, who had been afraid of retaliation, signed one of the union cards I always carried in my bag on the back of a church pew after we talked following the service.

Mostly, Richard and I bonded over our shared belief in the movement and the workers, our agreement that praying to Joe Hill, an organizer with the Industrial Workers of the World (IWW) and a songwriter who had been executed in a frame-up because he threatened corporate power, was the most reasonable religious practice, and—above all—our love of Phil Ochs. We shared inside jokes based on his song lyrics, singing along to "Draft Dodger Rag" in the car or insulting the Nissan-financed, completely co-opted ministers and leaders of civil rights and social justice groups by calling them names from "Love Me, I'm a Liberal." Our favorite song to discuss endlessly, and to call other people over to listen to, was "Here's to the State of Mississippi."

The pain and bitterness Phil Ochs' lyrics captured gave a cadence to the most haunting part of my job: sorting through the history of health and safety violations of the plant. In compiling a report, I called the affected workers to make sure they were comfortable with their names and stories appearing publicly. Sometimes, it was overwhelming, and I would slip out to privately cry over the ruined lives presented on these papers.

During house visits, workers told me stories about what working at Nissan had done to their lives. One man had spent months in limbo, trying to contact Nissan about the status of his leave and his insurance. He signed a union card and told me he hoped a vote would come before he was officially fired after a year out of work—an occurrence that had happened to other workers who had been injured on the job, as I had learned from previous conversations.

Committee member Eric Hearn, who was closer to retirement age than many of the other workers, had to get carpal tunnel surgery on both wrists; he did both at once so that he would be out of work for a shorter time. After the surgery, he came by the office every day with both hands bandaged to talk through campaign strategy and help however he could.

To my astonishment, the UAW lawyers refused to allow us to speak publicly about many health and safety issues within the plant, or to share other workers' stories. Afraid that Nissan would sue us for defamation if we spoke publicly about these issues, they struck passages from the report I was working on, censoring workers' firsthand accounts of their injuries.

I was outraged by this refusal to talk about such a critical issue. Nissan workers were quite literally in a fight for their lives: having a union would give them a say in safety issues, helping to save their lives, reduce the number of preventable injuries, and secure actual protections for workers who were hurt on the job.

**DESPITE THIS URGENCY, WITHOUT** the company respecting their right to organize, it was almost impossible to convince workers to overcome the fear Nissan and their anti-union advisers were instilling in them. I house-called a young white worker who was one of the beneficiaries of Nissan's questionable hiring practices. He was only a year older than me and had already worked at Nissan for two years, meaning he had been hired at eighteen permanently. He was sharing the house with another Nissan worker, also a maintenance tech.

When I asked about safety, he said he didn't have any concerns. Yeah, they could have put in better sensors, issued thicker gloves. But all businesses cut costs, he said.

"But what about the accidents?" I asked. "A man died on that floor, and there have been so many others."

"Oh yeah, accidents happen. But if I lose my job because we unionize, where else can I go and make what I'm making?"

Nissan workers knew things could be better, but the company's response made them feel that if they unionized, things would get much, much worse. Workers were afraid to join the organizing committee or sign a union card.

In her novel *O Pioneers!*, Willa Cather wrote, "There are only two or three human stories, and they go on repeating themselves as fiercely as if they had never happened before." Her statement certainly applies to anti-union campaigns. Creativity and fighting unions do not go together. Advised by anti-union law firms and consultants, companies had been churning out new iterations of the same leaflets, presentations, and talking points for decades, terrorizing workers from the same playbook.[20]

Had we pressured Nissan into signing the Fair Election Principles before going to a vote, workers would have been able to decide whether to unionize without a barrage of opposition from management. Had they held anti-union meetings, the union would have received equal time to hold its own meetings. If Nissan had violated the principles, they would have faced consequences from the public and their own consumers.

Instead, management ran their anti-union campaign with impunity. They regurgitated the same points over and over: The plant could move to Mexico. Workers could lose their jobs, their pay, benefits, lease cars, ability to become full-time Nissan workers. Nothing was guaranteed in negotiations. The company is not required to agree to any improvements the union may propose in negotiations. It can take years for a union to get a contract. Many never get contracts at all.

Managers rated workers according to their perceived union sympathies or lack thereof and made notes of who they'd seen talking to union organizers at the plant gates or hanging out with committee members. Based on that list, management divided workers into "pods," small group meetings that matched one undecided worker with an HR rep, a supervisor, and an anti-union worker to create a three-on-one dynamic. Union supporters were not allowed to attend meetings other than the ones they were scheduled for, where they were mostly grouped together to prevent them from talking to undecided or anti-union workers. Afterward, management would pull individual workers into additional meetings. One of our committee leaders, Chip Wells, was an Iraq and Afghan war veteran. He told me that these meetings triggered his PTSD.

The day before the union election, the governor of Mississippi, who had been campaigning against the union, posted a photo of a closed and crumbling factory on Facebook. "I hope the employees at Nissan Canton understand what the UAW will do to your factory and town," he wrote. "Just ask Detroit. Vote no on the union."

Nissan did not discourage that behavior, but the anti-union campaign they and their allies waged allowed an environment of fear to spread that led one caller into a radio show to say, just before the vote:

> If they get up there at Nissan, they will force Nissan out of Mississippi. And you Nissan people better listen because, you know, you were out there hoeing corn and picking cotton and plowing fields or digging ditches before, and you're going to go right back to it, because the union is not going to take care of you.[21]

Nor was this the only racist anti-union message in circulation. In the final days before the vote, a flyer began circulating around the plant. Workers pulled out their phones and showed me the image in their Facebook Messenger DMs. "Stop the Cultural Genocide Mississippi," the flyer said. "Yes to This," with images of a Confederate flag and swastikas. "Vote No" to a union at Nissan. The flyer was signed, "Sons of Confederate Veterans and Citizen Councils of Mississippi," evoking the worst of Mississippi's white-supremacist history.

Was Nissan responsible for this flyer? Was their notorious union-busting law firm, Littler Mendelson, which had sent dozens of lawyers dressed in the red polos and gray pants of Nissan workers into the plant to try to prevent unionization, to blame? Workers told me that some of the anti-union messages attempted to divide workers along racial lines, including asking white workers whether they wanted to be part of a majority-Black union.[22]

Some of the workers who got the flyer sent it to Nissan, asking them to disavow it. The company never responded. Whether or not the company and Littler had actually *created* it, they created the climate in which that kind of message proliferated, and, to my knowledge, they never discouraged or spoke out against it.

While leafleting the plant during a shift change with a flyer that showed the locations of all the Nissan factories around the world—noting that the only nonunion ones were in Tennessee and Mississippi—I stood in the middle of a driveway, speaking to people in cars as they were coming and going. Suddenly, a pickup truck appeared, plowing straight down the middle line toward me. I had to run to avoid getting hit. While many drivers reacted positively, including the unionized UPS drivers who honked their solidarity, other leafleters noted hostility.[23]

On July 31, I went out with the sign crew at 4:00 a.m. to put up more UNION YES signs along the roads. Later that morning, as I went out house calling with a coworker, I saw someone removing the signs along the highway exit ramp, as a Mississippi Department of Transportation truck blinked idly nearby. Looking closer, I noticed that the man yanking up our morning's work was wearing striped trousers beneath his neon vest. The state was using prison labor to try to help defeat the union.

Later that day, we went to the highway maintenance department office to try to get our signs back. The last time they had confiscated our signs, they reluctantly returned them. This time, a burly maintenance officer with a Confederate flag tattoo on his forearm said that he had gotten a call from higher-up authorities telling him to keep them for processing, which meant we wouldn't get them until after the vote. As we turned to leave, he told me and my coworker, "Now don't get shot. You know there's a lot of people out there that would like to . . ."

**I REMEMBER THE NIGHT** of the vote count vividly. It was a humid August night. My voice was hoarse from leafleting outside the plant for the past couple days, chanting, singing, waving a UNION YES sign as workers drove past us, going in to work. Richard had gone to the plant: The preelection conference and vote count marked the first time the union had had access to the factory. I was standing outside our office when Richard pulled back into the parking lot afterward. He got out of the car and went inside without saying a word, but the stern lines of his face said it all.

Morris Mock announced the results. "Well, I'd just like to thank everyone who put so much into this campaign. We came up short."

My eyes burned. I knew I wasn't supposed to cry in public, but I couldn't help it.

"But it ain't over! It ain't over! It ain't over! It ain't over!" Morris' voice had the cadence of a Baptist preacher's.

After the vote count, Richard told me later, he drove down to the plant and sat by the side of the road, staring at it. He had done the same thing the night his own first strike had ended, forty years before. He told me that when he finally returned to his hotel, which was down the street from the plant, some of the Littler lawyers, who stayed at the same hotel, were getting out of their party van. They carried bottles of champagne and anti-union yard signs, trophies of their conquest.

The next morning, as I drove back to Oxford, Mississippi, crying and listening to "Here's to the State of Mississippi" on repeat, it certainly seemed over. It was a life-and-death fight, and we had lost. How many more workers were going to die in that plant now that there was no chance for accountability? What did it mean that we had lost what we had called the biggest civil rights fight in Mississippi since the Civil Rights Movement? How much more emboldened would companies be to trample on workers' rights?

**THE SUMMER AFTER THE** Nissan campaign, someone asked me at an organizing training, "How can you organize in Mississippi?"

I didn't say what I was thinking, which was *How can you organize if you can't organize in Mississippi?*

Too many people wrote off our loss at Nissan as inevitable. *What did you expect? Organizing is so much harder in the South. Mississippi doesn't have a history of unions.* This kind of analysis was both counterproductive and ahistorical.

Instead of dismissing Mississippi, we should celebrate and learn from it. Even Phil Ochs missed the point. When he sang, *Here's to the land you've torn out the heart of, Mississippi, find yourself another country to be part of,* he ignored that the rest of the country had a great deal in common with Mississippi—which has become increasingly apparent.

Moreover, we didn't lose Nissan because it was located in the South; in fact, community support for the campaign was overwhelming, despite Nissan's best efforts at co-opting local groups. We lost Nissan due to a failure of the labor movement. Richard had taught me that every campaign needs two key components to win: a strong, representative organizing committee of workers, and a hammer to bring down on the company to pressure it into recognizing the right to organize. At Nissan, we had the committee; all we needed was the hammer. The UAW needed to make the company pay a consequence for what it had done by taking the fight to the dealerships, to reach the public and pressure the company through a boycott. With a union that had been willing to make Nissan pay a consequence for its union busting, we could have won.

Labor history is full of defeats that laid the foundation of future victories. The Knights of Labor's sugarcane organizing that the Klan brutally crushed at Thibodaux would resurface decades later in the Industrial Workers of the World's timber strike: The historian Philip Foner wrote of the "complete and defiant solidarity" lumberjacks showed in refusing to allow their bosses to divide them along racial or ethnic lines. The owners beat and deported the picketers and refused to recognize the union (though they did concede to many of the workers' demands), but the struggle was taken up by future Southern workers: The crushed IWW attempts contributed to the future successes of the Sharecroppers' Union, the Southern Tenant Farmers' Union, and the CIO campaigns across the South.[24]

In much the same way, the lessons of the Nissan campaign would emerge in future organizing campaigns, lending strength and strategy to struggles to come.

## CHAPTER TWO

# The Inside Organizer School

In January 1913, unionized workers with the United Garment Workers—overwhelmingly women, mostly recent immigrants—walked out of sweatshops across Rochester, New York, in an effort to win union recognition and workplace improvements. The strike marked a new era of solidarity among Rochester garment industry workers. Previous unions had either excluded or marginalized women workers, enabling the factory owners to use women as strikebreakers, causing huge gender wage gaps, and allowing for gender-based discrimination and rampant harassment. This time, women led the strike. They organized their own shops, coordinated a unified effort across the industry, and picketed the sweatshops that had not yet gone on strike, calling on the workers inside to walk out. These pickets were remarkably successful, shutting down a dozen additional workplaces across the city in the early weeks of the strike.[1]

On February 5, a group of strikers staged a picket outside a sweatshop owned by Valentine Sauter. Among the picketers was Ida Breiman, a seventeen-year-old worker whose engagement party was scheduled for that night. She had recently immigrated from Ukraine, where she and her family had been targeted by antisemitic pogroms. Ida was working to try to raise money to help the rest of her family immigrate as well. As the strikers called on the sweatshop workers to walk off the job and join their picket line, Sauter emerged, brandishing a gun. He fired into the crowd, killing Ida.

A grand jury failed to indict her murderer. The mayor of Rochester refused her union's application to sell memorial cards to defray her funeral expenses on the grounds that the cards said she had been "shot & killed by an Employer." Instead, the mayor demanded that the cards be revised to say she had "met her death." The union refused to make the edit.[2]

Ida's death galvanized the support not just of the labor movement, but of the community. Suffragettes and other local activists rallied to the cause, outraged by Ida's murder. Due to this public pressure, the United Garment Workers won their strike when the companies agreed to stop retaliating against workers who joined the union. By the mid-1930s, union density in the Rochester garment industry would reach 100 percent.[3]

**MORE THAN A CENTURY** later, in the spring of 2017, baristas at Gimme! Coffee in Ithaca, New York, began organizing. They got in contact with Workers United Upstate New York—a descendant of the United Garment Workers union—and with its dedicated, if multitasking, organizer, Richard Bensinger, whose connection with the union went back to his Head Ski organizing days. This was just before the Nissan vote, and for three months Richard didn't go home, commuting between Canton, Mississippi, and Ithaca, New York, working on both campaigns.

Sitting beside Richard at the shoved-together desks we shared in the Nissan office, I watched the videos he pulled up on his phone: workers giddy with happiness at winning their union election, talking about what organizing meant to them, and discussing what they wanted to propose in their first contract. They had formed the first baristas' union in the country, and the slogan on their local union's banner read SEIZE THE BEANS OF PRODUCTION.

This campaign wasn't just about Gimme!, Richard told me. It was a small coffee chain that capped long-term baristas at poverty wages. They were able to win significant wage increases in their contract, but winning other benefits, including health care, would require a broader plan to increase union density within the industry.

If all of the competing businesses were unionized, it would put an end to nonunion coffee shops undercutting unionized shops economically by paying lower wages and firing or threatening workers who tried to organize to secure better conditions. The industry's business model accounted for low profit margins by keeping labor costs low, paying minimum wage or just cents above it, and providing no benefits. When workers started an organizing campaign at another local coffee shop in Ithaca, the owners retaliated against the union leaders and forced them out. And then there was Starbucks, with its long history of union busting, operating two locations in Ithaca—one downtown and another just steps from the Cornell campus.[4]

We had to organize the whole coffee industry geographically, Richard said. Winning one shop meant committing to a strategy to win them all. Organizing one shop in a town would not provide enough power to restructure an industry built on low pay and thin margins. If we organized baristas across *all* the companies, however, then they could bring *all* the owners to the table and raise conditions across the board.

This was the Industrial Workers of the World's foundational belief. To take on industrial trusts, which consolidated corporate power across industries, workers needed to form industrial unions. Organizing into One Big Union would unite all of the workers into a fighting force. Narrow craft-based unions represented fragments of the working class, and their union contracts required them to continue working when their fellow workers in a different segment of the company went on strike. "Wobblies"—as members of the IWW were known—believed that industrial unionism was the only way to create the conditions for a general strike that would unite workers across companies, and even across industries, against the power of capital.

It was this vision that made the Wobbly-turned-Communist-labor-organizer William Z. Foster, known for his leadership on ambitious union campaigns in the steel and packinghouse industries, write in 1926, "The organization of the unorganized is a life and death question for the labor movement." Unions could not organize *some* workers and then rest on their laurels. If unions didn't commit to organizing everyone, he warned, companies would move production away from unionized workplaces or regions, pit unionized and nonunion workers against one another, and do everything possible to crush the power of existing unions. Moreover, the labor movement itself needed to move beyond its prejudice in favor of "skilled workers" and organize the vast numbers of "semiskilled" and "unskilled" workers, which would change the character of unions themselves, from social organizations designed to protect specific craft interests into a more militant and encompassing movement that could take on corporate power.[5]

In Foster's day, the "unskilled" workers in question were factory workers in industries like steel, meatpacking, electricity, lumber, agricultural machinery, and automobiles. Today—because those workers succeeded in unionizing their sectors—the definitions have shifted. Now, factory workers are more likely to be deemed "skilled," while service workers—baristas, cooks, housekeepers, laundry workers, and cashiers—are often considered "unskilled." These categories are a false and often arbitrary distinction: There is no such thing as unskilled labor. Jobs that are classified as "unskilled" often require as much or more training, craft, and emotional intelligence as many "skilled" positions. Unionization, not skill level, ensures that workers can win higher pay, job security, and respect on the job.

Winning an industrial union in the coffee industry would fundamentally change baristas' and other food service workers' lives, transforming public perception of the industry—and the workers' living conditions—from a so-called starter job that pays poverty wages and provides few or no benefits to a viable career. Knowing that the entire industry was based on a core business model of exploitation, we knew that organizing wouldn't be easy. Winning against companies that would do anything to stop workers from organizing would require a diversity of tactics.

But one tactic towered above the rest: salting.

**"SALTING IS HEROIC AND** righteous work. Anyone is to be commended for it," says Chris Townsend, the former organizing director of the Amalgamated Transit Union (ATU), describing the practice of getting a job at a nonunion workplace with the intention of organizing it.

One-upping legendary IWW organizer Bill Haywood, who famously quipped, "I've never read Marx's *Capital*, but I've got the marks of capital all over my body," Chris has acquired class-consciousness through both channels. He is never far from a volume of William Z. Foster's writings, a dog-eared *Labor's Untold Story*, or a collection of Mother Jones' speeches, and he lives by the slogan "The left wing must do the work." He salted in the 1980s, soon after joining the labor movement, and frequently contemplates doing it again.

"If you share the recognition that we need fundamental political change in this country, one of the only things you can do is challenge the dictatorship in the workplace. How do you organize workers in the absence of salting? Without salting, we're saying as trade unionists that we will stand on the sidelines and wait for the occasional Spartacus or Boadicea to pop up. That's preposterous. The dictatorship needs to be confronted immediately and on the widest scale possible."

No one knows exactly how this practice became known as salting, although there are many theories, ranging from the "salting" of mines by sprinkling gold in them to make them look more valuable to adding salt to water to make it boil faster. Regardless of the etymology, the tactic is unparalleled in its effectiveness.[6]

For decades, business groups like the U.S. Chamber of Commerce have attempted to ban salting. The Supreme Court ruled the practice legal in 1995; since then, Republicans in Congress have introduced multiple versions of legislation to outlaw it. They claim that salts are paid by the unions they work with; that they lack the motivation to be good employees; that their votes are inauthentic and shouldn't count in NLRB elections.

In reality, salts are usually volunteers: activists looking for a pathway to become involved with the labor movement and to learn how to organize; union members who've seen firsthand the difference a union can make and want to help nonunion workers fight for the same rights; people in need of a job seeking to maximize the impact they can have on society. Most salts work long hours at difficult jobs, striving to be excellent employees in the eyes of management and of their coworkers, and then volunteer their time after work to help build the union. They are not the vanguard of the revolution, but a catalyst; not the leaders of the campaign, but the means of identifying, inspiring, and teaching other workplace leaders.

Moreover, the lines between salts and "peppers"—workers who are already working in a shop and eventually become involved with a union effort—are often blurred. Since most people cannot survive without working a job somewhere, the distinction is in many ways moot. A worker who led the organizing campaign at a grocery store told me they decided to unionize during their job interview. Were they a salt or not? Trying to ban salting would essentially subject job applicants to a House Un-American Activities Committee–style questioning: Are you now, or were you ever, an aspiring union organizer?

In 2018, Chris Townsend was still working as the organizing director for the ATU. He was organizing a remarkable number of workplaces, but he was overworked and recovering from a heart attack. His staff needed training, and he decided that Richard would be the perfect person to help provide it. So, Chris arranged for the president of the union, Larry Hanley, to meet with Richard.

At the meeting, Larry asked Richard an open-ended question: "What do you want to do?"

"I want to run a salting school," Richard replied.

"Okay," said Larry.

Initially, Chris was concerned: He needed staff training, not a salting school. But he knew how important salting was to the labor movement, and he decided to create a program that could serve a dual function. Thus, with almost no budget, a revised name, and the sprawling, poorly managed conference-center headquarters of the ATU—formerly the AFL-CIO's National Labor College—for a home, the Inside Organizer School was born.

For several months, Richard had been kicking around the idea for the school on calls with me. We had kept in touch after the Nissan campaign. Many nights, when I was driving from Jackson to Oxford after a long day of volunteering at the Pink House, Mississippi's last abortion clinic, while he was driving from DC to Ithaca for a Gimme! Coffee meeting, we would talk until one of us pulled into our driveway. Mostly, we talked about Nissan. I was still meeting regularly with Morris, Travis, and other organizing committee members, and I would update Richard on what they had told me. We talked about the dealership boycott project. We should have done it before the vote in order to win the right to organize, he told me. But failing that, we needed to do it after the loss, to show companies they couldn't get away with union busting without consequences. He told me about how he hadn't left immediately after the loss, how he had stayed and talked to workers, ministers, and community groups. To his disappointment, the UAW eventually decreed that there would be no dealership campaign after the loss, either.

"I'm either going to become a capitalist or a Wobbly," Richard said to me on one of these calls, discussing his disillusionment with mainstream labor.

"If I have anything to do with it, you'll be a Wobbly," I said.

This proved accurate—Richard's turn Wobbly-ward was heralded by the concept that he shared with me on those calls. In 1989, he had started the Organizing Institute at the AFL-CIO in order to train hundreds of new lead organizers to spearhead union campaigns. Now, he said, what we needed wasn't staff organizers—it was salts. He wanted to start a salting academy that would train both students and activists looking for jobs and ways to make a difference and current nonunion workers hoping to organize their workplaces. This new school could help foster independent unions or even create a new and fundamentally different union. If it succeeded, it could revolutionize the labor movement.

**THE INSIDE ORGANIZER SCHOOL** (IOS), which hosted its first training in June 2018, was founded on a small set of core principles: The need for strong and representative worker committees that could lead unionization campaigns. The ability of workplace organizing campaigns to empower workers and create leaders, as opposed to top-down pressure campaigns without any worker ownership, which created new power structures and disenfranchised workers. The need for leverage—a "hammer"—to bring down on a company to win the right to organize. And the capacity of the labor movement to uphold and unite wide-ranging movements for social justice, because without class liberation no other liberation could truly be possible.

A collective of organizers, the IOS didn't belong to any specific union, instead uniting those who believed in union organizing and class struggle. Its mission was training salts—as well as nonunion workers—to win campaigns at their workplace and then turn around and train their coworkers to become organizers and to mentor succeeding groups of workers. The school's trainers were mainly former or current salts, ready to share the inner workings of the trade.

The curriculum of the school included case studies of organizing campaigns, giving workers and organizers a platform to share their strategies and lessons and inviting the audience to participate in discussions of how to move a campaign or bring down a union buster, and the nuts and bolts of organizing—from sequencing campaigns to getting hired at nonunion companies. It also featured a deep dive into corporate psychology.

"What kind of person do you think companies are looking to hire?" asked an organizer from the union UNITE HERE, who was a key member of the collective. "What kind of politics do you think they want someone to have?"

That was a softball question. Most of the people in the room already understood: Companies want people who believe they can pull themselves up by their own bootstraps, who want to move up within the organization and believe that being an obedient and loyal worker is the best way to get ahead.

"Do you think they want someone who is emotionally a rugged individualist?"

"Yes?" someone ventured.

No, the organizer explained, they most certainly do not. A rugged individualist would be too immune to their boss' praise or censure, too impervious to workplace dynamics. The ideal worker craves management's approval, yearns to be loved by bosses and coworkers alike, and will sacrifice their own well-being to receive that recognition. When companies are deciding whom to hire, the trainer continued, they're looking for codependent libertarians.

He handed out a packet of papers. "Look at this image. What does it make you feel?"

It was a full-page, glossy image of workers in a vending machine. Rows of identical cooks, housekeepers, repairmen, bartenders—each holding a stereotypical tool of their trade.

Underneath the image, the text of the ad read, "You shouldn't have to sacrifice quality for price," touting the staffing agency's ability to supply the hospitality industry with "the right people, at the right price, at the right time."

"This is how they see us."

The organizer paused to let the room reflect.

"This is who they want. They don't want personalities. They want people they can buy from a vending machine."

**THE CONTORTIONS REQUIRED TO** transform oneself into that kind of commodity, while also maintaining the gentleness and strength and empathy necessary to build relationships and trust and camaraderie with coworkers, is one of the greatest challenges of salting.

Just as organizers sequence a union campaign, salts must sequence their evolution within the workplace. No salt should ever dispense out of the vending machine and into the job and then suddenly present themselves as a flaming revolutionary. And yet, despite the necessity of obscuring their radical politics, or past union experience, or secret mission, salts must build trust with coworkers. It's critical to lie as little as possible—ideally, not at all—in order to create a smooth transition from the persona management thought they hired to the person that coworkers will get to know over the course of the campaign.

From creating carefully tailored résumés and cover letters, complete with corroborating references, to scoping out the workplace before applying, salts must prepare before even starting an application. They must then navigate personality tests designed to suss out the desired vending machine candidates—one must "strongly agree" that hierarchies are good, that only the most positive of emotions should influence one's work, that loyalty is the most important quality, and that hard work is the key to personal advancement.

Then, dressed nicely—but not *too* nicely—the salt follows up in person within a day or two of submitting an application. This gives the impression of eagerness—and of needing the job. For salts whose Google search results would reveal their past activism or union involvement, presenting a friendly, smiling, enthusiastic, carefully groomed, and eminently nonthreatening figure can stop management from using search engines. And nothing is more important than smiling!

Some managers will interview a prospective worker on the spot; others will schedule an interview. Often, going into the workplace to ask for the manager will help identify a key leader within the shop, who can put in a good word for the would-be new hire and provide insight into existing relationships and dynamics. You *can* "organize yourself a job," but it can take time, and follow-up is essential, both to get the initial interview and to actually land the job.

Interview answers should paint a picture of an overachieving and loyal worker. It is hard to lay it on too thick, just as it's impossible to smile too much. Praising the business and talking about what a good employee the candidate will be are critical. At the Inside Organizer School, we practiced possible interview questions.

- "What do you think of employees that gripe, gripe, gripe?"
  —*If they don't like their jobs, they should leave rather than dragging everyone else down with them.*
- "How important is seniority in getting a promotion?"
  —*Not important—the best worker should be the one who gets the job.*
- "Do you have problems with authority?"
  —*None whatsoever!*
- "If you know that one of your coworkers has stolen a candy bar from a hotel, do you think they should be fired?"
  —*Absolutely, if they would steal a candy bar, they'll steal anything.*

Once hired, salting becomes an exercise in being a quick study. The first concern is to become a good worker in the eyes of management. Learning the job is critical and enables one to graduate to becoming a good coworker capable of picking up the slack for others and building relationships.

These were lessons UNITE HERE activist Josh Armstead and his former coworker shared as they told the story of the Georgetown campaign, which successfully unionized the university's Aramark food service workers. Josh's fellow organizer, who had come to the labor movement through a profound sense of social justice anchored in his Catholic faith, was a salt. He talked about his first days on the job at a Georgetown café, including a harrowing moment when retaliation from a manager forced him to run up a steep flight of stairs with a trash can on his back in order to do his job without burdening coworkers. Josh, who had grown up watching his family struggle before organizing his own workplace and becoming a self-educated communist and unparalleled organizer, had been a pepper (i.e., not a salt) at the time. Josh described going on to salt another workplace, and then to lead teams of salts on subsequent campaigns.

**THE IOS WAS AS** much a retreat as it was a training. Each session took three days, and many of the participants stayed on-site, in the hotel attached to the conference center. The attendees ranged from lifelong organizers to college students; from Lush cosmetics workers to Canada Goose seamstresses to Target workers to Uber drivers. For the workers and potential salts who came, it was a break from the monotony of their jobs or an introduction to a new way of living; for the staff, it was a reminder of why the work mattered and a respite from the politics of navigating union bureaucracies. In between sessions—at mealtimes and late into the night—the participants gathered around cafeteria trays or drinks to talk strategy and labor history and get to know one another. Arguments ranged from the best way to pressure a company to sign on to the Fair Election Principles, to whether All Cops Are Bastards applied to the pro-union police chief, Sidney Hatfield, from the movie *Matewan*. Trainers shared their paths into the labor movement: The UNITE HERE organizer who had led the workshop on getting hired spoke eloquently about the moment he had realized the crimes—including murder—that companies were committing against unionizing workers elsewhere around the world and understood that companies would always behave as brutally as they calculated they could get away with, including against his coworkers and himself.

The first night of the training, I was nursing a double shot of Jameson in the basement bar when Gary Bonadonna Jr., the leader of Workers United Upstate New York, who had helped Richard put his coffee shop industrial union project into motion, came over to say hello. We ended up playing shuffleboard until one in the morning, talking about everything from coffee shop organizing and Nissan to literature and poetry.

From Richard's stories, I had gotten a notion of industrial unionism in upstate New York that made it sound like some kind of union paradise, where baristas would organize unions at all of their shops and then go out on a general strike that might not take down capitalism effective immediately, but would certainly send shock waves into the heart of the beast.

"What you're doing up there sounds like what the Wobblies wanted to do, but with teeth," I said to Gary.

"Good call," said Gary. "I like that."

Gary told me about how he had played football in high school but written love poems on buses back from games. He was an amateur pugilist and was delighted whenever someone suggested that he could win a fight against a union buster or CEO. His favorite writer was Kurt Vonnegut, but after a long discussion we had about Antonio Gramsci, he ordered a volume of his collected works and kept it on his bedside table. Most important, Gary recognized the genius and talent of Richard and gave him free rein to organize.

I spent the rest of the summer working with Richard on coordinating additional sessions of the Inside Organizer School and with Gary on developing a salting program for his region of the union and recruiting new salts. One of the attendees at the first IOS session was a Maryland native and long-term service industry worker named Cory Johnson. Cory had seen an ad that Richard posted on the forum of the local Democratic Socialists of America to recruit participants for the school and reached out. The two had met for coffee and talked for hours about salting, the labor movement, and the need to organize the coffee and restaurant industry. Cory also met Gary at the school and agreed to move to upstate New York to help with the organizing project underway. The first time Cory and I visited Rochester, the two of us drove up together, spending a couple days meeting with Gary and the union reps, exploring the city, and going to a tiny amusement park.

Thoughtful and enthusiastic, Cory was passionate about union organizing as a path to building a better world. He moved to Rochester and began working at a nonunion event center with a large but mostly seasonal workforce. To make ends meet, he got a second job at a local coffee shop chain, Spot Coffee, with a location down the street from his apartment.

In the meantime, I had gone back to Mississippi to finish my final year of college. My crew of advisers and fellow activists encouraged me to apply for a Rhodes Scholarship. I was concerned that the scholarship—founded by a colonizer and white supremacist—was antithetical to my radical values, but others convinced me that having that credential might be helpful to the movement. To our collective surprise, I won, which meant I would leave for the United Kingdom in September of 2019. But I was eager to get back to union organizing, and the summer after I graduated from the University of Mississippi, I joined Richard on a series of campaigns he was working with. I spent the next three months bouncing from picket line to picket line, attending committee meetings, talking to workers one-on-one, and attaining a deeper understanding of organizing.

The café Cory was working in was a hot shop, where workers were eager to unionize. He told me about a higher-up's proclivities for sexual harassment and stealing workers' tips; organizing provided the workers with a way to fight back. Cory and his coworkers quickly formed an organizing committee and took the company by surprise. In Rochester, Spot didn't fight the union hard. The company held a voluntary anti-union meeting that only one worker—Cory—attended, but did little else to attempt to dissuade the workers, who won their union election by a comfortable margin.[7]

Then, two Spot workers in Buffalo, Phil Kneitinger and Phoenix Cerny, reached out to Cory. "We've been talking about unionizing for years, and then Rochester beat us to it!" they said.

**CORY AND I DROVE** out to Buffalo for the first meeting. Phil and Phoenix shared an apartment and a passion for radical politics, particularly unionization. There was a Facebook group for Spot Coffee baristas from across the café chain. Phil told us about seeing the news article about Rochester organizing and deciding to message Cory.

"It was like, 'Holy shit, this is actually happening,'" Phil said.

Rochester had lit a spark. Workers in Buffalo realized, "If they can do it, we can do it."

Phil and Phoenix had pulled in four other workers from across the Spot Coffee Buffalo cafés in that living room: Kay Kennedy, Zach Anderson, Dave Mangan, and Lukas Weinstein. Cory had driven in from Rochester to join the meeting. He was exuberant to see the movement he had helped launch taking off.

The committee was small but impressive. Kay was a college student whose dream was to become a union organizer. Phil was a burly and passionate activist with a strong sense of justice. Phoenix was a longtime barista and committed leftist who possessed a vast knowledge of coffee and of the industry. Dave was easygoing and warmhearted, with a deep love of cats and the Ramones. Zach was remarkably earnest, with an innate desire to help others. And Lukas—an incredibly empathetic person with a love of poker, MMA, and his three (feline) sons—was also one of the world's most pro-union managers. We warned him that managers didn't have the same protections under federal labor law that other workers did, but he was eager to help in any ways that he could.

We left the meeting without definitive next steps. The workers would think about it and get back to us: They wanted time to make sure that they were ready to unionize, and to think over whether this was the right union.

Then, the firings started.

Lukas was first. We found out over email: He had been interrogated about who had been at the meeting and had refused to name names, knowing corporate would fire him instead.

Then, a few days later, Richard was on a phone call with Phoenix and Phil when they both got simultaneous texts from their managers, asking to speak with them.

"I bet I know what that's about," said Richard. "Turn your recorders on."

Union busting is often unsophisticated, but rarely does it reach Spot Coffee levels of incompetence.

Phoenix's store manager was on vacation, so the assistant store manager was forced to make the call. "I'm calling with bad news, unfortunately. I feel terrible, but Dan called me this morning and asked me to let you go immediately. I— Obviously, this is not what I want to do, and it's not coming from myself or [the store manager] at all, but I guess he's heard enough of the chatter of the union stuff going round and that's where it comes down to," she faltered.

Listening to the tape afterward, Richard chuckled. "Well, they're gonna get their job back."

Firing workers for unionizing is illegal, but U.S. labor law lacks consequences that might deter companies seeking to terrorize workers out of organizing from firing union leaders first and reinstating them later. In fact, companies have an incentive to make sure they fire quickly, before the union has a chance to build a majority. If a majority of workers have signed union cards before a company fires workers and chills the union campaign, the Labor Board can order the company to bargain with the union. But if the firings happen so quickly after the company learns about the union campaign that workers haven't had time to sign up their coworkers on cards, the Labor Board will not order the company to bargain with the union, even though the chilling effect can be even greater at that early stage.

We rushed to Buffalo to attend an emergency meeting at Phil and Phoenix's house. Many more Spot workers came this time, filling the room. Folks from the local labor community were there, too, pledging their support to whatever the workers decided to do to hold Spot accountable. The local labor federation even offered us the help of their intern, a fiercely dedicated, hilariously funny, and incredibly empathetic student named Yana Kalmyka, who became my constant companion during the campaign.

In the face of the firings, the workers signed the hastily scrawled-out committee sheet and signed their union cards, cheering one another on. It was an incredibly powerful show of solidarity and community defying the fear and division management had tried to sow. Then, the committee began planning an informational picket for the next day. It would be outside the Williamsville store, the location Lukas had managed. We stayed up late that night, sprawled out on the floor making signs and eating pizza.

I cleared my schedule to stay in Buffalo and help coordinate the picketing, since Richard had to fly to Martha's Vineyard for his mother-in-law's memorial service. I did not know that by staying in Buffalo I was becoming the lead organizer for the Spot campaign. When Richard informed me of this a couple weeks later, I protested vigorously, feeling I was not qualified to take on the responsibility of the campaign, particularly given the obligation to ensure we got the fired workers their jobs back.

How could we make sure we had these workers' backs? The NLRB process takes forever—if a company goes to trial and then appeals the case, reinstatement of fired workers can take years. By the time the workers win their case, they have often moved on to other jobs or industries. Additionally, Labor Board back pay settlements subtract any interim earnings, meaning companies often don't even have to financially compensate the workers.

Had the Spot workers relied only on filing charges with the Labor Board, the campaign would almost certainly have stagnated, eventually winning reinstatement for the baristas but failing to win a union, leaving the industry and the power dynamics within the company unchanged. Instead, Spot workers went on the offensive, demanding that the community hold the company accountable. We hoped that public pressure would force Spot to reinstate the fired workers and promise to end its retaliation against union organizers.

The picketing was successful from the start. The workers' organizing committee set up a consistent schedule to leaflet stores, and the Buffalo community responded with overwhelming solidarity and support. In fact, they almost responded with *too* much enthusiasm. State senator Tim Kennedy went out on his own in calling for a boycott of Spot Coffee, going beyond the workers' ask. But that call reverberated in positive ways: Even without a consistently enforced picket line, the Buffalo community bought their coffee elsewhere. Spot's profits plummeted, though the workers raised money at informational pickets to take "tip collections" inside to the baristas who were still working, to subsidize their lost income. We raised over $400 at a huge demonstration on July 4. Significantly, this boycott did not involve a strike: By staying on the job, workers managed to retain support for the union among less stalwart coworkers while bleeding Spot's revenue through payroll as well as lost sales.[8]

---

**CONVENTIONAL WISDOM MAINTAINS THAT** you can't hold a union election while boycotting a company. Undecided workers, the thinking goes, won't respond well to the stridency and attacks on the company that a boycott involves. Moreover, at Spot, many workers had seen their coworkers lose their jobs and were terrified of being fired if they got involved with the organizing effort.

A worker at the Transit Road location, where we didn't have a committee, told me that their manager had threatened to fire whoever had shared a list of workers with the union, and another worker there said she didn't think she was allowed to speak with me. At the Hertel store, nearly everyone had been supportive of the union prior to Phil's firing. Afterward, the fear was so great that many workers not only refused to sign cards, but also isolated Kay and Zach, the remaining union supporters. For them, going in to work every day became draining: They were forced to do their jobs with a target on their back and facing hostility from some coworkers. Burned-out by this treatment, Zach met with Yana and me to discuss taking a step back or even quitting Spot. Over a two-hour conversation, he not only talked himself out of quitting, but into remaining a leader in the union effort in order to make the company better for everyone in the long run.

The fear made it hard to build support in the stores where we barely had contacts, including the Delaware and Chippewa location. One worker there, Matt, agreed to meet me underground. Literally.

When I arrived at the dim and appropriately named Underground Niteclub, he was standing on the sidewalk smoking a cigarette.

"I'm who you're looking for," he told me, "but I don't think I should be seen talking to you. Too many people from corporate around."

A couple days after we met, he texted me a photo of the phone list in his workplace, giving me a better idea of how many people worked there and how to contact them. He went over the list, telling who would likely be open to the topic of unionizing, who was more hesitant, who had left, and who had been hired.

Over the next month, he became increasingly open about his support for the cause, even agreeing to house-call coworkers before the vote. After we won the union, he became his store's first steward.

In the meantime, the informational picketing and community-declared boycott were having a remarkable effect. The workers went out in all conditions, handing out flyers and talking to regulars. We held a mass rally downtown, showing the strength of our community support.

When Williamsville workers were called into a captive-audience meeting with corporate, they coordinated to wear their union shirts and ask pro-union questions. Workers from other locations protested outside, chanting, playing music, and waving a giant poster of Lukas, captioned WORKING CLASS HERO in giant letters. When corporate tried to hold a similar meeting at the Elmwood café, workers were so defiant that management slunk out halfway through.

It was becoming clear that Spot management's morale was dipping and that the boycott was working.

**MEANWHILE, WORKERS AT SPOT** Rochester had started bargaining with the company.

We had decided to present the Fair Election Principles—the same ones Nissan had refused to sign—as contract demands. We were confronted with another key strategy decision: whether to bring up the Buffalo firings in Rochester's bargaining session. If we did, it could derail progress toward a contract and create further hostility. On the other hand, we asked, did we have an ethical obligation to bring up the firings? Where was the line between unnecessarily agitating the company and standing in solidarity with other Spot workers? Wasn't this an audience with management that gave workers the rare ability to challenge the company's anti-union war just an hour down the road in Buffalo?

R. J. Stapell, one of the directors of the company and their primary negotiator, didn't think so. "Let's keep this about Rochester, please," he said.

But it was the same fight. I decided to talk about why the topics discussed in bargaining could not, in fact, be confined to Rochester, when workers in Buffalo were getting fired for trying to exercise the same right to organize a union that Rochester workers had already won.

RJ segued into talking about "putting potential prejudice aside."

He said, "I do not believe, fundamentally, that you're bad people, or that you represent a threat to our business, that you are anti-capitalism, or that you're all the bad things that people call unions. And therefore, I resent when I am characterized the same way."

(I showed great restraint in not commenting on the anti-capitalism part of his remarks.)

While much of what he said was dismissive—his response to my comments about the fired workers didn't stop at "let the NLRB decide," but also included patronizing praise for the "passion" of my letter responding to his—he was right about one thing. I did consider all capitalists the same, part of the system that oppressed workers.

Subsequent experience would teach me that, while all management representatives operated within the same system, they were not all identical. RJ was, in fact, interested in reversing Spot Coffee's union busting in Buffalo and engaging in a working relationship with the union. He told us that he might not agree with us about the need for a union, but that he supported our right to organize. He even claimed—and genuinely believed—that he had defended that right during his time as a helicopter pilot in Vietnam, since it was part of his greater mission to defend democracy. Despite the historical inaccuracy of his worldview, RJ proved key to winning a union at Spot. He was not ideologically anti-union, unlike some bosses who hate unions even more than they like money. When Spot management caved to the financial pressure of the boycott and signed the Fair Election Principles, it was partly because RJ told his fellow corporate directors to do it. In this, RJ was very different from executives like Starbucks' Howard Schultz. Having RJ at the Starbucks bargaining table might have spared workers years of scorched-earth union busting.

**AS THE SUMMER WENT** on, it became clear that many of our strongest committee members had expiration dates. Jen would be going to nursing school. Chris was getting a promotion into management. Danielle would be leaving. By late September, I, too, would have to leave for England and the Rhodes Scholarship. Finally, one night, Richard and I crunched the numbers. He had been focused on the boycott and winning the right to organize; I was laser-focused on the charts from each store.

In my mind, it was clear that we had to go to a vote. But, even operating on the premise that the bargaining unit was what we said it was—a premise backed not by labor law but by the increasingly defeated stance of the company—our margins were uncomfortably narrow. If we went for the stores where we had committee members—Williamsville, Hertel, Elmwood, and Delaware—I predicted a 39–27 vote in favor of the union. We only had 53 percent on card. But that number couldn't be swayed, I argued. Richard and I agreed that if we waited, we would lose any chance of winning once our supporters quit.

We decided to take the risk. The shop wasn't getting any hotter, and the effective boycott meant Spot was wavering. A few days later, realizing they were beat, Spot signed the Fair Election Principles, dropped their anti-union campaign, and made no effort to turn out "no" votes in the election. As a result, Spot workers won their union, 43–6. Unlike Nissan, Spot hadn't spent the last two weeks before the vote threatening workers about unionizing. Had they done so, we might well have lost.

The Spot campaign illustrates why winning the right to organize is the most critical element of any union campaign. With this right, all others follow: The power dynamic fundamentally changes. A campaign based around any other issue—like health and safety demands or higher pay—may be righteous, but is inherently limited: Once the bosses, however reluctantly, grant that single improvement, the campaign on the issue is won—but the broader fight to win the union fizzles, having failed to create a lasting shift in the power dynamic of the workplace.

Of course, unions can take action around specific issues or agitate around key demands to help *win* the critical but nebulous right to organize. But relying on the magnanimity of the bosses to grant key demands only leads to their giving with one hand and taking with the other, or—at best—to paternalism. For example, many companies will grant wage increases but then up productivity expectations or lower company contributions to health care. This is why the right to organize is the most fundamental demand: It gives workers the ability to win true workplace democracy and negotiate for their demands. The primary role of a union in an organizing campaign should be to hold the company accountable by wielding the pressure necessary to ensure it is safe and fair for workers to organize.

Once the Spot workers won the right to organize, they were able to win on many other key issues in negotiations. Phoenix gave an impassioned speech at the bargaining table when the company proposed giving small wage increases until it saw how it was recovering from the boycott. Instead, Phoenix argued, the contract should provide large wage increases and the union would promote Spot accordingly, as a company truly committed to social justice.

"Don't balance your budget on the backs of the workers," they said.

Convinced, Spot management ultimately gave the workers their initial wage proposal, signing a contract that increased wages by an average of $4 per hour upon signing, with some senior workers winning raises of $6 and $7 an hour.

The campaign also underscored the significant limitations of the NLRB. We submitted the recordings of management telling Phil and Phoenix they were being fired because of the union campaign, which was indisputable evidence. The NLRB issued merit determinations on Phil's and Phoenix's cases, and Spot agreed to settle with reinstatement and back pay. But Lukas' case was different. Under the NLRB, managers have no rights. Their only hope of protection is if they were fired for refusing to do something illegal. With Lukas, this was clearly the case. He had refused to give the names because he knew that would be ensuring the workers would be fired—a heroic act that should have been legally protected.

But the Labor Board disagreed. Lukas never got his job back, despite Richard's bringing it up for years afterward in meetings with management. To this day, Lukas remains a staunch union supporter, whose loyalty to his coworkers and the labor movement won the union at Spot and launched a revolution in the coffee industry.

**IN SEPTEMBER OF 2019,** just before I was supposed to leave for the Rhodes Scholarship, Gary Bonadonna offered me a full-time job as organizing director. I wanted to accept immediately, even when he promised to hold the position open for me until I returned. I had found the work I wanted to be doing and the union that would support ambitious organizing projects. What did the University of Oxford have to offer compared with that?

All of the people who had helped me win the scholarship pushed me to go. Eunice Benton, a wise, caring, and generous matriarch of the progressive community in Oxford, Mississippi, who had become my chosen mother, drove me to the airport and saw to it that I boarded the plane.

When I got to Oxford, England, I found that many of my fears were warranted. It was an extremely elite place: Many of my classmates were conservative not because they had been taught to punch down at the less fortunate, but because right-wing politics aligned with their own class interest. Consulting groups like McKinsey had full access to Rhodes House, holding recruitment meetings and promising big salaries. My history course emphasized "objectivity" and abstraction from real-world events and values.

Unmotivated by my coursework, suffering from seasonal affective disorder, and consumed by the feeling that I needed to be back in the movement and should never have left Buffalo, I came close to dropping out of Oxford. I started skimming reading assignments and writing papers based on what I wanted to read rather than what would fulfill the expectations of an academic system whose priorities were, I believed, misguided. Instead, I joined practically every reading group that existed: ones focused on feminism, critical theory, poetry, Marx's *Capital*, and revolutionary literature. I got involved with groups like Rhodes Scholars for Palestine, protesting the propaganda trips that took Rhodes Scholars to Israel to legitimize the occupation, and with community groups including the Boycott Israel Network. I attended their retreat, at a rented-out hostel in Ironbridge, where we made communal meals, strategized about ways to reach consumers, and hung out late at night talking about everything from anarchist practice to historic socialist labor songs. I made plans to go to Palestine the following spring with International Solidarity Movement.

I also found a small group of comrades who were similarly disaffected with the university's culture and determined to create a community there. Shruti Iyer, the only other labor activist in our Rhodes class, became my best friend. Her work focused on stonecutters and miners who contracted a lung disease called silicosis on the job, and what obtaining compensation for their illness revealed about the balance of power between the state, capital, and labor. Shruti was a brilliant natural educator who explained concepts like the Hegelian dialectic in ways that I finally comprehended. She was also a warm, hilarious, fun person to be around. She bought an Ottolenghi cookbook and sent me on quests to procure obscure ingredients for recipes she wanted to make. We made paella together and listened to a box of records featuring tracks like "The Witch Queen of New Orleans," while making plans for Shruti to visit me in Mississippi. When I realized that leaving early would impact her support system as well, I decided to stick it out for the rest of the year.

Over winter break, I worked on union campaigns in Canada and upstate New York, including helping workers unionize a small coffee chain in Buffalo. The committee was an impressive group: Mainly trans and nonbinary, they spoke of how the owner, a Florida millionaire, marketed the company based on their identities while consistently misgendering and disrespecting them behind the scenes. They talked for hours about the issues they faced, ranging from poverty wages and inconsistent pay to safety issues to short-staffing to management disrespect.

I watched the faces of the committee members as we talked about what they could do to change the situation, as they looked at one another and realized their collective power. There was Ember, enthusiastic and driven, with a commitment to leftist organizing. There was Sid, a Mississippi transplant like myself, with a litany of horror stories from their experiences working in restaurants that translated into a fierce desire to transform the industry. There was Frankie, fierce and thoughtful, Taylor, eloquent and outraged, and Courtney, funny and motivated. And there was Al Celli. They were a recent art school graduate who had worked in some of the museums around Buffalo, encountering the strange and exploitative labor practices of that sector, and spent the meeting making impressive doodles as they listened to others and shared their own experiences at the coffee shop. They were soft-spoken but unusually piercing, offering an incisive critique of both the individual experience of working at the company and of the broader norms of the industry. Their outfit was imposing and artistic, punctuated by a pair of exquisite and unusual earrings, their trademark accessory.

The committee got a majority of their coworkers on board quickly, but I was back in the United Kingdom by the time they launched their campaign. Richard called me with updates: They were encountering tremendous resistance from the owner and management, who made the workers' lives increasingly difficult. He asked if we should immediately boycott the company, demanding they sign the Fair Election Principles. Should we even go to an election if the company hadn't signed? We did go to an election, but even a decisive victory didn't stop the union busting; only pressure on the company could do that. Meanwhile, the coffee shop was pushing people out, including Al, who applied to Spot Delaware to work in a unionized environment instead. When the pandemic hit, the company laid off the unionized workers but continued to operate with a skeleton crew of managers, serving catering orders to the National Guard during the 2020 Black Lives Matter protests. Finally, the owner sold the business in a secretive deal; the successor company blacklisted the former workers who applied. This campaign illustrated the urgency and necessity of winning the right to organize early on; without it, arrogant companies would stop at nothing to try to crush the unions.

I also met with another barista, the former partner of one of the Spot Coffee organizing-committee members. Benny was working at the University at Buffalo Starbucks, one of the few corporate stores on a college campus. Benny wanted to organize their store for several reasons, but largely because they disagreed with the company's Coffee with a Cop initiative designed to "change perceptions of police." They were uncomfortable about serving cops, but any criticism of the policy could lead to termination. They had already talked to a couple of coworkers and began quietly reaching out to a few more about joining an organizing committee.[9]

Then, in January, just after I had returned to Oxford, Benny picked up a shift at another store. When an aggressive customer harassed them and their coworkers, Benny turned to one of their fellow baristas and asked, "Do you always have to deal with assholes?"

Management fired Benny, supposedly for cursing on the floor. In reality, Starbucks baristas cursed on the floor all the time without any repercussions at all. Management had to have found out about Benny's union activism. It would have been impossible to convince the Trump

Labor Board that the company knew about Benny's union activism, but we began making plans to launch a boycott of Starbucks and demand that they sign the Fair Election Principles. Richard got a *New York Times* journalist to agree to cover the story. Bernie Sanders planned to announce the boycott when he came to Buffalo to campaign in the New York presidential primary. I booked a plane ticket to return for the picketing and an Inside Organizer School we planned to coincide with the launch. Then, in early March, the journalist warned that the story might get cut because all of the media coverage was turning to a different topic: the coronavirus.

Everything was canceled: the Inside Organizer School, the picketing, the story, the New York primary, and, with it, Bernie's boycott announcement, and my upcoming trip to Palestine, which was supposed to happen later that month. Like most restaurants, Spot Coffee closed; I joined the bargaining sessions over the effects of the closure by Zoom at 2:00 a.m. UK time. Richard went into quarantine, and I debated whether to return to the United States, ultimately deciding that the risk of exposing Eunice Benton to Covid was too great.

The pandemic did grant me an extension on my thesis, and lockdown provided plenty of uninterrupted time to read. One of the key texts I used in my dissertation was Ralph Chaplin's autobiography, *Wobbly*. In it, the labor cartoonist and "Solidarity Forever" songwriter talked about his path to labor, his participation in union struggles and politics, the state crackdown on syndicalism, and his retrospective musings about what the successes of the movement had been. He wrote, within a discussion of messaging strategy, that in 1917 the Industrial Workers of the World had adopted the slogan "Get on the Job and Organize." I decided to make this my own personal mantra.[10]

The other book that absorbed my attention was Émile Zola's novel *Germinal*, about a French coal miners' strike. It was not the most uplifting read. Ultimately, the strike is crushed and many of the characters end up dead in a flooded coal mine. This made me cry. A lot. (I blame the pandemic.) And yet, at the end of the novel, hope emerges from the ruins—literally. The protagonist, Étienne, is rescued from the destroyed mine and heads off toward Paris, where, the book and its historical context imply, he would subsequently end up in the Paris Commune.

The last sentence of the book reads, "Men were springing forth, a black avenging army, germinating slowly in the furrows, growing towards the harvests of the next century, and this germination would soon overturn the earth." The word *germinal* was also the name of the first month of spring in the French Revolutionary calendar—the month, coincidentally, in which the Paris Communards found themselves when they revived the use of the calendar during their beautiful, if short-lived, revolution. I became obsessed with the word's lasting power: It had been a labor activist's last word before his execution by the Spanish government, which in turn inspired labor poetry and art.[11]

I graduated from Oxford in August of 2020 and returned to Buffalo a few months later, as the new Organizing Director for Workers United in Upstate New York and Vermont. The pandemic was raging, and a large percentage of our members were laid off.

I began thinking about applying to Starbucks. After seeing what had happened to Benny, I was more convinced than ever that Starbucks workers needed a union, and I wanted to work in the same industry I was organizing. On the other hand, getting hired would require open availability and reduce my ability to work on other campaigns. At the moment, however, there were no other campaigns—or even leads—and the pandemic made it even harder to meet or talk to workers without being proximate, within the workplace.

"What do you think I should do?" I asked Shruti.

"I think you should salt," she said. "You've always talked about wanting to do it, and you'll never have another chance like this, when you can actually do it without having to worry about too many other campaigns. It would be the most interesting and educational thing you could do, too, just on a personal level and as an organizer."

With that in mind, I decided to get on the job and organize.

# CHAPTER THREE

# Project Germinal

It was pumpkin spice season at Starbucks. The leaves had fallen across Buffalo and a chill was in the air.

After extensive Reddit searches and consultations with barista friends, I had determined that 10:00 a.m. was an ideal time to follow up on my application. I carried a manila envelope containing my curated résumé and cringy cover letter, which professed my excitement to "learn more about the work, expertise and care that goes into the crafting of every drink and to build relationships with customers and coworkers." I had practiced the art of doing what every job applicant does: telling my prospective employers exactly what they wanted to hear. With that in mind, I swung open the glass door of the Elmwood Avenue Starbucks and switched on the highest-pitched, best customer-service voice I could muster.

"Hi there, Jazzy Jaz!" said JP, the nine-year shift supervisor who had learned my name the first time I went in to inquire about a job and who made sure to comp my cold brew each time I came back.

"Is Patty in today?" I asked, making sure to smile behind my mask.

As JP went to get her from the back, I watched the baristas bobbing behind the bar. The hiss of steam from the espresso machines mingled with the sound of their voices calling out drinks and the sputter of a spent nitro keg. Their motions were smooth and constant: The espresso machines were never idle.

I could feel my heart rate climbing. *Is it even possible that Starbucks would hire me?* I wondered. One Google search and I would be found out as a union organizer, my cover blown.

I rehearsed my carefully crafted narrative. Before even submitting the online application, I had scrubbed my social media and set all platforms to private. I had pried the rusty SOLIDARITY, Y'ALL! tag from my car and crafted a narrative that hid my prior union work without lying outright.

Patty emerged from the back, an energetic figure wearing a green apron. "Hi, Jaz!"

Due to Covid, the café furniture was stacked by the front windows. Patty gestured for me to pull down a chair, and we sat down at one of the unused tables, where she began looking over my cover letter and résumé.

"Rhodes Scholar, that's nice." Then, looking down my cover letter, she murmured with approval, "'People-facing position,' I like that."

She told me that she had just hired a few other people and wouldn't be able to start me for a few weeks, and that she would call me in a few days to follow up.

She didn't.

I began thinking that Starbucks had found out I was a union organizer and that Patty was ghosting me accordingly.

"Keep following up," Josh Armstead told me. "Keep playing the role. They're not that bright, they don't know."

It took two months for me to actually start work—two months of constant second-guessing. I don't think I would have gotten hired without Josh as my salting coach. He had helped prep my résumé and cover letter, sharing examples of his and giving advice (including reminding me that it was pretty much impossible to be too enthusiastic about the company when I began questioning whether my exuberance had been a giveaway).

Josh believed I would get hired and made me believe it, too. Gary and Richard had their doubts. Would they google me? Was my lack of barista experience an issue? (It wasn't—Starbucks likes hiring people they can train their own way.) Why did Patty keep disappearing? Was this really a good use of time, or was there other organizing work I could be doing that would be more productive?

After each visit to the store or meeting with Patty, I would call Josh to debrief what had happened. He helped guide my next steps: how soon to go back for another coffee, when it was appropriate to follow up by phone, how to get an email address. He was always encouraging, always supportive, always providing reminders of management incompetence (hadn't they hired him, a union vice president, into what should have been a highly guarded food service target?) and, more important, of the mission and reason for salting.

Finally, while I was on a Zoom call with Richard—still deep in Covid quarantine—and Gary, discussing other organizing matters, I got a phone call from Patty: Starbucks was offering me the job. Even then, it was still weeks before I clocked in for the first time: Red Cup Day, Thanksgiving, administrative snafus, and other trainees kept pushing back my start day. Finally, on December 14, I went in for my First Sip.

Over Christmas blonde roast and lemon loaf, Patty told me about Starbucks' benefits and social responsibility practices, then sent me to the back room with the iPad to start my computer training. My favorite training video urged *partners*—Starbucks' term for workers—to "become one with the flow of espresso into the cup."

The next day, a coworker named Cassie Fleischer took over my training.

Cassie was perhaps the kindest person to ever work at a Starbucks. She was serious and thoughtful, with big blue eyes, wispy blond hair that she often dyed brighter shades, and a love of sunflowers that was evident from the tattoos on her arm. Thorough and by the book, she was incredibly caring and ensured things were done to standard without making anyone feel bad. She made perfect microfoam and artistic Frappuccinos and ensured that the iced tea backups always steeped for exactly five minutes.

I set about training with as much enthusiasm as I could muster. Steaming milk was fun. Sampling "dead" espresso shots to understand the importance of speed (which actually revealed the poor quality of our coffee, since high-quality espresso doesn't die) was less pleasant. Learning the customer support (CS) job rotations—ice, milks, sleeves, beans; rotating through cycle tasks of dishes, cold brew, backup making, bathroom cleaning, spot sweeping, front door cleaning—only to be summoned when the coffee brewer was empty: "We're out of Pike!"—was intense, but I tried not to let on. I was determined to be endlessly cheerful and eager to learn.

Right after I was trained, Cassie began training a new "green bean," the Starbucks term for a new hire, who hadn't reached the increasingly darker roasts that Cassie wryly told me she had attained. While I was washing dishes, Cassie came in the back without her green bean, looking slightly exhausted.

"How's it going?" I whispered.

"She keeps saying how overwhelming CS is. And I get it—but it's not going like it did with you."

At the end of my training, Cassie gave me a hand-decorated, Cricut-emblazoned tumbler with my name on it and a beautiful note about how training me had helped her to see the things she loved about the company again after the burnout of working through the pandemic. It was an incredibly thoughtful and kind gift. I teared up as I read the note, which Cassie made me open in front of her. Everything about Cassie was genuine, and she was letting me in on her life outside work as well.

I wished I could be open with Cassie about the fact that the second job I casually mentioned was actually with the union and about my hope of organizing our workplace. Even though I was afraid management would discover my background and I knew I couldn't risk talking about unionizing that early in my time at the company, I felt twinges of guilt about hiding key details. I knew secrecy was essential: Benny's firing had shown me how Starbucks responded to union organizing activity. Still, I wanted to be able to be as genuine with Cassie as she was with me.

**BEING "FULLY TRAINED" AT** Starbucks is a misnomer. None of our new hires at Elmwood, myself included, were ever given our certification tests, which were supposed to measure our ability to steam milk, sequence, and perform other tasks to standard. To compensate for the company's lack of training, I borrowed the deck of recipe cards and took them home with me, spending a few evenings memorizing and practicing remembering the correct build of each drink and the ratio of espresso shots and syrup pumps to cup sizes.

At work, I learned that different baristas had wildly different expectations and styles, and I learned to accommodate as best I could. Some were possessive of the sticker printer above their machine, while others appreciated their coworker grabbing stickers and helping out. One coworker was adamant that steamed chais tasted better with less water and more milk; I learned to make the drinks differently if I was working alongside them. One shift supervisor, concerned about my milk-steaming technique, got the glass from the back that was labeled with the lines to which foam should go for a latte versus a cappuccino and had me practice. I came in on my days off or came back after a shift to help cover for a coworker who'd called off from work. I was often frazzled—particularly when I was put in the more challenging positions that required juggling tasks and anticipating needs during peak—but tried not to let on, except by apologizing excessively. Coworkers attempted to break me of that habit, even joking about deducting a dollar per "sorry" from my tips, but to no avail. It became a running joke.

Meanwhile, Cory left Spot Coffee and applied to a Starbucks in a Buffalo suburb as a rehire with the company. During his previous stint with the company in DC, he had wanted to start a union campaign and even reached out to the United Food & Commercial Workers (UFCW), who ghosted him. They weren't interested in starting a campaign at Starbucks because they believed that it was too difficult: The stores were too small, the turnover rate too high, the scale of the company too massive.

There had been previous attempts to unionize Starbucks. In the 1980s, the UFCW had organized several of the first Starbucks cafés in Seattle. When Howard Schultz took over as CEO later that decade, he encouraged workers to decertify, or vote out, their union. He was ideologically anti-union, writing in 1999, "I was convinced that under my leadership, employees would come to realize that I would listen to their concerns. If they had faith in me and my motives, they wouldn't need a union."[1]

In 2004, workers in New York City tried to organize with the Industrial Workers of the World. They filed a petition with the NLRB to hold an election at their store. Starbucks tried to argue that rather than forming a union at that single store, workers had to organize every store in Manhattan. At Starbucks' request, the George W. Bush administration's NLRB agreed to impound the ballots until they could determine the bargaining-unit question. Realizing that the Board would almost certainly side with Starbucks, the IWW pulled their petition and decided not to file for any more elections. Instead, they adopted a strategy of directly advocating for workplace changes rather than seeking union recognition. They won the right for Starbucks workers to wear union pins, got the company to recognize Dr. Martin Luther King Jr. Day as a holiday, and pressured management to make some improvements and rescind other unjust policies.

But working at Starbucks had convinced Cory that baristas desperately needed a union to improve their standard of living—to raise pay and improve benefits, and to have protections and a voice at work. He was also aware that Starbucks baristas could pick up shifts at other Starbucks locations that needed additional coverage. He learned of the BuffBux group chat, a group of hundreds of baristas across Buffalo who would post pleas for baristas to come pick up hours or take their shifts, or to offer to do so, and got both of us added to it.

Picking up shifts would become a critical part of our organizing efforts. It allowed us to bounce around the district, meeting people, earning the respect and thanks of new coworkers, and learning which people might be interested in or important to forming an organizing committee.

After a couple of months at Elmwood, I got my first opportunity to try this out: a worker needed part of a shift covered to enable them to take a test. After my opening shift at Elmwood, I headed down to Hamburg, a Buffalo suburb, to clock in.

One of the workers there, Josh, was a regular at Elmwood, coming in most days to get their free food item and drink. They had been in my store that morning.

"Wow, you're a trooper, coming back for more!"

It was an easy shift, two hours on hot bar, my favorite position. A week or so later, Patty called me to ask if I would mind picking up a shift at Orchard Park. I didn't mind at all, calling Richard from the car to exult over how subversive an activity this was.

When I got to Orchard Park, they were in bad shape. They were so short-staffed that no one had had a break in six hours and the sanitizer bucket was dark with grime because no one had had time to change it. Omar, the assistant store manager (ASM), was afflicted with a migraine.

The drive-thru times were sky-high, and I was put on drive bar, which meant making hot and cold drinks at the same time. I spun from Frappuccino to pink drink to caramel macchiato to cold brew with cold foam as quickly as I could. It was my first time in a store with a headset. Someone showed me which button activated the outside speaker and which one allowed you to communicate with coworkers within the store, but I couldn't remember which was which and was afraid to find out. But I could listen to both channels: the customers at the speaker box outside placing their orders, and the internal conversations of my coworkers. A customer began a complicated order, with many steps and many extra toppings, and the migraine-suffering ASM was struggling to type it out. I started making it, signaling that he didn't have to input the specific directions, and I heard his sigh of relief as he laughed to the customer and said, "My team's got me!"

When my coworkers insisted I take a break (there was valor in working without a break, or in delaying taking one), I went to the back room, making sure to snap a picture of the phone list. A few minutes later, Omar came to the back, where he asked me about my store and told me about his. Sonia, their store manager, had trained at Elmwood; she, like Patty, was part of the Panera crew that had come over to Starbucks after David Almond switched companies and recruited his old team. David had been a district manager at Panera; now, he was managing one of the farthest-flung Starbucks in the market. I hadn't met him, but the people who loved him spoke of him as a legend.

"Panera's rough," Omar told me, while I nodded in agreement. "Starbucks is rough, too, but it's better."

I had been asked to come in for a couple hours to help them run breaks; I ended up staying till close, running trash, mopping floors, and earning the entreaty of the other shift supervisor who came in to help close: "Please don't let this stop you from coming back to pick up other shifts here. I promise it's not always this bad!"

Working at other locations not only brought with it considerable street cred, but also the gratitude of workers at those stores who would otherwise have been short-staffed. This gratitude also translated into flexibility around where I was placed: Since I came from a café-only store, I was seldom on drive-thru, and when I communicated that I was strongest on bar and weakest on customer support, I was usually put on bar for my entire shift.

Still, I didn't shy away from the less desirable tasks.

"You know you don't have to do the floors when you pick up shifts at other stores, right?" JP chuckled. "If I'm helping you out by picking up a shift at your store, you don't make me do the floors!"

But I did do the floors—on almost every shift I picked up. It was gross, heavy work, carrying the mats to the back and trying not to get splashed by the coffee-ground-and-strawberry-inclusion-studded slop they dripped. We would sweat into our masks, drenching them. But I was cognizant of the need to be a good worker. I was not the best—Cassie and Michelle Eisen could steam milk perfectly, sensing the correct temperature in the palm of their hands, a skill that took a long time to develop. But I learned the job—learning, too, that speed was more important than microfoam, not just to comply with corporate's profit-oriented dictates but also to ensure that my coworkers didn't endure the additional stress of customers demanding drinks that were still buried deep in the sticker printers.

I also tried to learn as much as humanly possible about the broader culture of Starbucks workers, joining Facebook groups dedicated to the barista experience, which were full of memes about batching Frappuccinos and the product shortages crippling our stores due to pandemic supply-chain issues. From vexatious customers to scheduling woes to dress code anxieties to TikTok drinks and obnoxious customizations to pandemic safety, Starbucks workers' concerns were largely universal, and the humorous, earnest, burned-out, and caring tenor of their posts largely translated into how Starbucks partners were in real life.

Salting was a lonely experience, a fact compounded by the pandemic. Working at Starbucks meant risking contracting Covid from a workplace exposure. When I was hired, vaccines were in the works, but they weren't yet available. We wore company-issued, thin cloth masks, which were not a particularly good defense against the virus. This meant it wasn't safe for me to go home and see Eunice over the holidays. Instead, Dave Mangan, my friend from the Spot Coffee campaign, invited me to his house for a beautiful Christmas filled with holiday cookies and cats. As it grew dark and we sipped coffee in his kitchen, a lake-effect snow band settled over the

Southtowns. Driving back home would be treacherous. But I had a shift early the next morning. Driving behind Dave's niece, I white-knuckled it slowly back, down whiteout roads. Every day, Starbucks expected workers to risk driving on unsafe roads to open its stores: We would get safety-text notifications from the state about staying off the roads, often while we were driving or already working our shifts.

I found ways to try to combat the isolation. Cory and I became close, inviting each other over to cook dinner, talk about work and life and philosophy, and watch TV episodes. He was a wise and comforting counsel: We spent hours troubleshooting workplace dynamics and strategizing about ways to increase our chances of winning a union. In between, I taught him how to sew buttons back onto his pants, and he initiated me into his love of MMA fighting. Lukas Weinstein invited me to join his poker group, which became a respite. Kay Kennedy, Al Celli, and I went for hikes and got coffee together. And I adopted an entire litter of cats.

Cats and union organizing go together. The Wobbly icon was the Sabo-Tabby, a black cat with its back arched, ready to pounce on the capitalist enemy. Louise Michel, the French anarchist who had fought on the barricades of the Paris Commune, adopted five cats during her time in exile. Rosa Luxemburg doted on her cat, Mimi, imbuing her with an anthropomorphic conscientiousness. Starbucks workers, and indeed service workers and young organizers more broadly, shared this love. Nearly everyone in the Buffalo barista bubble had at least one cat, and usually more. A friend told me about a newborn litter of kittens in need of a home. The first time I met the three tiny creatures, with claws like seed burrs that stuck in my sweater when I picked them up, I knew I couldn't separate the litter.

I had to go in for an opening shift at Starbucks the morning after bringing my cats home. This was the definition of alienation, I thought: having to say goodbye to the kittens batting at my apron strings and go to work. I named them all after union organizers: Big Bill Haywood, the long-haired, confident one, nearly double the size of his siblings; Frank Little, small and affectionate and, like his namesake, subject to Big Bill's bullying; and Lucy Parsons, timid but with the loudest purr, my "trans cat," whose gender had been incorrectly assigned. This trio became my emotional support cats. Independent enough to allow for my late nights in the union office and overnight trips away, they made the difference between an empty house and affectionate, purring companionship. I would come home from Starbucks and cuddle them until I felt my humanity return and my customer service voice recede.

**AS I INTEGRATED INTO** the social world of Starbucks partners, it became increasingly clear just how difficult organizing the company would be. The experience of guiding workers from the sidelines as an external organizer was very different from trying to start a campaign in one's own workplace. In theory, I knew the steps of organizing from inside:

1. Become a good coworker in the eyes of management and coworkers and begin building relationships outside of work.
2. Map the workplace.
3. Identify key leaders.
4. Build a diverse and representative organizing committee. This will be the group that will do the work of unionizing. Start by having conversations with the workers who are most likely to be supportive and able to keep a secret, then bring in others later, closer to the date of your first organizing committee meeting.
5. Have your first organizing committee meeting, where workers can ask questions and decide whether to form the committee. Try to make sure you've already talked to enough workers that there will be people there who are committed to making this happen, so that the meeting goes well and other workers see the optimism and enthusiasm of their coworkers.
6. Take the committee public with a letter to the company and launch the campaign's social media accounts and website.

7. Give the committee union cards to sign up their coworkers and try to reach as strong of a majority as you can.

8. Once you reach 65–70 percent or higher, file for an election with the National Labor Relations Board.

Putting these steps into action at Starbucks was far more challenging than I'd anticipated.

For one thing, turnover did turn out to be a significant problem: I would start making jokes about Che Guevara with a coworker or listening to them vent about work and the lack of respect from the company, only for them to quit a few weeks later. The pandemic, too, hastened many workers' exit, taking long-term key leaders out of the shop.

The small size and inevitable cliquishness of Starbucks stores was another issue. All workplaces develop social in-groups and develop rifts—between openers and closers, front of house and back of house, or other groups. At times, I worried that Starbucks workers were more annoyed with each other than with the company. My mental map of influential workplace leaders was constantly called into question by conversations with coworkers who would share their frustrations and concerns. I would listen to others' complaints about coworkers, trying to validate without agreeing, while panicking that someone I had identified as a key leader was actually perceived in a very different way.

From the beginning, we attempted to assess our stores and those we picked up shifts in, ending up with constantly evolving lists of coworkers and notes. Mine were not always particularly relevant to organizing, consisting partly of notes about coworkers' affinity or aversion to cats or houseplants, bullet points on arguments about football that happened on shift, what subjects they were studying in school, whose papers I could offer to edit. Cory's were more coherent: notes about which stores workers had transferred from, their social networks, who was likely to be a leader.

But mine were redeemed by the gems of information they contained:

- Told me we are not allowed to criticize any customer's order to each other etc when I said 15 pumps of syrup was a lot

- Really likes my chocolate muffins
- Likes bluegrass
- Likes cats but does not have
- Wears a lot of black, "how are people supposed to know I'm goth?"
- Used to be history major, focus on Russian history—1945 period b/c country modernized, story of Peter the Great
- Likes being my cold bar when I am hot bar
- Brought up 16 Tons, Pinkertons (also said history degree meant "you don't want to make any money")

Some of the observations were less humorous. I jotted down when coworkers brought up issues—from dietary restrictions that couldn't be accommodated by Starbucks' food offerings, to a history of management minimizing health issues or telling one coworker to "just fix" her depression, to concerns about pay and arguments between coworkers about whether being paid the same as new hires justified working like new hires. We were at work when the January 6th insurrection happened, and I listened to my coworkers' outspoken horror. Many of them had been in the Black Lives Matter protests the summer before, and I paid attention to which ones talked about confronting cops and helping organize events.

The most encouraging conversations revolved around other union campaigns; some of my coworkers were friends with Spot Coffee committee leaders, while others were paying close attention to current events. The previous November, Amazon workers had filed for a union election in Bessemer, Alabama, with the Retail, Wholesale & Department Store Union (RWDSU). Over the winter, they inched closer to an election, facing legal delays at the NLRB and fierce union busting from the company. Throughout the process, Starbucks workers were watching. Coworkers brought it up to me at work: "Do you think something like that could ever happen here?" At the time, I made mental notes and gave restrained answers: "That would be amazing!"

Our store maps shifted constantly, highlighting the difficulties of organizing small workplaces. One person's change of opinion about an issue could have wide-reaching effects that could turn a store of twenty-five workers around much more quickly than, say, a large manufacturing plant with thousands of workers, where one person's change would have far less sway on the entirety of the workforce.

By February of 2021, we faced a key strategic decision. Should we move on unionizing a couple stores or should we try to go for the entire city—including the far-flung suburban stores—at once? I began listing out possibilities.

There were many iterations of what the Starbucks campaign could have looked like. At first, we targeted stores that were close to the unionized Spot cafés. Knowing that Starbucks was a chronic union buster, we conferred about what "hammer" we could bring down on the company to win the right to organize. Only one tactic seemed to have enough power to accomplish this goal: a consumer boycott. Starbucks' customers were largely progressive, often seeking out the company because they believed that it was an ethical business that took principled stands on issues. We believed that the majority of them would support our right to unionize and help us hold Starbucks accountable.

Anticipating that we would be telling customers not to go to Starbucks until the company respected our right to organize, we wanted to be able to send customers to a union alternative. There was a Spot Coffee down the street from my store on Elmwood and from Cory's in Williamsville. Spot, which had remained closed for several months and involved workers in decision-making, had been devastated by the pandemic, and Starbucks, which had reopened quickly without any worker input, had taken many of their customers.

There was a possibility, we knew, that the campaign would never organize a single store anyway: If Starbucks refused to sign the Fair Election Principles and resorted to the behavior they had displayed the last time, firing Benny almost immediately and scaring the entire workforce, we might not ever gain enough support to go to an election. But we could show Starbucks that the Buffalo community would not stand for union busting, while ensuring that Spot reaped the additional profits as the only unionized café in town.

Then, there was the possibility of going for store-by-store elections. The newly installed, Biden-appointed NLRB was more labor friendly than the Bush Board had been during the IWW's earlier organizing attempt, and thus likely to allow single-store bargaining units. After working in stores across the district, we had learned how different each store was from the others: Each had its own culture, its own cliques, its own relationship to its manager and to the company. While some would be hot shops where workers overwhelmingly supported the union, others certainly would not. We joked about putting so many salts in one store that we would guarantee the result of an election—a tactic Howard Schultz would later accuse us of using. But we worried that going for single-store elections would allow Starbucks to isolate stores and put our campaign in a weaker position.

Starbucks had divided the Buffalo region into two districts. We also considered organizing by district, learning which stores were part of each. One of them contained far more of the likely pro-union stores than the other. However, this plan had huge drawbacks: The districts weren't tidily organized, partners could pick up shifts between districts easily, and unionizing one district would exclude the strong stores in the other.

Lastly, there was the citywide, industrial-union strategy. There were twenty stores across Buffalo and the surrounding towns, from Niagara Falls to Hamburg. After a few months of picking up shifts, Cory and I had identified possible leaders in many stores and gotten phone lists from across the city. We visited additional stores on our days off or after our shifts, circling Buffalo, ordering coffee, and chatting to other partners. At the beginning of the pandemic, Starbucks allowed us to mark out one free drink and food item per day; this policy subsidized our visits. There was an instant credibility in going into a store wearing the flimsy company-provided black cloth masks and giving your partner numbers. Clocking in to work alongside the baristas as a borrowed partner lifted the credibility to camaraderie. This was winnable, we decided. But if we wanted to have a shot at organizing the whole thing, we needed more help. There were too many stores, too many workers, too many shifts to pick up, for the two of us to be able to map the district efficiently enough. Moreover, turnover meant that our efforts were constantly unraveling.

We decided to delay preparations for launching a campaign for at least a few months and focus in the meantime on finding additional inside organizers willing to get jobs at Starbucks. To that end, I wrote up a job posting for UnionJobs.com, which was designed to be obscure enough to fly under the corporate radar yet interesting enough to attract the right class-conscious workers. I named our program Project Germinal because it was both sufficiently secretive and rooted in my own love of labor history.

Plus, the name Germinal featured built-in damage control: If the campaign and the project came crashing down on our heads, I said, many times, we would still have accomplished the planting of seeds for some future struggle—and we would inevitably end up better off than dead in a French coal mine. It would be hard to set a lower bar!

"We believe," the ad stated, "that the best way to help workers—and the best way to learn union organizing—is through a focus on inside organizing and building strong worker committees. When you join us as an intern through Project Germinal, your commitment to us is to help build the movement in upstate New York. Our commitment to you is to help train you as an organizer and to work together to build a more just world for the working class."

To my astonishment, people responded. My email inbox swelled with a small avenging army of applicants.

Many of them were already interested in labor, but weren't sure how to get involved. "Working as a union organizer has been a dream of mine but I never knew how I would begin doing so," Brian Murray wrote. "I have wanted to join the labor movement for a long time," said Casey Moore. James Skretta decided to drop out of their PhD program in saxophone and music theory to become an inside organizer. Bill O'Malley, a retired lawyer seeking to learn organizing, moved to Buffalo to join the campaign.

Interviewing the new applicants was a heartwarming experience. They exuded energy, joy, and solidarity. And they were eager to get on the job and organize.

"How soon do you want me to get there?" Brian asked me.

"How soon can you come?"

He was available almost immediately, driving out to Buffalo to visit the city. I took him on a driving tour, showing him sights ranging from the swamp in the outer harbor, my favorite spot to go for walks, to the various unionized and union-busting coffee shops across town.

Housing the salts posed an immediate problem. Month-to-month leases were hard to come by, and determining who could sign a longer lease without locking the salts into a yearlong contract was confusing.

"Well, I have a guest room and a couch," I finally told the first three interested salts who wanted to come. "We'll figure it out!"

James arrived first. In the couple of days they stayed at my house, before they were able to move into the co-op house a mile down the road, they fixed the broken bathroom door, prepared delicious tacos, and shared excellent Scotch. Brian was next to arrive, with a small arsenal, a pile of books, and a love of picking up and draping Bill the cat around his neck.

Once James moved into the co-op house, Brian—who would soon be hired on the spot during his Starbucks interview—installed himself in the spare bedroom. Then, Zachary arrived—the night before his first shift at Starbucks. He was the best of us. Recruited by Robert Sarason, a labor lawyer in Syracuse and lifelong friend of Ginny Diamond's, Zachary had joined our initial Zoom interview with a REFUGEES WELCOME flag in the background, then immediately swiveled his screen to show his IWW flag as soon as he saw mine and knew it was a leftist safe space. Upon his arrival in Buffalo, Zachary's accommodations consisted of my $15 thrifted couch, which was far from luxurious. For two and a half months, he slept on the couch, waking up for opening shifts and coming home still unbelievably kind and considerate, cooking gourmet dinners and keeping everyone in the house in good spirits.

My pandemic isolation abated with the arrival of these good-hearted troops. Brian had brought his blender and love of tiki drinks and commandeered my mason jars to concoct new syrups for his bar. Every night—even before opening shifts—our tiny group stayed up late, drinking mai tais or piña coladas and arguing about history and theory and organizing strategies.

While my mental health had improved, my wrist was suffering the consequences of Starbucks' speed requirements. Making the drinks required constant repetitive motion: pouring milk, pumping syrups and Frap bases, wielding steaming pitchers and blenders. And then there were the drink shakers. Iced teas, iced matcha lattes, refreshers, and Doubleshots on ice were made and then shaken in tall vessels with lids we had to hold on and then pop off. The constant motion of that and the speed we were supposed to work at—I was told we should be making six drinks a minute—soon began to send pains through my wrist, which got increasingly painful over the spring and into the summer. Many long-term baristas I knew had developed carpal tunnel during their time at the company. With a union, we hoped we could fight for better health and safety policies and more reasonable speed expectations and staffing levels.

When Richard came back to Buffalo for the first time since the pandemic, I was wearing a wrist brace 24/7 to help with the injury. I couldn't pick up my cats with my right hand, and overcompensating with my left hand was causing the same issues to creep into that wrist, too.

"Maybe you should just quit," Richard said, his worry masked with gruffness.

But I couldn't quit. Part of my effectiveness in recruiting salts was that I was salting, too. More important, if I quit and tried to organize from the outside, I would lose the credibility I was building with my coworkers, both at Elmwood and across the district. I would be someone who couldn't hack it.

So I continued working. My coworkers noticed and helped me out. Kyli Hilaire would try to preempt me from carrying the heavy kegs of cold brew up from the back of house. Patty let me wear the brace on the floor without asking any questions or requiring a medical note; other managers made it difficult for workers to wear braces and required official diagnoses. JP stopped assigning me to work the positions that put the most strain on my wrist. Thanks to his accommodation, my wrist stopped getting worse and then, slowly, started to get better.

Working at Starbucks was difficult, but it was also fun. I loved opening the store with my coworkers and cherished the jokes and banter and community among our team. Coworkers constantly brought in treats to share, from Cassie's cookies to Em's lavender syrup to Angela's banana bread to JP's rare and exquisite bag of Jamaican Blue Mountain coffee. We gave each other rides and met each other's pets—JP gave me bags of his own cat's favorite treats to feed to mine.

At the beginning of my salting career, I thought that I needed to do everything possible to ingratiate myself to management. I was so successful in this effort that Patty asked me to let her know when I was going home to visit Eunice so that Patty could write her a letter about how much she liked working with me. I did get the letter, although I felt guilty that I also wanted the letter so that if Starbucks fired me later, it would be easier to prove that it was retaliation for organizing.

But, a few months in, I learned that my coworkers feared I was too much of a goody-goody. Knowing what Starbucks' excuse had been for firing Benny, I never cursed at work; I was generally a rule follower. Then, I learned that people weren't telling me things because they thought I might talk to Patty. Some of my coworkers thought I was a teenager, which further detracted from my credibility. So, I decided to change things up, introducing swear words back into my vocabulary and making edgier jokes.

One incident in particular helped me build trust with my coworkers. We consistently looked out for one another in uncomfortable situations. When rude customers came in, we didn't have a lot of options for dealing with the situation: We weren't allowed to refuse service, and it was nearly impossible to get customers banned from the store, even when they sexually harassed us. We did the best we could; when creepy customers came in, we covered for coworkers so that they could hide in the back of house and avoid contact. But the best means of retribution was petty but immensely satisfying: decaffing customers.

When one customer screamed at a coworker who didn't have his order ready the second he came in, calling her a bitch and threatening her, I vowed never to give him caffeine again. He came in every day for his triple caramel macchiato; every day, I pulled three decaf shots. When Patty caught me, I began explaining what had happened. The coworker who had been cursed at intercepted: "Oh, that's just an accident. Here, I'll fix it!"

"I don't want you getting fired!" my coworker said afterward.

"It would have been worth it!"

The decaffing incident helped me win over my coworkers, showing them I was willing to break rules for their benefit. Meanwhile, I continued to be friendly with Patty, dodging her questions about what exactly I was writing and working on outside of Starbucks while helping put together our store's collective gifts for her.

While I was endeavoring to thread this needle, we continued to recruit more salts.

**GINNY DIAMOND SENT US** Colin Cochran, who moved to Buffalo after graduating from William & Mary, bringing a love of bird-watching and his incredible archaeologist partner, Kat. They would soon add Juniper and Mackerel, a bonded pair of cats, to the growing feline population of our union. They also became among our most levelheaded advisers. As a green bean at the struggling Walden and Anderson store, Colin quickly became a leader, even turning down a promotion to shift supervisor within the first couple of months. Later, we determined that this had been a mistake: He turned it down because he felt that longer-term coworkers might resent him for moving up. That consideration, we would learn, was less important than having him in a position of greater authority, which would have given him more weight with coworkers later in the campaign.

In May 2021, a former Gimme! barista and longtime union activist, Will Westlake, texted me, "Hey Jaz! How are you? What are you up to?"

"Hi!!" I wrote back. "I'm good, just pretty busy in Buffalo with a couple campaigns and a lot of inside organizers! How are you?"

"Great! Just finished my semester and graduate in December. Was curious if there was something to work on this summer through WU."

"Would you be willing to go into Starbucks in Buffalo?"

"I'll apply right now."

And he did, writing a cover letter that encapsulated his history as a barista—but not as a unionizing barista—over the past five years. In 2016, as an eighteen-year-old student working at Gimme! during summer breaks, Will had been skeptical: Some unions were wonderful, he thought, but others could be equally bad. In preparation for his meeting with the organizer, Richard, Will typed up five pages of questions on an iPad: What is the structure of the union? How is the bargaining committee decided upon?

Who decides which grievances are taken up? How much are dues? How much do you make? How much does the president of the union make?

In his four-hour meeting with Richard, Will got answers to his questions and decided to ensure the union effort succeeded, joining the committee and pulling many coworkers with him.

After Will and his coworkers won their election, he became a leader on the bargaining committee, occasionally infuriating his coworkers with how broad-minded and generous he was, and how willing to find ways to get proposals through. He was indispensable in actually getting the contract to a tentative agreement. Then, on the day the contract was to be ratified, he was unjustly fired.[2]

Many of his coworkers wanted to go on strike to protest Gimme!'s retaliation against him. "No Will, no contract!" they chanted.

But Will insisted the union must come first, urging his coworkers to ratify the contract anyway.

Will's dedication and selflessness hadn't wavered in the five intervening years. He had worked at two other coffee shops, working to get organizing committees formed and helping lead a boycott of a particularly egregious union buster. Whenever I was in Ithaca for work, Will and I would meet up. I was impressed by his insight and wit.

Will's passion for and expertise in coffee—he was so skilled that he could make complicated latte art designs with the clumsy, rounded Starbucks steaming pitchers—got him hired on the spot as a barista at the Camp Road Starbucks, one of the farthest-flung locations and one where we had not yet made inroads.

**OF ALL THE NEW** salts, one applicant in particular proved my limitations as a judge of character.

After graduating from college, Casey Kennedy Moore wrote in her application, she had moved to Texas with a friend. They had collaborated on a series of videos about bridging the political divide between Democrats and Republicans. I watched them, alarmed at the stereotyped view of Texas and naïveté about the two-party system that they included.

"I'm just worried she'll fall for Starbucks' anti-union campaign if they say what a great and progressive company they are," I said. "I don't want to have to worry about our own salts."

"I don't think that will really be an issue," said Richard, "but you can probably ask an interview question that would get at that, right?"

On Zoom, it was immediately apparent that Casey was a remarkable person with the requisite eagerness, friendliness, and fiery dedication to make an ideal salt, and moreover with an unparalleled capacity for getting things done.

"Do you think that companies can ever be truly progressive?" I asked.

"Under capitalism? No."

That settled my doubts.

In the meantime, the salts had moved out of my house and into the "salt house," an apartment they decorated with Brian's extensive flag collection and revolutionary posters. Casey, upon moving in and looking at the Karl Marx, James Connolly, and Fidel Castro decor, promptly ordered posters of Mother Jones, Lucy Parsons, and Dolores Huerta to add more gender equity to the space. We started holding campaign strategy meetings there, and the circle of chairs around the table continued to expand to make room for new salts, joining our small band from various routes.

Danny Schleyer, a laid-off leader of the Spot Coffee union and the creator of the Strong Coffee, Strong Union design, lived around the corner from me. Iconoclastic and scrappy, Danny was constantly remixing music, planning a bonfire, adopting a kitten, exploring mystical traditions, or indulging angst by listening to Townes Van Zandt on repeat, a habit they passed on to me. During the Spot Coffee campaign, Danny had fried me a pork chop at two in the morning when they found out I was homesick for Mississippi. They possessed a certain part-hippie, part-rebel air that occasionally conflicted with their underlying wholesomeness and desire to look after others. For several weeks, we discussed the possibility of Danny applying to Starbucks, and eventually they decided to try.

The first thing they needed was a résumé and cover letter. Their seven years at Spot Coffee spoke for itself. The cover letter took a little longer, but the final result was a work of art. All of the salts laid it on thick in their cover letters—Will even went so far as to invoke his mother's memory, describing her nonexistent love of Starbucks coffee—but Danny's was the pinnacle.

"When I was in first grade, I told my teacher I wanted to be an ice cream truck driver. When I was in third grade, I told my teacher I wanted to be a teacher. Only in 12th grade, when I started experimenting with Starbucks Sumatra in a Bodum French Press, did I realize I had a future in coffee," Danny's letter opened.

They got the job.

An alumnus of our inside organizing program recommended his friend Olivier, fresh from the University of Virginia and a BB&T bank internship. The son of a factory owner, Olivier turned out to be a true class traitor. Endlessly upbeat, he charmed everyone from the hotel night-shift front-desk worker, who confided her troubles to him, to his coworkers. We decided to keep Olivier undercover, not participating in the committee or in public organizing conversations, meaning his experience was more isolating than the other salts', especially as he arrived on the scene later than most. But he constantly sought out new ways to help, editing flyers and performing what work he could do in secret.

One night in May, Brian returned from a Tinder date gushing about how incredible his date's roommate was. "Oh my god, they're so cool! They have, like, this entire radical library! And they are really good at organizing and have all this background! They're so fucking cool!"

Brian continued to go on dates with his Tinder match in order to hang out with Arjae, eventually convincing them to join Project Germinal. Arjae had been working as a metal spinner, in extremely hazardous conditions, and seeking to organize their coworkers around workplace issues and eventually into a union, though there was not sufficient interest at that time. Inspired by the example of Leslie Feinberg, the Buffalo-based butch lesbian, transgender activist, and communist, Arjae had joined the Workers World Party. They applied for a job at the Genesee Starbucks, strategically holding their hand over the hammer and sickle tattoo on their forearm during the interview, and got the job on the spot.

---

**WITH THESE ADDITIONAL SALTS** in place, launching a citywide campaign seemed possible. We were now able to fan out to all of the stores, covering greater ground and obtaining phone lists from nearly all the stores that we had been unable to crack. While a few—like the Niagara Falls drive-thru location—remained impenetrable, our networks and connections continued to grow. I knew Josh Pike and Marcus Hopkins because they were both regulars at Elmwood. They worked at the far-flung Camp Road and Depew stores, but lived close to Elmwood and came by on their days off or in the morning before a closing shift. They were also both drag queens. One day, Marcus was scheduled to work at the time of a show.

I offered to pick up that shift, even though it would mean working a sixteen-hour day, opening Elmwood and closing Depew.

Marcus was extremely grateful, texting me: "Hmu anytime I owe you one ❤."

When I reached out a few months later, they would respond almost immediately.

We integrated into the social circles of our stores. Friendships were blossoming across the city between bright-eyed and hardworking inside organizers and coworkers. Casey—who hated state fairs—went to the Erie County Fair with her coworkers. Brian went out drinking with his coworkers, transgressing the boundaries of salting by discussing communism and then inviting some of them over to the salt house, which we had collectively decided was off-limits due to the need for secrecy. Cory went for a walk in a cemetery with some of his coworkers, texting me ahead of time to comment on the strangeness of the activity and to ask if I thought it was too early to sneak in a "if we don't fight capitalism, we'll end up here one day" (it was, I texted back).

Our preparations for launching a campaign intensified. In unionspeak, a *blitz* is a brief period of intense house calling designed to build an organizing committee in the shortest possible time. Historically, most unions had sent one or two staff organizers to start talking to workers. Sometimes, they leafleted the plant, which blew their cover; other times, they slowly met with workers, dragging out the time frame to the extent that the company often found out about the organizing activity. If a campaign did launch, unions would send lots of staff in at the end, just before the election.[3]

This formula was backward, Richard said. Unions needed to condense the time frame of building an organizing committee. The period before the union campaign was public, but after workers had begun talking about unionizing, was risky. If management found out, it could begin union busting and retaliating against workers. It was also more difficult to prove company knowledge to the Labor Board if a campaign hadn't yet surfaced: Companies claimed they had no idea workers were unionizing, and that firing workers or changing business practices was purely coincidental. To avoid this, and to balance the need for secrecy with the need for communication, organizers needed to have as many conversations with workers as possible, as quickly as possible.

The blitz model was evolving. The pandemic was still raging. The workforce was more transient, making it harder to find accurate addresses, and young, which made it less likely that people would answer the door even if we did obtain the correct information. As a result, house-call blitzes didn't make as much sense. The campaign at Pavement Coffeehouse, a Boston chain that Richard and I had helped organize via Zoom calls from my dining table in May, helped us visualize what an alternative blitz could look like. Pavement workers' first organizing committee meeting was poorly attended, with only some of the stores represented. We decided that this fledgling committee would visit all of the other stores that weekend, tell workers about the campaign, and invite them to another meeting. The strategy worked: The next meeting had enough turnout to launch a public campaign, and the workers won voluntary recognition within a few days.

We decided to run a similar blitz at Starbucks, visiting stores across Buffalo and talking more openly to workers for a few days before we held our first organizing committee meeting. We debated when that meeting should take place. Some of the salts wanted significantly more time to build relationships in their stores, while some of us—myself included—were afraid our key leaders were about to quit and take with them our hopes of a strong organizing committee. We ended up compromising on a mid-August launch.

"It's going to be really intense once the campaign gets going, so I thought we could all use a vacation ahead of time," Will said, and invited us to his family's cottage on Lake Ontario.

When we weren't visiting lighthouses or getting ice cream, we were sketching drafts for logos and cartoons for the campaign. We experimented with various sirens and coffee cup motifs. Then, one morning, Will came out onto the back patio wearing his Gimme! Coffee union shirt. It depicted a union fist holding a moka pot, coffee splashing artistically from the spout. I was still wearing my carpal tunnel brace, and we joked that instead of a moka pot the Starbucks version should show the drink shaker, which exacerbated wrist strain. Quickly turning the design around on his laptop, Zachary turned the concept into a logo that would become synonymous with the campaign.

In the meantime, we created a time frame for talking to coworkers about the union, working backward from our tentative first-meeting date. First, we would approach those we thought would both be supportive and able to keep the secret. Then, around a week out, we would approach the key leaders we needed to get on board and the coworkers we were fairly sure would support the union but who lacked some of the pull of the key leaders. In the last three days before the Sunday committee meeting, we would talk to the majority of our coworkers and also circulate around the city, picking up shifts or ordering our drink markouts, and invite likely supporters to the meeting.

In preparation for my first union conversation, I learned to crochet. Or intended to. Despite my desire to learn, the chaotic nature of the union campaign meant that I never got beyond the first lesson, and my cats took advantage of the unattended ball of yarn. In the months since my training shifts at Starbucks, Cassie and I had become closer friends. She had been to my house before, bringing a giant cardboard box of tea ingredients to teach me how to make creative blends and books on astrology to explore our charts, and she had seen my labor decor, commenting favorably. She had asked me if I wanted to learn to crochet and I agreed.

In late July, after a trip to Joann's to buy yarn, Cassie agreed to come over to my house to make old-fashioneds and give me my first crochet lesson. I decided to bring up the union for the first time during our meeting.

When Cassie got to my house, I made the drinks—which ended up being overly strong and not quite right. We talked about cats and her new roommate. There wasn't a great opening to shift into the union conversation, but she'd mentioned that she was tired from opening so I asked how that had gone. She was concerned about favoritism affecting everything from promotions to workload.

As the whiskey swirled through my head, I tipped back in my chair a little. "I've been thinking about this, and I wanted to get your thoughts on organizing a union at Starbucks and whether you think it might help solve some of these issues."

Cassie replied that she had basically no understanding of unions, other than that they help people not be fired. She had read about organizing Starbucks on Reddit, she told me. "But people who try to do that seem to end up not working at Starbucks anymore."

"Say more," I said.

"Well, people either leave of their own volition or Starbucks finds a reason to fire them."

I did mention Benny quickly, saying I'd seen that happen once, but that it seemed to happen when workers didn't have the backing of a union or talked to a lot of people in an undisciplined way.

"Let me back up," I said. "I worked with Workers United during the Spot campaign, where I was the lead organizer, and I still work with the union. We can do this, and we'd have the backing of a union from the start."

Cassie's demeanor shifted a bit. "Wait, they were successful, right?"

"Yes, and they got a four-dollars-an-hour wage increase in their contract. If Spot can do that, Starbucks should be doing way more."

Cassie told me she was still afraid of getting fired, how she couldn't afford to lose her job. Starbucks was a much bigger company than Spot, she pointed out, and would fight harder. "Wouldn't we have to unionize the whole company?"

I said we could organize a single store if we wanted to, but that we would have the most power if we organized Buffalo-wide.

She asked what issues the union might solve, saying that she thought it could help with wages, and possibly with benefits, although we already had those, but that she didn't think it would help with favoritism. I said that it would be able to help with that because we would be able to bargain about how promotions happened and also be able to take action if people were discriminated against or treated unfairly. Cassie said that she had tried to call partner resources before, but that went through the district manager. I tried to explain that a union would be our own independent organization.

Cassie brought up how Patty was behind on big things, like posting schedules, and little things, like not holding votes for partner of the quarter or ordering a partner appreciation corkboard. I tried to redirect the focus to corporate, saying that Patty was also overworked and that all the issues with short-staffing and scheduling really seemed to be coming from the top, and emphasizing that we needed to keep Patty in the dark for her own protection.

Finally, I asked Cassie if the union was something she would be willing to get involved with. She said that she wanted more information about what organizing a union meant and what our goals were and asked me to send her something because her mind was going blank and we were drinking.

Regretting my decision to integrate the old-fashioneds into this get-together, I asked if she thought there was anyone else in Buffalo who would be interested, and she said that she used to know the whole district but didn't anymore, but that she and Angela were the ones at our store who wouldn't talk about it to others.

"So, do you want to crochet now?" Cassie finally said.

She taught me how to start, from the slipknot to creating the first chain. But my mind was still on the union conversation, and I was disappointed. Going into our meeting, I had known Cassie might not support the union, but I had been hopeful. I knew she wouldn't tell anyone, but we had become friends and I had wanted her support on a personal level, too.

**OTHER CONVERSATIONS WENT BETTER.** On Will Westlake's first day of work, a shift supervisor named Gianna Reeve had told him not to be overly concerned if he clocked out after gathering his items and taking off his apron. "Partners rise up, take their money in wages," Gianna said.

When the time came to begin talking about unionizing, Will invited Gianna to the Spot Coffee in Hamburg for a conversation.

"I wanted to talk to you," Will began, as they sat down at the table.

"Is Starbucks unionizing?"

"Yes, that's exactly what's happening. How did you know?"

"I've seen things on Reddit about how Starbucks is unionizing and thought that's what you needed to talk to me about, because it was either that or you were trying to kill me."

Gianna painted an optimistic picture of the organizing landscape at their store. Josh Pike had recently held a birthday party for Karl Marx and had talked about wanting to unionize Starbucks before. Gianna was confident they could sign up a strong majority of their coworkers on cards.

Will wanted to invite Gianna to the weekly meetings at the salt house. I drew the line, saying that would be an error, and that even if Gianna was trustworthy, it would become too complicated, as other salts might want to invite their coworkers, too. We could all meet at the first committee meeting.

My next conversation was with Angela because I knew she would keep the secret. She had already told me, as we ate our breakfast sandwiches at the table in the back room, that she had been working since she was eleven, helping her mom with her cleaning business.

"Sometimes it feels like slavery," she told me. "I probably shouldn't use that term, though."

"Well, you know, wage slavery is a thing."

"I know—we need to have an uprising. The rebellion is coming. You and I are the catalysts."

As a result of these previous comments, I had high hopes for our talk. We met at Tipico, a craft coffee shop down the street from our store.

"Why wouldn't I support this?" she asked, when I brought up the union.

"Well, there's really no reason to be opposed to it, although Starbucks might try to talk us out of it. But all we want is to make the company better."

But it was harder to get her to join the committee.

"I don't want to do anything wrong," she said.

I pressed her on what she meant by that. She shared that she couldn't take the risk of getting fired as she was independent and didn't drive: Her apartment was just a few blocks away.

I tried to be as reassuring as possible, eventually leaving the conversation with a strong pledge of quiet support and recommendations of other coworkers to talk to.

Meanwhile, I began trying to get in touch with workers from other stores. I had texted Marcus about meeting up to discuss something work-related, and although they texted back immediately, it was hard to pin them and their partner, Josh, down on a time, between their Starbucks shifts and drag engagements. Accordingly, Will and I made plans to track them down at one of their shows, ignoring that the show started at eleven and we were both scheduled to open our stores the next morning.

When we got to Club Marcella, the room was dotted with Starbucks workers. During a break between sets, one of my Elmwood colleagues drunkenly talked to me about work, which coworkers he thought were cool, and how much he loved his job. "I could make more down the street at any fast-food place," he told me. "I've stayed at Starbucks because I care."

Marcus, aka Tara Bishop, was resplendent in blue and silver. I talked to her as she mingled with the crowd.

"Oh, I already heard!" she said. The coworker who'd mentioned it had said that he didn't think it would ever happen, she added. "I said, 'Why not? It's 2021.'"

Hiding my anxiety that the cat had gotten out of the bag, I asked if Tara and Pamela B. Carnes—Josh's drag alias—would join the committee.

"Of course!"

The next set was beginning. Tara slipped backstage. Will and I crushed closer to the front. A few minutes later, Pam waved at us from the wings, gleefully.

"She knows," Will whispered.

She managed to sneak up behind us shortly after and threw her arms around us.

"I'm ready to help!"

After the show, we talked outside on the patio. Josh was eager to organize. One of their higher-ups was a key problem. He was openly biphobic, had fired three trans workers in two months, and said hateful things like "homeless people are disgusting" and "should burn in a volcano." When he started bullying Josh for not being able to make it to a shift after a flight cancellation, Josh began recording him secretly at work and reporting those conversations to Starbucks internally. So far, Starbucks had done nothing, Josh said.

"As soon as we announce our campaign, our manager will get fired," Will predicted.

"Good," said Josh.

I warned that we needed to make clear that we weren't just organizing because of bad managers.

"Oh, of course," said Josh. They had even talked to Gianna about organizing a union before. "Now we are actually doing it!"

Josh talked about other people they knew across the city, and their vision for how the union could make Starbucks a place to work without fear, without abuse, and without insincerity. They told us about their depression about the situation at Starbucks and how the talk of a union was giving them hope.

"There are two kinds of people who work at Starbucks," said Will, "those who fear management, and those who—"

"—are ready to stand up," Josh finished Will's sentence.

With their contacts—under the names of Pam and Tara—filed in my phone and with plans to follow up in person again soon, Will and I eventually left the club and went to his house to make quesadillas, write up a report on the meeting, and decide whether it was worth trying to go to sleep.

After napping for an hour, we groggily went in for our opening shifts. Four blonde ristretto shots didn't do much against the exhaustion, and JP looked at me keenly: "Everything all right?"

"All good! Just a late night!"

Some of my conversations went remarkably well. Stephen, a fifteen-year partner, told me about their love for the company and their conflicted feelings about unionizing as both the best thing they could do for Starbucks and as a perceived betrayal—and then signed a card and joined the committee. Kellen, a long-term partner who had worked at Starbucks throughout school and had found a chosen family in his coworkers, talked about a negative experience with a prior, health-care union—and then said, "But that was that union. This will be our union, and we can make it what we want it to be—both for Starbucks and for our whole industry. I'm down."

I met with Kellen immediately before my meeting with JP, the meeting I was the most nervous about. I was afraid JP would be an anti, and if he was, he could influence a lot of people. My goal was to get him onto the committee—if we got him on board, we would get the store—but even ensuring that he didn't campaign against the union would be a win. Kellen gave me advice for approaching the meeting, recommending that I emphasize my background with organizing Spot Coffee and speak bluntly about JP's leadership within the store.

JP and I sat down at the Elmwood Spot and talked for nearly two hours. He was friends with Lukas from Spot and familiar with the organizing there—and with the earlier IWW attempt in NYC.

"That didn't go well," he said. "Starbucks can just replace us if we go on strike."

"This is different," I said. "We're trying to create a positive, true partnership. And we can be pro-Starbucks and pro-union."

A Wobbly myself, I found it difficult to say that I was pro-Starbucks—although I would repeat the same line to the media countless times once our campaign was public. But it was strategically invaluable to position our union effort as a positive and collaborative force rather than a threat to the company. More important, it was what Starbucks workers themselves wanted, and what they believed their union would provide.

JP told me that he worried that the Buffalo district was too small and not a priority for Starbucks, even though he agreed that the Buffalo community would strongly support a union effort. I told him that the small size of the Buffalo district made it perfect, because it was possible to organize the entire thing and build power across the region.

"But they're opening two new stores a day in Toronto, and there's thousands of stores in New York City," he said.

Still, he acknowledged many of the issues that existed within the company. After his nine years with the company, he was paid the same as a brand-new shift supervisor. Starbucks had told him the only way he could get a raise was to move into management, which he didn't want to do. A business and economics major, he kept reiterating that Starbucks had treated him fine.

"You're a hard worker," he told me repeatedly. "You're good on bar." Going into the conversation, he thought I wanted to talk about becoming a shift supervisor and kept telling me to apply even once I'd brought up organizing.

He asked if I thought I should be paid the same as a coworker who didn't work hard, and also what Starbucks had done to me to make me want to unionize. I said they hadn't done anything to me, but that I thought it was a misconception that unions were for workers who had gripes—Starbucks could be better, and since Starbucks was the industry leader, we could raise standards across the board.

We argued in long circles about whether it was possible to unionize at as big a corporation as Starbucks and about seniority pay versus work ethic. I told him how workers had been reaching out ever since Spot organized, and that I thought we could get a committee of seventy-five to one hundred people.

"Show me the bodies," said JP. That was shift-supervisor talk, about staffing the store with sufficient people. To me, it was an indication that he was relenting. He kept going back to how I was new and he'd been there forever.

"That's exactly why I need you to be able to do this," I told him. "You know exactly what would be effective here and what we need to make the job work." I asked him if he would join the committee and help us if we got the people together, and I told him about the meeting.

"I'll help you," he finally said. He gave me names of people to reach out to, but said he didn't want his name used. I asked if one of his close friends would be interested.

JP shook his head and laughed. "This isn't him. It's not me, either, but I'm going to help you."

Leaving that conversation, I felt that my months at the Elmwood Starbucks had been worth it. I may not have gotten him onto the committee, but I had gotten his support. And while we had been debating the pros and cons of house calling internally, I didn't think anyone else who had house-called JP would have gotten the same result. The organizing conversation had to come from a coworker he knew and respected. If he hadn't seen me as a hard worker or a good barista, my arguments would have fallen flat. JP saw himself as a mentor and supporter for baristas, whose job was to help us. His offer to help me fit into that view of his role, and I left feeling secure about our chances at Elmwood.

And there were pockets of interest at other stores across the city.

**FOR MONTHS, RICHARD HAD** been talking about a worker at the Genesee store, where he had been a regular customer during the Spot Coffee boycott because he stayed at a hotel by the airport. This worker, he said, had always supported unions; she had gotten to know Richard, and they had talked about organizing Starbucks. She had been up for an assistant manager promotion, though, he cautioned; he wasn't sure if she might now be in management. Worse yet, he had misplaced her contact information.

By picking up shifts, we got the Cheektowaga phone list; by talking with other workers there, Cory ascertained that Lexi was a long-term partner who had been up for an ASM position but hadn't gotten it. Richard was pretty sure that was the right person. On August 16, I braced myself and texted the number that we *thought* was the right one. It was the first time I had used the word *union* in a text message to a Starbucks worker—I wanted the best chance of getting a reply.

Two minutes later, I got the best possible response: "Hi! That is so awesome to hear. I've been advocating for us to unionize for years. I would love to sit down so we can chat!"

In those days, Starbucks partners identified one another by our masks: We all wore the oversize black cloth masks that the company issued (the second generation of Starbucks-branded masks were two-ply—more tenured partners often wore the one-ply masks the company had made at the beginning of the pandemic, which were later discarded as ineffective against the virus).

I had never met Lexi before, but I knew immediately who she was as she walked up. She had long hair, an artistic and dark-hued aesthetic, and sleeves of tattoos on her leg and arm, and she was wearing the mask.

We sat outside on the patio at Caffe Aroma, just around the corner from my store, and talked about work. Lexi was a year younger than me, but had worked at Starbucks since she was seventeen and had worked in

Florida before transferring to her Buffalo store. She knew every aspect of the company and delivered the quintessential "Starbucks experience"—she knew all of the regulars and was universally beloved.

Then, we ran through the names of her coworkers. Lexi predicted their universal union support. As I made notes in my sketchbook, I gently questioned her confidence. Surely there would be more hesitation or fear?

"I know my partners," Lexi said. "They'll all sign up."

Two weeks later, Genesee Street would file with 100 percent support on union cards.

In the days leading up to the first committee meeting, however, it seemed that the hottest shop was the Galleria mall kiosk, where workers faced issues ranging from sunburns caused by working under a glass roof to a lack of air-conditioning to stalkers following them to their cars in the parking garage at night. This harassment was so continuous that all the workers collectively decided to stop wearing name tags to try to hide their identities and cut down on unwanted social media requests from customers. James and Brian had become regular borrowed partners at the Galleria. I had worked there once, and it was an incredibly high-volume store. Customers were also more unkind and less likely to tip.

Sam Banaszak was a twenty-year-old shift supervisor. Starbucks had been their first job, and they were determined to make it better. After James broached the topic with them, I followed up and we got lunch at the Panera across the street from the mall. They described a small but angry group of workers at their store, ready to take action against Starbucks. They agreed to rein in that anger, agreeing that the "pro-Starbucks and pro-union" messaging was more universally appealing.

I tried to emphasize the need for secrecy, but the Galleria was soon abuzz with interest, and workers were soon speaking openly—far too openly—about organizing, on the floor. Sam put me in contact with other workers, including Róisín Doherty. We met for coffee at Spot Elmwood, and I was instantly blown away by Róisín's breadth of knowledge, which encompassed every detail of the IWW's campaign and a play-by-play analysis of the strategic shortcomings and relevant overlap of that effort. For a moment, I wondered if Róisín was also a salt from some other union, but it seemed unlikely.

The Galleria would certainly be up for organizing, I thought. As we continued to have these conversations with workers across town, it became clear that some stores were hotter shops than others; that there was considerable fear; that we might not be able to win the entire city. But I insisted that we continue to talk about that and plan for that as the goal. The time to switch to a store-by-store strategy, I argued, was the day of the first committee meeting, if it turned out that we didn't have enough people to go for the whole district.

This ended up being exactly what happened. There were downfalls to the plan: Since the whole district did not go for the union, some of our salts were working in stores that ultimately didn't file, so those were not the most strategic locations for them to be working in. However, the plan did provide a district-wide network that kept us informed about what was happening at each store in real time. That the plan was somewhat idealistic didn't make it any less adaptable: It is much harder to scale a plan up than down. Aiming high doesn't preclude revising to make the plan more realistic, but aiming too low creates tunnel vision and limits the possibilities of what we can accomplish. This is why James Connolly, the revolutionary socialist leader and Wobbly who helped lead the fight for a free Ireland in 1916, responded to critics advising him to be more moderate in his demands by saying, "Our demands most moderate are—we only want the earth!"[4]

**WE ONLY WANTED THE** earth in the form of credit card tipping, I explained to my coworker Em as we sat on the grass in Delaware Park in August of 2021, eating take-out tacos. She agreed: Most customers paid with cards and few carried cash. The ability to tip on credit card transactions would provide a significant boost to workers' paychecks. Em was a ray of sunshine, a cat lover who made herself matcha lattes and bought bouquets from the farmers' market and took me to street markets that sold batik clothing and vintage magazines. When I came out to her about my history with the union, she laughed and teased me, "I love it! Jazzy, our little spy!" Her insights were incredibly helpful in writing the letter to the company that would announce our campaign. She wanted a voice in the company, and she wanted a union that emphasized the positives—of working at Starbucks, of organizing, of coming together as coworkers.

"We are forming a union to bring out the best in all of us," the final version of our letter read. "Our organizing committee includes Starbucks partners from across the Buffalo region. Many of us have invested years of our lives at Starbucks, while others have recently become partners. We all have one thing in common—we want the company to succeed and we want our work lives to be the best they can be."[5]

The letter was peppered with references to Starbucks' mission and values statements, statements Em had brought up during our conversation. "They shouldn't say all of those things if they don't want us organizing!" she had said.

She was right.

Starbucks workers overwhelmingly supported the union because they had taken Starbucks at its word. It claimed to be "a different kind of company," one that did good in the world, that lived up to its progressive principles, that created a safe space for marginalized individuals. Starbucks workers were overwhelmingly women (about 70 percent) and LGBTQ+—so much so that I would have to argue with (male) event organizers about whether the lack of men on panels composed of worker organizers was actually a diversity and inclusion issue.[6]

Another Elmwood coworker, Michelle Eisen, personified the type of person who had applied to work at Starbucks because of what she believed it stood for. She had been with the company for over eleven years, and at Elmwood for six. A stage manager with a performance background, Michelle had been a regular at Starbucks long before applying, seeking the health benefits Starbucks promised to part-time workers.

At first, I wasn't sure whether she would support unionizing and held off on talking to her until less than a week before the first committee meeting. The signs were mixed. A coworker had told me she was one of the most progressive people they knew and that there was an 85 percent chance of her supporting the union. But if she didn't, she was close to Patty and I worried she might say something. She had told me, too, that she wanted more roundtable meetings with the district manager, and about how proud she had been of the letter Howard Schultz had sent to partners the day after the 2016 election, urging togetherness. Most concerningly, from an organizing time-commitment perspective, she had demoted herself from a shift supervisor to a barista because she didn't want to take the job home with her.

Michelle was clearly a leader within the workplace. She was wonderful to work with, effortlessly flexing into support positions to help anyone who was struggling, without making them feel bad. She started every shift with a coffee tasting, guiding us to discover the distinct flavors, and kept up workplace jokes and banter, including serving as a delightful foil to JP. She was also a mentor, especially for younger workers who came to her for advice on surviving at Starbucks. She would tell them, "Starbucks is a good company, but you have to use it as much as it's using you—and it is using you."

When a stolen catalytic converter crippled my car, Michelle texted me to ask if I needed a ride and then picked me up before daybreak for our opening shift the next morning. As we sat in the car in the cold morning, she told me about how much she loved opening: how, throughout the year, the sun had never quite risen as she went into the store, and how much she loved coming into the stillness and getting things ready for the day.

I finally arranged to meet Michelle outside the store for a talk after she got off work. Because of the cryptic nature of my messages—and because I had suggested meeting at a different coffee shop, a weird request particularly in a time when Starbucks still gave us free coffee daily—Michelle assumed I was seeking her advice on trying to become a shift supervisor. I got to the point quickly: What did she think of organizing a union at Starbucks? We walked around the side streets of the Elmwood Village as she told me about her experiences with her current union, the constraints of her theater schedule, and the confidential fact that she was planning to leave Starbucks in November, after her stocks vested.

Not realizing the extent to which union election time frames had changed for the worse under the Trump NLRB, I told her the campaign would move quickly: "We should have an election in twenty-one to twenty-eight days, so that would put us in September, or worst case in October, and you wouldn't have to stay for the contract fight—it would just be great if you could stay through the vote, and that shouldn't be an issue!"

Michelle told me she was always pro-union and that she thought a union made sense for Starbucks, which wasn't the same company she had started with. "I might not be here for much longer," she added, "but I want to make a union for the partners who will come after me."

I would think of that line many times in the coming months as I listened to Hazel Dickens' "Fire in the Hole," with its similar lyrics, on repeat in the car, a habit I had formed during the Spot Coffee campaign as a way of processing emotions and regrounding myself in the true reasons for the struggle. The line became even more profound to me after Michelle told me about her family's roots in Harlan County, Kentucky, and her childhood summers spent there: It wasn't just a free association, but a traceable path between the struggle of her ancestors and the fight we were in.

Michelle warned me at the end of the conversation that she didn't have a great deal of time to commit to the campaign. She was willing to sign the committee letter, but between theater productions and her actual Starbucks shifts, she was limited in what she could do. She told me she was going to Boston for the weekend of our committee meeting; I promised to keep her in the loop.

Later, working backward, Michelle would figure out that she was one of the last people I had talked to; even later, she would admit that, given my reasoning, I had made the right decision with the information I had. Still, had I made the request slightly earlier, we could have been off to an even stronger start.

**IN THE MEANTIME, OUR** ADHD-riddled team of organizers was making last-minute preparations for our meeting and the launch of the campaign. We decided to rent an office. The one that we had was too small to fit a large committee (and was decorated with a few too many American flags for comfort—actually, any American flags were too many for my comfort and didn't fit well with the iconoclastic and radical bent of the Buffalo barista bubble).

Cory spent a couple of days searching out places, then invited Richard and me to ride around and visit them with him. We ended up renting a large room on the fifth floor of the Tri-Main building, the old Ford plant that was now home to everything from art studios to refugee-services nonprofits to the area labor federation. Our office had no air-conditioning and was brutally hot in the summer and freezing in the winter, but it had large windows reaching to the ceiling on two walls and plenty of space to hang giant union banners. This office would become our new home for the coming months.

We did a micro-blitz in the first days before the meeting, driving to stores before sunrise to chat with workers, frenetically picking up shifts, meeting workers for lunch to answer tough questions about unions, and sending GroupMe messages and texts to promising contacts. We printed Q&As, attempted to source pins and shirts, and ordered union cards.

I was up early the morning of August 22, the day of our first committee meeting. Brian and Zach sourced coffee and doughnuts from Spot, while Richard wrote out the meeting agenda on a flip chart in the office and I scrawled the names of workers who had already confirmed they would be on the committee but wouldn't make the meeting. Then, the first workers began trickling in. Katie Cook from Walden and Anderson. Róisín Doherty and Sam Banaszak from the Galleria. Gianna Reeve from Camp Road.

We ended up with about ten workers in the circle of chairs. Richard tried to be reassuring: "It's a morning meeting, there are always more people at night."

As agreed upon beforehand, we started on the most positive note possible: "What do you like about working at Starbucks?" Richard asked.

Most of the workers in the circle said some version of "my coworkers." I talked about how I found steaming milk extremely satisfying. "What could be better?"

People talked about issues that ranged from a flood in the back room to scheduling issues to broadly wanting a voice on the job.

"Starbucks has been nonunion for the past fifty years," I said, when it came to me. "I just think about how great the next fifty could be if we had a union."

At the climax of the meeting, each worker stood up and signed their name and contact information to the sheet of paper on the flip chart. Then, we signed our union cards together. Sam and Gianna cornered me as we signed around one of the tables off to the side.

"So now that we get to know, you can tell us: Did you come here to do this?" Gianna asked.

"You definitely did, didn't you?" added Sam.

I wanted to tell them the whole truth, but it was still risky. Instead, I said, "No, I didn't, but I would organize any workplace I ever worked at."

The evening meeting was better attended. There were enough people to fill rows, instead of a single circle. There was something heroic and moving about the meeting: People were delivering on their commitments. Lexi arrived like a small general, leading coworkers Caroline and Danka into battle. From Orchard Park to East Robinson, Depew to Del-Ken, workers came from across the city. Josh and Marcus were quarantined with Covid, but Gianna, Will, and Kathryn Bergmann held down the Camp Road fort.

It was hard not to feel good as I looked around the circle of smiling, optimistic faces in the room. The spark had been lit: Starbucks workers wanted to organize. At the same time, I was disappointed there weren't more people here. Perhaps it had been optimistic, but Cory and I had predicted that we might have between seventy-five and one hundred workers on the committee when we launched. Instead, we had just under fifty.

"If Starbucks said they would sign the Fair Election Principles but we had to go for the whole district, would you take the deal?" I asked Richard, who had had a conversation with Starbucks executives years before in which they had told him privately they would not engage in union busting if he tried to organize baristas. Starbucks had the chance to prove it was a "different kind of company" by recognizing the right to organize; maybe the company would agree to sign.

"That's a very interesting question," he mused. "I like the all-or-nothing approach. I'd have to think about that."

The new organizing committee left the meetings with stacks of union cards to take into their stores for coworkers to sign. Initially, we debated exactly when we should go public: There could be an advantage to trying to sign up our stores before management really knew what was going on.

The next morning, I decided to pick up a coworker's closing shift to get a read on how things were going at Elmwood and to try to sign up coworkers. Then, in the newly created group texts, the texts began pouring in.

"They're calling all the shift supervisors into a meeting!"

"My manager has been on a Zoom call all morning with a lawyer and won't let me see her screen."

Anxious that Starbucks was about to try to make the shift supervisors managers or take some other underhanded action, and hurrying because I needed to go to work soon, we decided it was time to take the campaign public.

I logged in to the Starbucks Workers United Gmail account and, shaky with nerves and excitement, uploaded the PDF file of our letter, announcing the campaign and asking management to sign the Fair Election Principles.

"Dear Kevin," I typed. "We are proud to announce the formation of SBWorkersUnited in the Buffalo region. The organizing committee includes but is not limited to the initial signatories of the letter attached."

Then, as soon as it was sent, we posted the letter to Twitter and I rushed to Elmwood to clock in.

When I got there, Patty was in the back room with the shift supervisors. It was slow. In between customers, my coworkers and I talked about the union. Kat, a new hire who had previously come into work wearing a KILL YOUR MASTERS hoodie, was immediately in. Jayden, a seventeen-year-old barista, enthusiastically signed his union card on the espresso machine counter and asked me if I'd already spoken to Maya, his fellow high schooler. "She's an activist," he said. "She'll be really into this."

The next morning, I got a text from JP. Michelle had returned from her trip to Boston and was energetically talking union. I gave her a stack of union cards and she returned all of them, signed. Across the city, we were all signing coworkers openly on the floor, leaving our shifts with signed union cards in our apron pockets and taking them to the office for safekeeping. Store managers almost never worked early in the mornings or at night. Gianna Reeve was pulling her closing baristas off the floor to go to the back room, read the union leaflets, and sign cards. Lexi Rizzo did the same thing at Genesee.

The Galleria got to 50 percent first. I talked to Róisín, who was confident they could get another card or two quickly. The Galleria had the fewest number of employees, though, so if even one person quit or changed their mind, it would be a huge swing. Richard and I began talking about which stores to file.

When Lexi came in with the last union card, which put her store at unanimous support, Richard suggested filing for just Genesee. It would focus the world on one store: the baristas, led by Lexi, versus the billionaire Howard Schultz. Plus, it might draw some of the focus away from me and our salting, which we were trying to keep under wraps, fearing that Starbucks would try to delegitimize our union effort by labeling us "outside agitators."

"We have to file Elmwood," I argued. Partly, I was sure we would win: I knew my coworkers, and I firmly believed we would hold our cards. But I also felt a deeper desire to file for my own store.

Ultimately, Richard pointed out, it didn't matter how many stores we filed for. "We only have to win one," he said, a phrase that became a slogan of the campaign in those early days—and that, to me, evoked the Irish Republican Army's famous line about only having to be lucky once. If we won one, we would show that the workers wanted a union. Then, we could unite the whole labor movement around the fight of these baristas to win the right to organize and a fair contract.

On August 30, a week after we sent our letter to management, we decided to file for Genesee, Elmwood, and Camp Road, which had also gotten to an 85 percent majority. Other stores across the city were hovering at 30, 40, 50 percent. We could file for them at any time, we thought. But we needed to start the clock for the first elections.

The next day, Rossann Williams, president of Starbucks North America, was on a plane to Buffalo.

## CHAPTER FOUR

# Corporate Terrorism

Rossann Williams, president of Starbucks North America, swung open the door of the Elmwood Starbucks and walked in, flanked by Allyson and Deanna, the regional vice president and the new regional director.

Michelle Eisen and I were sitting at a high-top table, sipping coffee. She was filling me in on how things had gone at that morning's "listening session," Starbucks' term for captive-audience meetings designed to deter workers from unionizing. Management had told us not to report for our scheduled shifts; we would receive our full pay for the day if we attended the meeting instead. Corporate brought in workers from the Niagara Falls Boulevard store to run our store instead.

We watched as Rossann, in her crisp blazer, walked down the bar, patting partners on the back and chitchatting with them. Then, she walked to the register and ordered her signature drink: a venti, extra-dry cappuccino.

Making that drink required steaming two pitchers of milk and scooping out the foam with a spoon. When the barista handed her the cup, Rossann took the lid off and ran her finger through the foam, testing it.

Then, while Deanna swept and Allyson wiped up the trash bin in the lobby, Rossann tied up the bag of recycling and took it to the back, then reemerged with a spray bottle and some paper towels and headed to the bathroom.

One of our store's regular customers turned to Michelle and asked, "What happened to everybody?"

"We're all supposed to go to meetings with corporate," Michelle explained. "These partners don't know our store, and now they're having to deal with this, too."

The customer looked around and shook his head. "This is insane."

**ON AUGUST 23, OUR** organizing committee had emailed Kevin Johnson, Starbucks' CEO at the time, the letter announcing our campaign. The next day, the two district managers, David and Shelby, were in our stores. David, looking dapper in a fancy suit, asked my coworker Em—already running a short-staffed shift—what he could do to help. She looked at him blankly. He went into the back and grabbed the ice bucket. At other stores, the district managers ran trash, washed dishes, or swept the lobby—behaviors we would see them repeat all over the city.

A couple days later, the manager at Walden and Anderson told partners they were getting an additional store manager to "help with hiring." Then, he told them that Allyson and Shelby would be coming "to help us celebrate the Fall Launch"—a celebration that consisted of their standard performance: going behind the bar, introducing themselves, and taking out the trash.

Meanwhile, at Elmwood, I wanted our manager, Patty, to know that we still loved her. The night we went public with our campaign, I had called her and left a message, but she had avoided talking to me. Meanwhile, we learned that store managers were being summoned to countless Zoom calls with higher-ups and lawyers, directing them on what to say, what not to say, and how to start pushing back against the union.

One morning a few days later, Patty was changing the trash bags while I was on hot bar. I asked if she'd gotten my message and told her that our organizing campaign wasn't about her at all.

"Hmm, well, none of this would be happening if there wasn't some kind of disconnect, right?" she said, barely turning to look at me.

"I don't think there's a disconnect at all. People just want more of a say in the company, but that's about corporate, not about our store."

"But it is. If there's a union, I won't be able to help you on the floor anymore."

"That's not true! I'm not sure what they've told you, but we'll be the ones negotiating the contract and we would never agree to something that would hurt us or hurt you."

"Well, if you did, you'd be shooting yourselves in the foot," Patty said.

"We won't. We all love you. If they try to do anything to you, the whole store will strike."

"Well, we'll see." Patty turned and trudged to the back of house with the trash bag.

**STARBUCKS CORPORATE'S FIRST PUBLIC** response to our union campaign was a statement they gave to the media shortly after we went public: "While Starbucks respects the free choice of our partners, we firmly believe that our work environment, coupled with our outstanding compensation and benefits, makes unions unnecessary at Starbucks. We respect our partners' right to organize but believe that they would not find it necessary given our pro-partner environment."[1]

At our Tri-Main union headquarters, we debated what Starbucks' statement—which we later found out was recycled verbatim from the statement they had issued on the IWW's organizing effort in 2006—meant for our campaign.[2]

Richard was cautiously optimistic: "They could still sign the Fair Election Principles."

"They're not going to," I said.

One of the baristas on the organizing committee made a meme, filling in the text of Starbucks' response alongside the template of someone applying clown makeup.

This was Richard's first meme. When he saw it, he leaned back in his chair and laughed until he cried.

"Now I can die happy," he told me. "For fifty years, I've watched companies say this same shit—and now one of the workers has exposed it for exactly what it is. These workers are special—the corporate-speak doesn't work on them."

The other workers in the office made many more memes. The group chat exploded with them. Never had memes been met with a more grateful and receptive audience than they found in Richard. Partly, it was the novelty of the situation. Partly, it was the absurdity of the corporate newcomers juxtaposed with the wry humor of the terminally online baristas. Oprah distributing trash runs, SpongeBob personifying corporate burning a copy of the Fair Election Principles, Mean Girls graphics—"Get in partners, we're unionizing"—Drake disapproving of listening sessions and nodding toward the union. Many of the memes were lost on me, such as one depicting Barbie with a Starbucks apron in her closet, referencing a movie I hadn't seen. These memes helped us highlight the more hilarious aspects of Starbucks' union busting: humor helped maintain morale, while posting the best ones on social media showed the world what was happening in our stores.

From the beginning, Starbucks workers controlled the campaign's media strategy, from setting up interviews to crafting social media posts. Each initial organizing committee meeting included a segment on media training, where we practiced our key points, taught our coworkers to deflect questions that were going off track, and emphasized positivity and solidarity. From online content to printed leaflets to *The Partner* magazine, our campaign materials reflected the wry outlook of Starbucks workers, the lived realities of our jobs, and the issues that mattered the most to our coworkers.

To be sure, there were pitfalls. The biggest one was that I had used the Spot Coffee Union Instagram account for the Starbucks campaign to retain the Buffalo community supporters who were already activated. I saw the Starbucks campaign as a continuation of the industry project and was afraid that it would take too long to build public support. But I was wrong. I didn't realize that Spot workers would see this as a takeover of their campaign. They were right: Workers should have kept control of their accounts and run them, along with their union, autonomously.

There were other, smaller issues: When workers forgot which social media account they were logged in to and began liking non-union-related posts from the official SBWorkersUnited account, we had to ensure that those with access were responsible about checking which account they were using. Occasionally, someone did an interview that deviated wildly from the consensus-derived talking points. Managing the union group chat was a special headache for me, as I had to call the most talkative workers and beg them to take off-topic posts and venting to different chats because it was driving some people away from the campaign and impacting others' emotions. But these were good problems to have: they reflected the messy realities of running a truly worker-run and autonomous campaign.

**I CONVINCED PATTY TO** send me to Starbucks' first "listening session" in Buffalo, which took place on September 2. Rossann started off by trying to explain her sudden arrival in town. She told us that she just happened to be on the East Coast, visiting Deanna. "And when I found out she was coming to this market, it gave me the perfect reason to come out and celebrate with you and the team, to get to know some of you."

I recorded the meeting, holding my phone under the notepad on my lap. New York is a one-party consent state for recording, meaning you can record any conversation, as long as you are physically present when it happens, without notifying or getting permission from the other people in the room. We wanted to document how Starbucks was fighting our union, even as corporate spokespeople told us and the media that they weren't in Buffalo because of the campaign.

Deanna talked about how normal it was for Starbucks to have meetings like these. Milk-crate conversations, they called them. Because in the Pike Place store, which was the first Starbucks, the partners used to pull up milk crates to talk during their shifts. A couple of workers pointed out that these meetings were not normal, that they had never seen anything like them.

Rossann was in Buffalo anyway, she reiterated. Partners had raised their hands and asked for help. Sure, this meeting would be a little different because an outside group, a union called Workers United, had filed petitions for elections at some of the stores. There were some things corporate couldn't do, some things they couldn't say. They were still learning the law around unions themselves.

"But we do want to hear from you," said Deanna. "Want to know how you're feeling and what's going on in the stores because that's what this is about. We're Starbucks partners, and this is, you know, again, our long-standing tradition. So, what's on your mind, how are you feeling?"

Then Casey chimed in, "You guys said this was an honest conversation.

So, like, we all know you're here because of the union. You can't really look us in the eye and say that's not the thing. Like, there hasn't been one of these in, what—five, six years? So we all kind of know that that's why we're here. So I think what's on our mind is, why Starbucks hasn't signed the Fair Election Principles?"

Deanna launched into a rambling answer. Finally, Rossann summed up, "Whether the union is a part of the reason or not part of the reason, listening to each other and making this a greater company is what we've always been about."

The rest of the meeting covered everything from call-offs to turnover to TikTok drinks to bees to customer-connection scores to training to which law firm Starbucks had hired to advise them on the union (which they declined to answer).

Rossann brought up that she had heard the Elmwood store had a carpet in the back room, which she said was shocking. "How did that get by? I've never seen a store with a carpet in the back room before, in seventeen years."

Throughout the meeting, Rossann fluctuated from declaring, "When you say 'corporate,' that's me," when discussing certain matters, to weakly saying, "I can't say on behalf of Starbucks because it's just me," when asked if the organizing committee could have equal time for a union meeting, as the Fair Election Principles demanded. When Rossann said that the union would be speaking for us, I knew I needed to get a comment in and felt my heart rate rising.

Eventually, Róisín pointed out I had had my hand raised for some time. I couched what I wanted to say in the gentlest language I could muster: "The most recurring theme that I've heard from all of the other folks on the organizing committee is that we love Starbucks and all we want is to make it better. And I think we want Starbucks to see it not as a threat or as anything detrimental to Starbucks or to Starbucks' reputation, because all of us think Starbucks is great, we just want to make it the best it can be. And we think that, honestly, it won't change many things, like these kinds of conversations will still happen. And honestly, union negotiations wouldn't look that different, because the thing I wanted to go back to is you said something about the union speaking for us. And that's not how unions work—it's basically just a way for all of us to be able to speak for ourselves and to make sure that there's accountability, and, like, if a district hasn't had that kind of conversation in years, we can negotiate labor/management meetings to make sure that this kind of conversation happens regularly. And then we're actually making the most of the partnership."

Casey picked up where I left off, segueing into the supply shortages plaguing our stores and talking about how mean customers were when we were out of key items.

"Be the hero," said Rossann. "If you're really disappointing someone, just say, 'Look, it's on us today.'" She turned to Casey. "Does that make sense?"

"Yes," said Casey.

"And do you feel empowered to do that?"

"I mean, honestly, we're out of so many things. Like, we would just end up giving everything away. We would just be constantly giving things away. I mean, I appreciate the sentiment. I don't think that's really, like, a practical solution. But I appreciate the support, I appreciate making the effort."

Then things took a turn. Rossann snapped, "I wish there was something else I could do besides just close all the stores and not have jobs for anyone until things are back in stock. And there's all sorts of things we could do that we're choosing not to do."

She continued, at length, into a discussion of customers pulling up TikTok videos on their phones and showing them to us baristas at the register as they ordered the trending drinks. She suggested that this was a helpful method to ring in beverages, which Casey managed to turn into a comment on why having store partners empowered to make decisions through a union was so critical.

Hearing this, Róisín voiced her fear of retaliation—despite Rossann's adamant assertion that Starbucks had a firm anti-retaliation policy—and worried that Starbucks would close the Galleria store. The Galleria had issues, like fruit flies and the lack of a roof to prevent workers from getting sunburned under the glass ceiling of the mall, that were fixable, but which Starbucks might use as a pretext for their retaliation.

"So I do want to respond to that," said Deanna. "I know we're still getting to know each other, but I'm going to let you in on a secret. So when I go to stores, I tell every single store that I go to, I'm, like, 'Pop your collar, walk, you know, with some pep in your step because you work at this store, this is the most important store.' So if I were at your store, I would say, 'You work at the most important store, you work at the Galleria. So pop your collar, walk like you're the most important store in the entire world, because your store matters.'"

After the meeting, as partners broke off into smaller debriefs, emotions ranged from nervousness to exhilaration. "Did she threaten to close all the stores?" we wondered. Sure, Starbucks was going to try to stop us. But our numbers were clearly growing. Mellenia, a barista from the Del-Chip store who had talked about her woes around training, came up to me and Casey after the meeting, introduced herself as a member of the committee, and asked for union cards for her partners to fill out. Meanwhile, the workers began to come in for the next session: Michael Sanabria asked for a debrief as he came in, and Cory—who was getting off his shift—came over to hear how it had gone. The camaraderie among Starbucks partners had never been greater.

**EVERY DAY IN THE** weeks that followed, partners from across the city came into the office with handfuls of newly signed union cards—the tangible proof of that camaraderie. Support soared at Walden and Anderson, where Colin had recruited a fearless and upbeat shift supervisor, Katie Cook, to lead the committee. As they dealt with issues ranging from flooding to a manager known for favoritism and for his Spotify singles (baristas initiated new hires into the store by playing his signature track, "Keep Fucking," for their amusement) to a bee infestation (four workers had been stung in one week), partners came together to demand better. At the Transit Commons store, Michael, Loretta, and Roger pulled their coworkers together, creating a TikTok showing everyone on the shift wearing union pins and signing up an overwhelming majority on union cards. Other stores slowly grew their numbers: Delaware and Kenmore, known for chaotic shifts, cliquishness, and lines that extended far down the street and often caused traffic accidents, reached a slim majority.

A few days after the first committee meeting, I went into the Depew store and asked if Angel Krempa was working. A couple other workers had mentioned how important they would be to winning the store. After a moment, Angel came out from the back, a four-foot-eleven powerhouse in an apron streaked with whipped cream and mocha.

"Have you heard about the union stuff that's been going on? We could really use you on the committee," I said.

"I'm so down, homie. Come on!"

They led me into the back of house, where we chatted about their coworkers and the broader effort. "I've been waiting for something like this," they said. "My degree is in Russian history, this is kinda what I do."

Our committee kept one another informed, via the group texts, on where the corporate swarm went. I was working at Elmwood on a farmers' market Saturday, two days after Rossann's first listening session. This was the busiest time for the store, when our wait times were frequently upward of thirty minutes, our nitro machine was constantly breaking down or overheating, the number of orders exacerbated the shortages, and enforcing masking was near impossible as customers thronged the lobby.

Around 9:00 a.m., in the midst of the chaos of our morning peak, Rossann, Allyson, and Deanna came in. I was on handoff, giving customers their drinks and struggling with the nitro machine, punching the button to reset it again and again. It had overheated and wouldn't work; even the cold brew wouldn't come out. Customers impatiently leaned over the bar or took their masks off to eat their cake pops while they waited.

At the register, Rossann ordered her extra-dry cappuccino and $100 worth of gift cards. Then, she came behind the bar and started touching baristas on the shoulder or the back, introducing herself as our partner. She got to me and the handoff plane. "Hi, it's nice to see you again! I had to come to your store to see the carpet!"

"Good to see you again, too," I said.

She looked at the customers, leaning on the walls. "How long have people been waiting?"

"The machine's broken. Some people have been waiting for a while."

Rossann went back around to the lobby and started asking people what they'd ordered. Then, she would come over to me.

"Do you have the nitro for Julie?"

"No, I can't get the keg to work."

"I need the nitro for Julie!" Rossann said to me, then turned to Julie and handed her one of the gift cards. "Sorry about your wait!"

When her extra-dry cappuccino hit the counter, Rossann lifted the cup disapprovingly. She took the lid off to examine the foam and shook her head, then went over to where Allyson and Deanna were standing with Patty in the lobby. Rossann asked who had made her drink.

A few minutes later, I was doing a milk run to restock the fridges. As I hurried to the back room, Rossann was deep in conversation with Stephen, the longest-term partner on the organizing committee. Stephen was telling her how grateful they were to have the opportunity to talk to her.

"I'm just here because I wanted to listen and hear from partners like you," said Rossann. Shockingly, no mention of the carpet.

I made a note to follow up with Stephen afterward.

On my lunch break, my background in defending the last abortion clinic in Mississippi came in handy. At the Pink House, I had learned how to engage with the antiabortion protesters to distract them from yelling at our patients. Now, I transferred these skills to corporate.

I ordered coffee and a breakfast sandwich and headed to the back room. Within a couple of minutes, Rossann followed me, hovering over me as I ate. I didn't have time to start recording on my phone, but I hid in the bathroom for a few minutes afterward to jot down the conversation.

"Thank you for your time in the listening sessions," she began.

"Of course!" I said brightly.

She told me this was her first time in Buffalo. "Do you like sponge candy?"

"I've never had it."

"Well, we tried it, and it wasn't really my thing, it's really sweet, you know. But our Uber driver, he was born-and-bred Buffalo, and he told us, if you're in Buffalo, you have to try it. And he didn't have any teeth. Maybe that was because of the sponge candy."

This went on for some time.

Then I tried to steer the conversation back to the union, knowing her guard was down.

"You've been going to a bunch of stores, right?" I asked, in the kindest possible voice.

"Oh, yes. So many."

"How has that been?"

"Well, we've been out visiting the stores following up on the problems that you all told us about."

"Are there any changes you think make sense in Buffalo?"

"What do you mean?"

"I just meant, in terms of what you all have been following up on, what do you think is needed?"

"Oh! Well, we're trying to address the issues that you all told us about—things like scheduling and staffing, facilities problems—the reason we are at Elmwood is the carpet," she reiterated.

Maya came into the back to grab paper towels.

"And then there's training issues, like where people are not adequately trained and then thrown on bar," Rossann said. Turning to Maya, she asked, "Do you think you got the training you needed for bar?"

"I guess not," said Maya, "it can definitely be kind of overwhelming."

"Exactly!" said Rossann. "And then the customers aren't happy, and the partners have anxiety. Like, my cappuccino wasn't right, but you weren't trained to make it right, which is on us."

As Maya went back to the floor, Rossann turned back to me. "And of course, we're trying to meet as many partners as we can, which is what we do in every market visit."

Rossann talked to me for nearly forty minutes, then looked at her watch. "Oh, did I keep you your whole break? Oh, don't worry—take a few more minutes if you need!"

I was ten minutes late punching back in, turning to JP apologetically to explain that I had been commandeered.

"They're doing whatever they want to do," he agreed.

**ROSSANN'S TEAM WAS DOING** whatever they wanted in stores across the city.

"Rossann sighting!" one partner would type.

"My shoulder has been touched twice already," another would complain.

Rossann and her team would pull partners off the floor into meetings or conversations, leaving their coworkers even more short-staffed.

One night—over Labor Day weekend—Michael Sanabria, Richard, and I were working in the Tri-Main office. Richard had been filming since before the campaign even launched, talking about how he was going to make a documentary about it. Michael, a barista at the Transit Commons store, had enthusiastically joined the project, convincing Gary Bonadonna to buy him a fancy camera and asking the corporate visitors to appear in the documentary.

During one of Michael's conversations with Rossann about this, she suggested that he make a documentary about coffee instead of working with Richard on a project about unionizing: "I see the sparkle in your eyes when you talk about coffee, but that sparkle goes away when you talk about making a documentary for someone else."

Getting Rossann to go on camera became a bucket list item for Michael.

As we sat there, chatting, the group chat started pinging. Josh Pike announced that Rossann was at Camp Road, at 8:45 p.m. on a Saturday during a holiday weekend. We had already been talking about filming Josh for the documentary.

"We should go!"

Michael grabbed his camera and we raced down to my car. I drove as quickly as I could across the Skyway and down to the Southtowns.

When we got there, Michael needed a moment to pep himself up: "I think I'm going to throw up. There's only been three times in my entire life I've been so nervous I've thought I was going to throw up, and this is one of them. Who else is in there?"

We watched through the big open windows at the front of the store as Rossann leaned across the bar and the other corporate people hovered behind her. Another woman came out from behind the bar and went to the handoff plane.

Then, they started walking toward the door.

"They're leaving!" I said.

"It's now or never," said Michael, and started the camera rolling.

We threw on our Starbucks masks and jumped out of the car as Rossann, Allyson, and Deanna walked out.

"Hi, Rossann," said Michael.

"Good to see you, Michael!" said Rossann. "I just emailed you, I really don't feel— What are you doing?" Her tone changed as she noticed the camera.

"We're actually interviewing somebody else," said Michael.

We went into the store and talked to Josh, who said they could go on their ten in a couple of minutes. Meanwhile, after getting into her car for a minute, Rossann came back into the store under the pretext of using the bathroom. She watched us and circled back around the bar.

Michael, Josh, and I went out onto the patio. Michael filmed Josh, and I filmed Michael filming Josh. A couple minutes into the interview, Rossann walked by, staring intently, and got back into her car. The car circled the parking lot, then parked farther back, headlights on, with a direct view of the patio.

Josh talked about working at Chipotle and walking out over the working conditions. They had gone across the street to Starbucks, applied, and gotten the job. They admitted they hadn't realized their store was one of the first to file for a union election, and they had approached Will to ask how they could make their store one of the unionizing ones. "Josh, we are one of the stores, " Will had told them.

"How did you feel about Rossann visiting your store?" I asked.

"I felt weird. She asked me about my drag, and I showed her a video, and she was nice, but we all know why she's there."

"Did you bring up the drag?" Michael asked.

"No. They knew who I was, they'd looked up my Instagram, they know who we are. I'm worried, I need the job."

"They're going to be super-nice to you," I said.

"They're going to be super-nice to me for the next three months," Josh said. "They know all the names on that list."

Michael asked if Josh thought corporate's attempt to fix issues in the store and respond to what partners were saying in listening sessions would work, dissuading people from unionizing.

"I know my partners," said Josh. "People at my store are gonna vote yes. It's not gonna work."

**OVER THE DAYS AND** weeks that followed, Rossann's forces swelled as other members of corporate and managers from across the country joined her in Buffalo. Denise Nelsen, the senior vice president in charge of U.S. operations, arrived with a wardrobe of high-end Canada Goose jackets and vests. She told me she was in town to supervise the remodel of the Elmwood store. But she didn't limit herself to just our store, instead joining the corporate entourage.

In some ways, corporate's invasion backfired. As work became more intense, partners turned to each other for support, comfort, humor. The memes continued. Support poured in from the community, including regulars like TR, who brought bags of union pins into the store; Tom, who would walk through the store and tell each of us individually that he hoped our day was beautiful; and Bradley, who drove half an hour nearly every morning to don a union pin and come wish us success. Orders for "Union Strong" and "Union Yes" decorated our handoff counter.

One of our staunchest comrades was Sara Nelson, the president of the Association of Flight Attendants. She had joined our second-ever committee meeting via Zoom, tearing up on the call as she told us what our campaign could mean for the labor movement. She wore our union pin constantly, in every interview and public appearance she made. A charismatic, dynamic, and caring leader, Sara showed what the labor movement could be at its best.

Starbucks Workers United had endorsed Buffalo's progressive mayoral candidate, India Walton, almost immediately after launching its campaign. It was a symbiotic relationship based on shared goals and solidarity: Baristas knocked on doors for her campaign, and she included us in events, arranging a meeting with Alexandria Ocasio-Cortez when she came to town for a rally. Later that fall, our organizing committee was thrilled when Bernie

Sanders called in to the campaign office to wish us luck in our election and hosted a livestream with workers from the unionizing stores.

Meanwhile, more workers across the city continued to reach out and step up, encouraged by the momentum and jubilation behind the campaign.

Our campaign was so effective because it was genuinely partner-to-partner. We joked that the organizing effort was just Richard and one hundred–plus Starbucks partners in a group chat. My coworkers knew that I worked for the union as well as at Starbucks, but they also knew that I understood the struggles of working short-staffed, dealing with irate customers, and shaking iced matcha lattes, which were among the least fun drinks to make. With partners running social media, press outreach, and the email account, and fielding inquiries from new partners interested in joining the organizing committee or the GroupMe chats, we maintained an authenticity that enabled us to build trust with partners who were initially hesitant to become involved.

**DUE TO HER SCHEDULE** as stage manager, Michelle had been unable to attend any of the first union meetings. Two weeks or so later, she talked to me about arranging a meeting with Richard at the union office.

"How involved are you willing to be?" he asked.

"How involved do you need me to be?"

From that moment on, Michelle became our de facto leader. Later, she would tell me she had realized this was going to be a fight, and that she needed to get more involved.

We could never have won Elmwood without Michelle. She was the rock of the store, the voice of experience and care, the unassailably perfect worker. She was fearless in confronting management, but in a way that was never strident, always motivated to protect and defend her coworkers. She was also perfectly poised: Her theater background had prepared her for the unglamorous and demanding minutiae of organizing, which dovetailed with her stage-managing expertise, as well as for the seemingly effortless interviews she could give, where she turned bullet points into perfect sound bites, thanks in part to her training in performance. She was always the most thoughtful, the most prepared, the most kind. She brought sandwiches to meetings to make sure no one forgot to eat, planned perfect birthday surprises, listened empathetically to anyone's concerns, and did her best to serve as partners' human shield. Cassie nicknamed her our "security blanket" because Michelle's presence at any meeting—from captive-audience meetings to union events—made attending less daunting.

This was particularly important because the "listening sessions" continued, with particular intensity at the three stores that had filed for union elections. Michelle and I devised a system for divvying up the meetings, attempting to ensure that none of our partners faced corporate's union busting alone. Starbucks scheduled most of them outside our availability, but Michelle was able to attend the earlier ones before having to go to the theater.

I gave Angela and Stephen a ride to the first Elmwood-specific meeting, at the hotel next to the Genesee store. On the ride over, Stephen told us about their conflicted feelings.

"Rossann Williams, Denise Nelsen—these people are heroes to me, like, legends. And they're telling me they want to hear from me. And I know why they're here—we all know why they're here. They wouldn't be here if we weren't unionizing. But at the same time, this is the only chance I'm ever going to get to talk to them, and I feel like if I take that, I can make the company better for everyone. Which I know is what unionizing is trying to do, too. It's just complicated."

Angela talked about how the store was short four people as everyone drove across town to go to the meeting. "I don't want to go. Nobody wants to."

The psychological upset became physical, too. As soon as we pulled up to the curb outside the hotel, Angela climbed out of the car and threw up into the mulch. "I'm just really anxious," she apologized.

"I hate that they're doing this to us," I said.

Rossann and her team were late to the meeting, claiming they had mixed up the times. After doing our Covid check-ins with the overly peppy corporate representative—another person we had never seen before—we sat together in a semicircle. I switched on my phone's recorder before corporate arrived and slid it into my back pocket.

Finally, Rossann, Allyson, and Deanna came in, carrying French presses full of sludgy coffee. Allyson and Deanna wore combat boots and militaristic jackets—Allyson's was even camouflage. Rossann had swapped out her customary blazer for a dusty-pink sweater.

"Let's spread out some!" said Deanna in a too-cheery tone.

Reluctantly, our semicircle shifted. Angela ended up sandwiched between Rossann and Allyson and looked extremely uncomfortable throughout the meeting.

Allyson poured sample cups of burnt-tasting Pike Place coffee from the French press. Angela declined. I took one and awkwardly held it through the coffee tasting, as the corporate executives vied to see who could make the loudest slurping noises. By way of introduction, Rossann talked about her wife and their fancy trips to Europe on official Starbucks business. Deanna talked about getting Frappuccino chips stuck between her teeth and about her wife. Allyson—who did not have a wife—took every opportunity in the listening sessions to talk about being a fan of k.d. lang and the Indigo Girls. ("She is not going to out-lesbian me!" Elissa, one of the Camp Road partners, announced in the organizing committee group chat.)

Deanna talked about the changes they were implementing in the market, then handed off to Allyson.

"Now, I want to talk just a little bit today and have a conversation around the union petition in your store," Allyson said. "We want to have an open discussion about that. And I want to make sure that we are answering all of your questions so that you can make the very, very best decision for you. You need to make sure you have all the facts. And we respect your decision, but we want to make sure that you have all of the information you need, and we don't believe that unions are—have a place at Starbucks."

Rossann jumped in to talk about how many other markets she had held listening sessions in, and how it was her obligation to bring the market up to standard.

Then I—softly—said that I didn't think any of us were organizing a union because there were specific problems, or that any of us had even said there was a specific problem. "I think it's more that we want partners to have an equal relationship," I said.

Afraid of seeming confrontational, I spoke so quietly that Rossann had to ask me to repeat what I was saying.

She responded with something about unions being third parties, then pivoted to the issues she was allegedly here to address. Including the carpet. Especially the carpet.

"We've heard that there have been some facilities issues, and I'll have to admit, I've never seen a carpet in the back room like I saw at your store, Jaz. I mean, really. I was like, 'What is a carpet doing in the back room?' I've been all—literally all over the world working at Starbucks, and I've never seen a carpet in the back room."

Angela talked about how corporate had rewarded a customer who had called to complain after we told him, kindly, he needed to wear shoes if he wanted service. She talked about how upset she was that corporate never listened to us: They sided with customers every time.

Stephen talked about their idealism. "I feel, and have for a while, very disillusioned. And I think it's, like, the hardest thing for me. Because, like, I actually love this company, like, a disgusting amount. Like, a lot. A lot."

They described the isolation they had faced after blowing the whistle on an inappropriate colleague during their time as a store manager, and their determination not to leave Starbucks despite feeling they hadn't experienced the "best shift ever" Rossann spoke of in an unacceptably long time.

Cassie talked about how she wasn't given the resources to appropriately train and then shadow new partners, and about partners' concerns about retaliation when they took mental health days.

At the end, I tried to ask again whether corporate would sign the Fair Election Principles.

"We have to wrap," said Rossann, after reiterating that if we wanted "equal time" for a union meeting, we could meet with partners off the clock. "We're still learning, but we will take all your questions and get back to you."

"Our emails are on the board," Deanna said, nodding.

After the meeting, Stephen started talking one-on-one with Rossann. Cassie came over to me and told me she was surprised at how much she had spoken up.

"That was amazing," I said. "And needed to be said—you're so right about mental health days. You know, when we win, it would be really great to have you on the bargaining committee—that's exactly the kind of insight we need."

After my initial conversation with Cassie about the union, I had worried that our friendship might change or become tense: I still wanted her support for the union, while she wanted to avoid the topic. After she told me she didn't want to sign a union card, I had dropped the subject. We chitchatted during opening shifts and she sent me videos of crochet tutorials; we went out for dinner on her birthday and attended a coworker's drag show together. Deep down, I still hoped she might come around.

We migrated to the hotel lobby, and our conversation shifted to making plans to go to Stephen's drag show that weekend. Then, I saw Lexi and some of the other Genesee partners.

I ran over to hug Lexi. "How's it going?"

"I just came from getting tattooed. My head hurts, and I'm in pain."

I learned that a higher-up had called her in the middle of her tattoo appointment and told her that if she didn't go to the listening session that afternoon and wasn't able to attend the next one, which was scheduled on a day when she would be out of town, she would face discipline.

We advised the Genesee partners not to let corporate divide them, even if they told them to spread out, and wished them good luck as they went down the hall to the conference room.

Then Stephen rejoined us, talking about how they were both starstruck—Rossann had offered to get coffee!—and saddened—they saw through corporate's pretenses.

**AT WALDEN AND ANDERSON**, things other than the beehive in the drive-thru were abuzz. At the beginning of September, partners had enough support to file for a union election at their store. Eighty-five percent of them had signed union cards, and nearly everyone on the floor wore a pin on their apron.

Then, a bee stung a customer.

Management closed the lobby and the store was drive-thru only for the rest of the day, which was unheard-of. Partners had been dealing with bee stings for months, and management had done nothing. Shelby visited the store with a couple of facilities people to look at the beehive.

Two days later, the store manager told the partners their store would be closing to the public for several weeks, "to provide a full retraining for all partners new and old, and to have professional work done to clean and remove the flying insects that we have."

Colin and his coworkers were confused. Sure, some new hires hadn't been adequately trained, but other partners were long-term or already excelling at their jobs. Partners were told not to come in for their regular shifts and to wait for a new training schedule. At night, fumigation crews set off bug bombs to try to eliminate the bees and fruit flies.

Two days later, the partners returned to a closed store. In between deep-cleaning sessions, partners rewatched *Barista Basics* videos and practiced steaming milk with Tito, a store manager from Rochester. They had discussions about diversity and mental health and took lots of breaks.

"It feels like Starbucks summer camp," said Colin. "They've just decided to make our life easy for the next few weeks to make people forget how stressful it is to work here."

When customers drove up to the closed store, managers would run out to meet them and offer them a free iced coffee. Most of the regulars, however, migrated to other stores. Some of them were higher maintenance than others. One person came into Elmwood every morning to order a grande nitro cold brew, in a venti cup, with a side cup of ice, a side cup of almond milk with cinnamon dolce powder shaken in, a small cup of Frappuccino crunchies, and a pup cup—an order forever seared into my memory.

On September 8, the day after their first "retraining" shifts, Walden and Anderson partners filed for their union election, along with Transit Commons, which had also reached a strong majority.

The Regional Director of the No Labor Rights Board, as Richard called the NLRB, was a Trump appointee and, subsequently, a Biden appointee who was married to a management lawyer. When we filed for these additional stores, Starbucks requested that the NLRB consolidate the new petitions with the first three. That would effectively restart the clock on the original stores' election time frames, postponing the unit determination hearing to add in the next two stores and giving Starbucks management additional time to union bust. The NLRB sided with Starbucks. Frantically, I called committee leaders at Walden and Anderson and Transit Commons to discuss our options.

Ultimately, partners at the two stores voted to pull their own petitions to avoid delaying the first three elections. Richard's phrase "We only have to win one" summed up our strategic belief that winning an election at one store would be enough to rally the labor movement around our right to organize and prove that organizing Starbucks was possible. If we won, other workers might look at our store and think, "If they can do it, we can do it." If the NLRB forced us to start over, our chances of winning that one store would significantly decrease.

Simultaneously, partners at the Galleria mall store, across the freeway from Walden and Anderson, were experiencing much of the same treatment from corporate. Rossann had visited the store and gone behind the bar, asking the partners what was on their minds. One worker mentioned that management had ignored repair tickets for their oven for a long time. The next day, September 2, facilities crews brought and installed a brand-new oven. Then, a couple of days after Walden closed temporarily, management told the Galleria partners that their store, too, would close for a week, for retraining and deep cleaning. Partners spent a week scrubbing the store on their hands and knees while facilities people brought in new equipment. At the end of that week, management told the partners the store would remain closed for another week, to hire and train new partners for the store.

On September 25, the partners returned to the Galleria for what they believed was a store reset with the district manager, to go over details of the reorganization and ensure everything was up to standard before they reopened. Róisín came in early to meet with her store manager and go through the career-development paperwork to start becoming a shift supervisor. The other workers began trickling in for the meeting.

Then, Shelby and Mark, the new district manager, came in a few minutes early and pulled the store manager into a private meeting, telling Róisín and her coworkers that they could join after ten minutes. When the partners went upstairs, they found their store manager crying.

"I know it's surprising, but we're going to close Walden Galleria," said Mark.

He claimed the store was costing the company too much money, that they were struggling to pay rent and pay the workers for cleaning. He handed out transfer request forms.

None of this made sense to the workers. Starbucks had just hired people, trained them, deep-cleaned the store, and brought in new equipment. It didn't add up.

After Mark left, the workers turned to their store manager. "Are you okay?"

"I literally found out about this three minutes before you did," she said. The workers saw how miserable and terrified she was. She had serious medical issues and was suddenly out of a job.

Panic rippled through the organizing committee group chat.

"I'm sure people have heard me say I'm going down with that goddamn ship like the band on the *Titanic*," Sam wrote. "With that in mind, I've decided to quit. I'm signing out of all the socials and deleting these GCs but if you guys ever need help with anything please let me know! I wish all the best for y'all and the effort."

Other partners texted me, terrified. "Our store is also infested with fruit flies—do we need to worry?" "Are we next?"

We decided that the best thing to do from a strategic standpoint was to downplay the closure and avoid making it a focal point. But the Galleria partners floated around the district, transferring into new stores or—for those whose transfers were denied or stalled—picking up shifts. Their presence and shared experiences were a constant reminder to their new coworkers of Starbucks' retaliatory and arbitrary power to disrupt partners' lives. The company was also closing stores for remodels, often for long periods. When they closed Niagara Falls Boulevard to redo the floor, those partners also flooded into Cheektowaga, except for the days that they worked at other stores while the partners attended captive-audience meetings.

The Galleria partners were joined in this migration around the district by their colleagues from the Walden store, which management turned into a training store. Some of them were sent to Genesee Street and Camp Road, flooding the stores. A few partners—the barista trainers—would return to Walden, to help train "pods" of new partners alongside Starbucks managers brought in from around the country. Colin Cochran was one of the trainers.

He kept us posted on the progression of the new hires. Some of them, seeing the contrast between their barista trainers and the corporate managers, bravely donned union pins before they even got to their new stores. Colin connected me with Kaleb, one of the new hires, who was still in training.

Kaleb complained about how corporate had switched managers and trainers at random: "Training was great until they had that lady from Seattle come and train us instead. Then it was definitely a 'let's focus on company' training. I loved Tito [the previous trainer] and out of nowhere Tito was gone."

Kaleb was going to be working in the Del-Ken store, which hadn't had enough support to file and which had become increasingly tense as the corporate presence grew more overwhelming. I asked if they wanted me to connect them to the committee members there.

"Yes, of course, I'd love that," they said. "Especially 'cause I don't think I'll be comfortable asking when I get there. The training made me think it's hush-hush about anything other than working."

**ACCORDING TO CORPORATE, THE** swarm of managers had come to Buffalo to fight problems like carpets, bees, and fruit flies. In reality, they were there to create the exact impression Kaleb had gotten: that partners needed to hush about the union.

Dustin Taylor, a store manager from Georgia, was Elmwood's first "support manager." Starbucks' pitch was that leadership in Buffalo had let partners down and that outside support would help get the market back up to standard. In reality, corporate wanted to increase the managerial presence to keep an eye on workers and try to prevent us from having conversations at work. Each store was open about one hundred hours per week. A store manager worked about forty hours per week, and many store managers didn't spend much time on the floor. Bringing in additional managers was a key method of surveillance.

One morning, I was visiting the store on my day off to order coffee and check in with everyone. As I was talking to Angela and ordering my drink, Dustin came up and said, "Hi, Jaz!"

I was not wearing a name tag and had not introduced myself.

He hovered over Angela's shoulder, making it impossible for me to keep talking about the union.

Michelle gave me the rundown as soon as she could: Dustin had just gotten in from Georgia the night before. He was stationed in our store "until sometime in October," he thought, but they hadn't given him an exact time frame. And he was already rearranging everything in the store. Dustin's main demand was that the partners putting away the order unpackage everything immediately, and he gave strict orders about back-room storage standards. Nondairy-milk cartons in boxes were anathema to him.

JP was annoyed. "He's trying to tell me I don't know how to do my job!"

Patty had been confiding in JP and Em. She had told them back in August that as soon as corporate found out about the union campaign, they had locked her out of the hiring portal, taking that power away from her. Now, Dustin was taking over scheduling and throwing his weight around as a longer-term partner than Patty, coaching baristas and talking about Starbucks "standards."

One or two baristas told me they liked or were becoming close to Dustin, who adopted strikingly different postures toward different partners. But most of the store united around Patty. Sure, she had seldom given us our schedules more than a couple of days in advance and had strung partners along about promotions. Nevertheless, she was genuinely kind, empathetic, and sweet and—unlike most of the managers in the district—worked alongside us on the floor and tried to make our store function cohesively and well. Moreover, if corporate fired Patty, partners would have blamed the union and said that it would never have happened had we not tried to organize. So, to protect Patty as well as our store, we coordinated our talking points for captive-audience meetings from the very first listening session, emphasizing our love for her to protect her from the fate store managers across the district were facing, as corporate scapegoated and fired them.

But Patty was getting annoyed. She began venting to Michelle as well, expressing her exasperation as Dustin tried to take over store operations. One day, Patty mentioned having to adjust the schedule for another meeting.

"Is that for the whole store?" Michelle asked.

"No, it's another of these 'listening sessions,'" Patty said, rolling her eyes.

JP warned that this was taking its toll: "Patty told me she is thinking about walking."

That would have been catastrophic in ways that paralleled corporate firing her, in terms of the hit to morale, the ripple effect of other partners quitting, and the backlash against the union. Our organizing committee brainstormed ways to remind Patty we loved her. Kellen identified the best place to buy her a gift card. Recalling a conversation she and I had had about chocolate preferences, I went to the candy shop and got a box of her favorites. Michelle gave her our collective offering and reported back that Patty had teared up.

Not long after Dustin's arrival, I came into the store to find Patty talking to another "support manager" newcomer. She introduced him as Matt, who had just arrived from Boston.

For all of his flaws, Dustin was at least capable of doing the job. Matt was not.

"Did you know he used to work at the Apple store in the mall and then just went over to the Starbucks?" JP told me.

"I'm getting him to fix all of my devices," said Maya.

I came in for a shift one morning and ordered my drink. Matt was on bar. The drink had regular shots instead of blonde, and I could tell they were not ristretto shots. I said something to Em.

"You should ask him to remake it," she told me.

I walked out onto the floor and held out the drink to Matt. "This is not blonde."

He remade it.

JP and Em were laughing in the back when I returned. "That's the first time you didn't say sorry," they said.

"I only apologize to people I like." Not to mention, I was still half-asleep. But it was a sharp contrast.

Michelle and I had agreed that our strategy would be to treat Patty as the only store manager and the others as intruders. We didn't go to the newcomers with scheduling questions or anything else. But Matt—unable to do many jobs in the store other than handoff—set himself up as the go-to person for getting promotions.

Cassie wanted to become a shift supervisor. Em wanted a remote job. Angela wanted to finally become, as promised, a barista trainer. And so on. Matt pulled people into one-on-one meetings in the lobby to hold what Starbucks called partner-development conversations. He strung them along, scheduling subsequent meetings to discuss interview questions and role expectations.

**IN THE MEANTIME, THINGS** were dragging on at the NLRB. They had scheduled the unit determination hearing about voting store-by-store for late September, nearly a month after we had filed.

I had promised Michelle that we would have an election by September or October. Under the Obama NLRB rules—the rules that had still been in effect during Nissan, Spot, and every other union election I had experienced prior—this would have been true. But the Trump NLRB rules were still in effect. In fact, the Biden Board had not even begun attempting to change them. This meant that instead of holding an election within three to four weeks, which the Obama rules required, the NLRB enabled Starbucks to delay our elections indefinitely by litigating the appropriate bargaining unit prior to the election instead of afterward. Starbucks announced that instead of allowing us to vote store by store, they were going to ask the Board to hold an election of the entire market.

Starbucks knew they weren't going to win the unit-determination hearing. If we had said we would go for the market election, they would have asked the NLRB to make us vote the whole region. Moreover, NLRB precedent was on our side. But Starbucks' goal wasn't to win; it was to delay. To drag things out, Starbucks spent thousands of dollars in legal fees arguing losing cases in order to stall and give corporate more time to disrupt our stores.

Companies have two critical tools in fighting the union: fear and delay.

Delay augments the fears and doubts management tries to plant in workers' minds in captive-audience meetings, one-on-ones, and slick leaflets. We had filed with unanimous support at Genesee and overwhelming strength at the other stores. Therefore, Starbucks was willing to do whatever it took to drag things out and buy themselves time to try to influence the Buffalo partners.

It wasn't always like this. Despite the limitations and exclusionary nature of the NLRB, which had been present since its founding, it was clear on a critical point: The company should not be a participant in the election. The choice was supposed to be up to the workers: a choice between a union or no union, not between the union and the company. The framers of the NLRA wanted to forbid companies from influencing unionizing, but fear of a conservative judicial backlash forced the law's authors to change the word *influencing* to *interfering*, giving companies greater power. Nonetheless, NLRB elections (versus other methods of establishing majority support for unionization, like petitions or out-of-board votes) didn't become the default method for determining whether workplaces were unionized until much later; in the 1940s, management pushed for changes that would give them the ability to go to war against unions in the period leading up to a vote. The Starbucks hearing process showed exactly how far a company could push the limits of labor law to become not just a party, but a roadblock, to an election.[3]

Prep for the hearing was intensive. We subpoenaed workers from all three stores, and because we didn't know when they would each need to testify, all of us camped out in a conference room at our union lawyers' office, while the witnesses testified upstairs about how our stores actually operated as independent units. Michelle was our first witness. With her long tenure, poised demeanor, and patient delivery, she delivered smoldering hits to the company's facade through her commonsense credibility. The crew in the conference room cheered when she shot down particularly ridiculous insinuations during her cross-examination, as the mild-mannered board agent, Tom Miller, attempted to referee.

As we sat in the conference room in the lawyers' office, our phones began to buzz. It was Starbucks. The text read, "Starbucks Partner Update:

Buffalo Partners: Your voice matters. Check your e-mail or Partner Hub for an important update from Allyson Peck today. Thank you!"

"The last time Starbucks texted me was in a hurricane when we had to evacuate and they were trying to make sure everyone was okay," said Lexi. "And I think they texted us at the beginning of the pandemic."

"I've never gotten a text from them," several other partners said.

The hearing was our first definitive confirmation that Starbucks' union busters were from Littler Mendelson. Starbucks had a long-standing relationship with Littler; the firm was the two-time recipient of Starbucks' Excellence in Diversity and Inclusion award. The lawyers the firm assigned to the Starbucks campaign had experience in fighting unions; one of the duo who represented the company at our hearing had been assigned to fight the UAW's unfair labor practice charges at Nissan four years prior. The other one—Alan Model—was older and given to frowning into his Littler-branded coffee cup on the Zoom screen, perhaps for the benefit of the reporters who thronged the livestream. I was surprised that so many reporters logged on; it brought home that the nation was watching what was going on at our little cafés in Buffalo.

**WHILE THE ORGANIZING COMMITTEE** was sequestered in the lawyers' office, listening to Starbucks' "decision scientists" discuss how the company relied on algorithms, not store managers, to run their stores, the "support managers" were wreaking havoc in our stores. They were there around the clock. Some shifts at the Genesee store consisted of one or two baristas and six managers, creating an unfamiliar and overwhelming environment for the workers. Corporate took advantage of our committee's absence to have one-on-ones and to try to sow doubt with our coworkers. When we were in the stores, we could clarify their misinformation and lies; shift supervisors could assign work in such a way that partners were less likely to be forced off the floor into anti-union conversations.

The hearing took the union leaders out for a week; making matters worse, Lexi was scheduled for surgery the following week, meaning that Genesee would lack its most effective organizer. Through remodels and store closures, Starbucks had already seen that dividing and scattering workers was effective. Now, they began to invent creative ways of removing pro-union workers from their stores. If organizing committee members coughed or sniffled, a support manager was likely to send them home and place them on a mandatory fourteen-day Covid isolation period, even if they tested negative. At Genesee, Danka and Caroline were sent into quarantine; Will was banished from Camp Road on the same basis.

"We're openers," Michelle said. "If you don't feel a little weird at five a.m., something's wrong with you."

She and I agreed that we could never admit to so much as having a headache at work for fear of getting sent home.

In addition to the support managers, we still faced visits from roving bands of corporate executives. Rossann and Denise were frequently in our store, often with new corporate officials like Adam Modzel, the newly promoted community engagement director from DC.

In October, Elmwood shut down for a one-week remodel. Some partners were forced to work at other stores. I visited Cassie while she was working at Genesee. She found it to be a flustering experience, mainly because the support manager was so stressed about half hours with far lower customer volume than we experienced at Elmwood. Other workers went to Delaware and Kenmore, which was an even more intense and stressful environment. To try to bring the store together and help shore up support, I invited my coworkers to a bonfire at my house. I also spent the week visiting stores across the city. One day, after seeing a message that Rossann and Adam were at Sheridan and Bailey, I headed over to get a cup of coffee.

An organizing committee leader was on register. They were wearing a union pin and were clearly annoyed with the corporate presence. "We'll talk later," they said.

I got my drink—grande iced latte, quad, blonde and ristretto, with oat milk—and sat down in one of the chairs in the lobby.

Within a couple of minutes, Rossann wandered over. She didn't ask to sit down, and I didn't stand up. Instead, I awkwardly looked up at her as she hovered over me. The partners behind the bar could observe how uncomfortable the situation was. I made eye contact with my friend at the register. This was yet another illustration of the discomfort corporate was causing. Plus, I could try to get information.

Rossann brought up how excited she was for us to see our store after the remodel.

"Are all of the stores in Buffalo getting remodels?" I asked.

"All the stores that asked for it."

"Did Elmwood ask for it?"

"Yes—partners were mentioning needing more space behind the bar, so the bar has been pushed back a foot."

A few minutes after Rossann left, Adam came over and adopted the same hovering position above me. I craned my neck to look up at him. Once again, he made no effort to sit down.

"I haven't really met you," he said. "Let me introduce myself."

He volunteered some info, telling me that he was the new community support mobilization person.

I played along and asked brightly how long he'd been in that role.

"Two weeks." Before, he was a regional manager in DC. He kept talking about how DC had had problems and corporate had sent in a whole bunch of people to support them, just as they were doing here, because he'd raised his hand.

I asked if he knew how many "supporters" were in Buffalo.

"I don't know, I've only been here three weeks," he said. But corporate was responding this way because Buffalo raised their hand and he was here to make sure all partners—"including you," he added—have the Starbucks experience.

I asked who in Buffalo raised their hand.

"Well, the partners."

"Would this have happened if we hadn't been unionizing?"

"Well, if we knew about the issues, then, yes, definitely."

He asked how long I'd been a partner and why I came to Starbucks. I said almost a year and that I came because I was burned-out on grad school and wanted to get back to actual work. I added that I knew the industry from working at Panera and this was definitely better. He laughed and said he hoped so. Then I asked him the same questions. His story was that he came to Starbucks hoping to become a rock musician. When that didn't pan out, he decided that he really liked working at Starbucks.

He also talked about the Elmwood remodel and how great the store was going to be afterward. He explained the new digital screen for mobile orders and how it would improve conditions for bar partners and for customers alike. He said that Starbucks was currently testing these screens in stores with high mobile-order volume and in an ASL store in DC, where many of the partners were hard of hearing.

I could tell from talking to him that Adam was more skilled than Starbucks' standard-issue union busters, and therefore more of a threat. He was familiar with baristas' jobs, suave and engaging, with a dapper overconfidence and the ability to project a friendly and concerned presence.

This was in contrast with many of the other corporate executives, who were often cold, strict, and stiff. Joana was an unfriendly presence across the Elmwood, Genesee, and Camp Road stores, often hopping on the floor to grab cold-brew kegs and interrupt partners having union conversations. She tried to tell Genesee workers they couldn't take union flyers from coworkers who came in off the clock to hand them something to post in the back of house, even though exchanging items had been allowed prior to the campaign. She watched vigilantly for organizing committee members visiting stores and greeted them loudly, hovered nearby, and hurried them out the door.

Some of the support managers began making efforts to blend in. I overheard Dustin telling a colleague where to find the BuffaLove face masks at Wegmans. One of Rossann's first stops in Buffalo—after she realized we were making fun of her preppy outfits—was at the Bills merch store, where she acquired a T-shirt to wear under her blazer as she cleaned our bathrooms. (Partners were trained to call in messes with bodily fluids for specialized cleaning, but Rossann cleaned diarrhea in the Hamburg bathroom and vacillated between sweeping lobbies and mopping bathrooms at the other stores.)

At night, Rossann and her crew would get drunk at fancy downtown bars. Unbeknownst to them, the bartenders were friends with our committee members. We learned from one of them that some Starbucks executives referred to us as their "little peasants" when they thought no one was listening.

That attitude trickled down to many of the other managers. Painted nails were forbidden under Starbucks' dress code, which claimed they violated the health code. District managers started working on our floors wearing acrylics. They claimed that because they were DMs, the dress code didn't apply to them, even when they were handing out drinks and doing barista work. Another DM refused to do any work on the floor, citing her rank, and spent her time making calls or going to other stores to resupply us with oat milk.

Starbucks directed the warehouses to redirect product to Buffalo to help solve the supply shortages, in hopes that would placate partners. The unionizing stores started getting extra shipments every week. We joked that other stores around the country were probably becoming hotter shops as corporate sent us their cinnamon dolce syrup and strawberry acai base, leaving them to deal with angry customers and Uber Eats orders for things they didn't have in stock.

Despite corporate's actions, however, we were not unionizing because of product shortages. We weren't unionizing because of insect infestations or flooded back rooms or understaffing. But corporate couldn't disentangle their egos from the reality of the situation.

## WAS STARBUCKS THE WORST?

No—not by a long shot.

That was never the point. We told Rossann that in the first listening session, and I reiterated it—no longer for Rossann's benefit, but for my coworkers'—in meeting after meeting. The point was—why not the best? The point was—"partners" should be partners, not with the Bean Stock grants of shares in the company that Starbucks claimed made us partners, but with a true voice in our workplace. We wanted to shift the power dynamic and put partners on an equal footing with corporate. The point was—a company should not be able to systematically crush any organizing attempts for more than thirty years and then pat itself on the back for being "progressive."[4]

Howard Schultz and Rossann both took unionizing as a personal critique—hadn't they tried to create a company that showed a "third way," a human form of capitalism that was so good it didn't require unions? The point was—with unflinching optimism and carefully crafted reiterations of their love for the company, Buffalo baristas were going to challenge corporate power and see whether workers in the United States actually had the right to organize, or whether that right was a meaningless platitude, the National Labor Relations Act a dead letter.[5]

If we could succeed, I thought, we could show it *was* possible. That corporate dictatorship, strong as it was, was not absolute; that a small group of workers could launch a challenge from a dining table or an un-air-conditioned office that could challenge a global company.

We were organizing for everything from credit card tipping to trans rights, for a say in matters as small as playlists and syrup options and as large as sustainability, ethical sourcing, and health and safety protections. Partners were living paycheck to paycheck, but their biggest demands were not usually economic.

"Our store is closer than it's ever been," Michelle Eisen said. We had been in a Covid bubble with one another through the pandemic; as a union, our community would now gain the legal right to bargain with Starbucks for the things we already knew we needed.

Starbucks corporate spent most of their anti-union speeches trying to convince us that we were not the union.

At the big anti-union meeting at Elmwood, the only one to which corporate invited the entire store at one time, they brought in Chris Stewart, a licensed stores partner-relations manager from Atlanta. He had worked at McDonald's with Allyson before moving over to Starbucks.

He told us that his time there had taught him what unions were like, especially Workers United's parent union, the Service Employees International Union (SEIU), which had attempted to organize McDonald's. "It won't be you at the bargaining table," he said. "It'll be SEIU lawyers."

"That's simply not true," I said.

The meeting became increasingly intense.

Michelle, our clear leader, sat in the middle of the long table, surrounded by partners who felt comforted by her presence. As she pushed back against the propaganda of the "union expert" from partner relations, she became physically larger over the course of the meeting, unconsciously pulling her feet up into the chair and shifting upward.

Erin, the shift supervisor from the Galleria store who had been bouncing around the district and was hoping to transfer into Elmwood, spoke up about the hardship of having to make her own schedule and beg stores to take her.

"We're so sorry that happened, we're here to fix everything," said Mark, one of the district managers.

"You keep saying you're here to fix things that happened before," said Michelle, "but this happened on your watch. This was you."

As she spoke, her smartwatch dinged, showing the toll these meetings were taking: Her heart rate was unsafely high, and the watch recommended cutting the stress.

When Em tried to speak up, Chris cut her off. Toward the end of the meeting, she stormed out. Kellen was emotional afterward as well. But support came from unlikely quarters: One of our new, young partners spoke up about conditions in New York City, asking why corporate hadn't been there. JP joked about Howard Schultz's penthouse.

Chris had brought a water bottle to the meeting that was covered in stickers. One of them showed the iconic I AM A MAN picket sign.

"Even the union buster has a pro-union sticker," I pointed out to Jayden.

Chris saw me and jumped into the conversation. "Is there something on my bottle you like?"

"Yes! I was just saying how even your bottle shows unions are good, because that sign is from the sanitation workers' strike in Memphis."

"I never said unions weren't good, in some cases. They have their place, and that was a good strike. But we don't need unions here at Starbucks."

"Isn't that what management would have said to the sanitation workers?"

Chris tried to pivot back to third parties and SEIU lawyers, but, watching my coworkers, I saw it wasn't working.

As the campaign intensified, I became increasingly worried about coming off as strident. Corporate made our stores stressful. Coming to work was triggering partners' anxiety. My partners blamed corporate for how uncomfortable the captive-audience meetings were, but they dreaded them and wanted them to stop. No one knew when the next support manager would appear, who would be dress-coded for wearing the wrong shade of blue, who would get pulled off the floor into a one-on-one meeting, what would be rearranged at the whim of a new facilities-and-operations person, which store would be remodeled next and where those partners would be scheduled.

"Our stores don't feel like our stores," said Lexi.

Starbucks was responsible for creating this environment, but corporate tried to gaslight partners into blaming the union campaign for the tension they felt. In letters mailed to our homes, the company told us to vote "no" to return our stores to normal and put an end to the stress of the campaign.

This was one of many ways in which Starbucks weaponized partners' emotional and mental health against them. In our majority–Gen Z workplaces, workers frequently talked openly about mental health, and many of them utilized company-provided therapy services. (These therapists, coincidentally or not, constantly advised partners to quit Starbucks—we begged conflicted coworkers, "Please don't quit before the vote!") If partners were anxious and conflict-averse, management would confront them. If partners were particularly empathetic, managers complained about the stress they said the union campaign was causing for them and demanded comfort.

Corporate claimed that they had flooded our market to support us, to help us, because they hadn't known about the issues we were facing, because we "raised our hands." In captive-audience meetings, corporate presented their anti-union propaganda as objective facts and constantly reiterated how they were "still learning about unions." This set up a difficult dynamic for us to navigate. Pushing back against their narrative and their misinformation risked appearing confrontational to our coworkers, who wanted as little additional stress as possible.

Early on, James had taken an iconic selfie in front of Rossann sweeping the lobby of their store. We posted this on Twitter and it went viral, showing the world the absurdity of corporate's response. Then a few of our coworkers started texting us. A small but influential and critically important number of our union leaders felt that we were being too disrespectful: "That's somebody's grandma!" "She's just doing her job, we shouldn't be making this about her personally."

I tried to explain that we weren't attacking Rossann as a person, but as the face of the anti-union campaign. Moreover, what she was doing violated federal labor law. Companies weren't allowed to move managers and execs in from across the country and flood the stores. The National Labor Relations Act outlawed companies from having any managerial presence that was greater than normal because it surveilled workers and made it harder to organize.

This had more weight when my coworkers could read it in print. In early September, Lauren Gurley, then at *Vice*, wrote the first story on Starbucks' anti-union activity in Buffalo. Coworkers brought up the article on our shifts: Seeing the public recognize the realities of what Starbucks was doing to us was priceless.[6]

In November 2021, we filed our first unfair labor practice charges against Starbucks with the NLRB and held a press conference at our office where we talked about the swarm of managers that had descended on our stores and talked about our hopes for accountability.

"If it's against the law, that's different," said a coworker who thought we were being too hard on Rossann. "I didn't realize she wasn't supposed to be doing that."

The NLRB has no real ability to punish companies, and its process is slow. When a union or a worker files an unfair labor practice charge against a company, the Board takes statements, called affidavits, from witnesses and reviews evidence from all parties. Eventually, it either finds merit in a charge or dismisses it as baseless. If the NLRB finds merit, a board agent will ask the parties about their willingness to settle. If they don't settle, the NLRB changes from an investigator to a prosecutor. It issues a complaint, formally charging the company with violating labor law, and takes the company to trial before an administrative law judge. If a company wants to appeal the judge's decision, it can—first to the Board in Washington, DC, and then into the federal courts. It can take years for anything meaningful to happen, like the reinstatement of a fired worker or the payment of unfairly denied benefits.

But filing charges and going through this process did serve a valid purpose. It helped expose corporate malfeasance to the public, and it corroborated our experiences. Now, it wasn't our word against Starbucks'. Lawyers, government workers, and ultimately federal judges were telling us this wasn't normal or legal or right.

That didn't stop Starbucks.

**IN OCTOBER, NEW HIRES** began clocking in at Elmwood. They had been hired after significantly heightened screening: Starbucks had brought in four recruiters, who gave some prospective partners the runaround while expediting others' onboarding. The new hires had trained at Walden and Anderson, where they hadn't even learned how to operate the ovens, since Starbucks wasn't getting food orders at the closed store. Once they arrived in our stores, we had to retrain them ourselves. Some veteran partners were frustrated with them, both because they hadn't been properly trained and because the managers began cutting our hours to accommodate the many new workers who had arrived. With mixed success, we tried to redirect this annoyance toward corporate: They had failed our new coworkers.

Despite their best efforts, management had also failed to properly screen our new coworkers. Cortlin had applied because he wanted to be part of the union effort; he asked for a union card and a pin on his first shift. I met Natalie for the first time at the job-fair-like anti-union meeting at Elmwood, which took place on her third shift. A swarm of managers descended on her: "Have you signed up for health care? Do you know about Bean Stock? Have you signed up for the 401(k)?"

"I've been here for three days," said Natalie.

But while it may have taken her some time to navigate the company, she quickly became a key player within the union, including helping to get other new hires on board. Starbucks also transferred in a new shift supervisor, Bridget Shannon, from a store in Cortland, New York. While she wasn't eligible to vote in the election because she came after the NLRB had scheduled our election, Michelle and I worried that she had been hand-selected to try to convince others not to unionize. Like any worker who needs a job, she had told Starbucks what it wanted to hear before the transfer. They believed she was a corporate supporter. But she quickly became one of our biggest union advocates: Her tenure at the company had taught her how important having a voice on the job would be.

Most of the new partners were Black. My new coworker Cortlin and I observed Starbucks—working with Littler Mendelson—adopt different talking points and ways of interacting with different workers to try to prevent us from unionizing. This reminded me of my experience at Nissan, which had also worked with the same firm and used many of the same strategies. Now, some managers told the new workers, "Look at the leadership of the union. Do you really want to be part of a union that's so white?" All we could do was attempt to befriend, assist, train, and support the new partners, hoping the workers would see through what they were doing and join with us. Almost immediately, Cortlin became a key union leader. He asked me for a meeting outside work, bringing up the whiteness of the organizing committee and his desire to become involved with the wider effort as one of the new Black partners. He helped convince many coworkers to support the union.

As more new hires showed up in our store, Michelle and I became increasingly nervous. Elmwood was our "firewall"—the store that we were still holding the strongest, the one we were the most likely to win. When the NLRB scheduled an election date, we would get a cutoff period, meaning no workers hired after that point would be eligible to vote. But the NLRB took its time scheduling our election.

Finally, in late October, we learned that the Board would probably release its decision and set our election date on Friday. Starbucks had evidently gotten the same news. Thursday night, they released major news: For the first time in its fifty-year history, Starbucks would be granting seniority pay to workers across both the United States and Canada. This was a big deal and a key demand. We had urged workers to avoid naming specific issues, aware that Starbucks would take every opportunity to remedy grievances and grant new benefits. But the lack of seniority pay was so blatant—and spoke so fundamentally to the issues at stake—that we had made an exception. Michelle Eisen had spoken eloquently about how, after her eleven years with the company, she was making just sixteen cents more than a new hire. As an organizing committee, we responded to the news by taking credit on behalf of the union—Starbucks would never have done this otherwise—while also emphasizing that we would now be negotiating based on Starbucks' new wage structure. But Starbucks used this carrot as a stick, promising new benefits while threatening to withhold them from unionized stores. There was one unionized store in Canada.

"Those partners can't get these benefits because they're covered by a contract," execs began telling us in captive-audience meetings.

The press called Starbucks' announcement a billion-dollar investment in its partners. It was an investment largely designed to provide the union busters with one devastating talking point.

While Starbucks was willing to use any available weapon to try to stop our union, the center of their anti-union campaign relied on creating a never-ending cycle of stress. They played upon partners' anxiety. They pulled us into one-on-one meetings, rearranged our stores, scrutinized our every move, and interrupted our conversations. No one knew when Rossann and her crew would be in our stores, whether Joana would hop onto the floor, how many support managers we might expect to encounter in a single shift.

It was exhausting. Making matters worse, the company blamed the union and the organizing committee members, saying, "The union has brought so much tension to our stores. Vote 'No' to end the tension."

At the Genesee store, Lexi Rizzo was bending over backward to try to turn her partners' experiences around. She was working through her breaks, helping coworkers out, being kind to the support managers, trying to advocate for everyone, making playlists to help elevate the mood, and checking in on everyone. Because so many partners from other stores and so many support managers were working at the Genesee store, corporate began slashing partners' hours. Lexi asked Rossann for a meeting and got it. She pled with Rossann to restore the hours and stop punishing partners.

"It was a deal with the devil," she told me, "but it worked." Genesee partners began getting their full hours again.

Lexi sent me long screen-capture videos of partners attacking her as a proxy for the union, asking why she had brought this on their store. She responded to them with remarkable grace, empathy, and optimism, assuring them that she had only been trying to improve conditions and that she would continue to be there for everyone regardless of where they stood or how they voted on the union.

"I don't know if this will work," she told me, "but I care about them, and the only way they might come around on the union is if they see that I'm only doing it because I care about them."

Captive-audience meetings remained one of Starbucks' key weapons. They brought in "union experts," partner resources execs, senior vice presidents, operations coaches, and many others. They put together a PowerPoint presentation that they showed at store after store that talked about the Workers United constitution, told workers they could be put on trial for violations of union rules, and warned them that the partners trying to "sell them on the union" might not have their best interests at heart and might not be around for the long term.[7]

In every meeting, I tried to cloak my pushback in the gentlest terms. Rossann and the other corporate officials had to look like the aggressors and the unreasonable ones. We, the committee, had to come off as both nonthreatening and moderate, appealing to our undecided coworkers.

So I put on a dress.

**AT THE TIME OF** the Starbucks campaign, I was in the process of coming out as nonbinary—language I had not grown up with and was still acquiring. *The Partner*, the Starbucks Workers United newsletter, was the first place I used *they* pronouns.

"Congratulations, Jazzy!" Em told me when she saw my bio. "I didn't know! That's super cool!"

But utilizing my normally unhelpful ability to appear femme—or, even less desirably, to code-switch into the earnest, Christian homeschooler vibes of my childhood—came in handy in captive-audience meetings. On two occasions, I showed up at the meetings in a dress and low heels, carrying a purse, to make my presence as demure as possible in contrast with corporate's antagonistic pushiness.

This strategy worked. At one meeting, I reiterated that we were not organizing because of facilities problems or bad management: "Nothing has to change about these structures, and, like, you know, any organization of anything always has things that could be better. That doesn't mean that it's terrible. But I think, 'Why is Starbucks so afraid of us?' Like, we— I'm telling you we want to be partners. We're not telling you we have a problem. We're telling you we want a voice, and we want to be able to go through existing channels. But if those channels aren't working, or if we want different channels in terms of being able to have our voice or empowerment, why is Starbucks so scared of empowered partners?"

"We're not scared at all," said Allyson. "In fact, we think it's really about embracing what we already have. And I think in this market, parts of it may have been missing. And so we want to get the market up to standard so every partner can experience the kind of partner-to-partner connection that should exist. And so it's really not at all about fear. It's about embracing our culture that we have today."

"But everyone would be part of that culture," I said. "Because if it's really about connecting, then it wouldn't be something that would change."

"I think it's just about understanding what a union is," said Allyson, going into the third-party spiel. She added that a union could only bargain about wages, hours, and working conditions and that Starbucks had full control over the issues we were discussing.

This response backfired.

Josh Mendez, one of our partners who'd been on the fence about the union, mentioned that he was in the military and talked about how his unit was also having problems with communication. "So it's like, when the chain of command is failing, we need to enlist somebody else, of course, right? Like, their leadership failed. So I agree with Jaz. I think we should have somebody to carry us up if others don't—that's if I can talk to my sergeant, I talk to my staff sergeant, and then et cetera, et cetera."

Rossann's response was that partners should hold her accountable to fix the things that were "owned by Starbucks," like communication and leadership problems. "A third party's not going to fix communications for you. They're just speaking on your behalf. And they're negotiating a contract with you, your employment contract. It's speaking on your behalf. If something in your store is not working on your shift, that's us. You're going to call us."

"They won't let us put up our decorations anymore," Kellen started.

"I don't know who *they* is," said Rossann. "I heard, 'Well, *corporate* won't.' Okay, well, I'm corporate."

I tried to gently push back on the Starbucks narrative about third parties disrupting communications and coming in to negotiate for us by talking about how partners were organizing to be able to look after each other.

"There's a therapy component to the job because we're all checking in on each other and making sure everybody's okay," I said, as sweetly as I could. "And that's what the union would look like, too. It's partners checking in on each other, and then having the ability to make sure accountability exists. Because I think this is the fundamental vision. Power doesn't just come down. It comes up. And a union is just a way of making sure that that truly exists, instead of being something that we hope exists. It doesn't change anything about, you know, if we want to call any of y'all up. That would still exist. But if we also want to sit at the negotiating table and make sure that certain ground rules exist, then we would have that ability, too. And, like, no union people are going to come in and negotiate. Like, we would decide what we want for ourselves."

Rossann was visibly upset. "I have to emotionally respond to that. The reason that I love working at Starbucks is there's no power from the top down. I've never lived that way in my entire life. There's no big structure at Starbucks that says Kevin's got more power, or I have more power, or— The whole reason that we love the company we really have and the reason we call ourselves partners is because from the very, very early days, if you've read any of Howard's books, he wanted to build the kind of company where partners knew they already had a seat at the table, because of what happened to him and his family."

**HOWARD SCHULTZ, WHO HAD** stepped down from his second stint as CEO in 2017 but had remained centrally involved with the company, first came to Buffalo in September, holding a private meeting to rally the store managers against the union. Then, in November, about a week before the NLRB would be mailing out the ballots for our union election, Starbucks told us they would be closing all of our stores early for a meeting with a special guest. This was unprecedented: twenty stores closing at three for all the workers to attend a meeting at the Hyatt downtown.

Speculation proliferated. A support manager dropped a hint it would be Britney Spears, newly free and an idol to several Sheridan and Bailey partners. Another manager mentioned that the last time Starbucks had made an announcement like this it had been Oprah. Richard posted in the GroupMe that he thought it would be Taylor Swift, whose promotional drink (a nonfat caramel latte) was about to launch in stores.

One of my coworkers called me, crying. "I just don't know what to do. If Taylor Swift tells me to vote no, I don't know what I'm going to do. I would have to do what she says. I mean, it's Taylor."

It was not Taylor, although my coworker stayed up all night worrying about the possibility.

The morning of the meeting, as my coworkers and I were clocking in at five in the morning, we all received texts through Starbucks' emergency-contact system. The message was a link to a video of Deanna announcing the special guest: Howard Schultz.

"Of course it's Howard," said Michelle. "Did you really think they would get someone cool?"

I headed to the Hyatt early, taking my backpack to join Kellen as he did homework. We sat at a high-top table in the courtyard and watched the managers begin trickling in. They filed up the escalators to the second floor, where a big BuffaLove banner was hung. Some of them posed for photos in front of it. Eventually, some of them spotted us. One at a time, they came and peered over the banister, looking down at us. Rossann was among them, scowling.

"Don't they have anything more exciting to look at?" Kellen asked.

They didn't.

Meanwhile, others were getting ready for the meeting across the city. There was a tense excitement among the partners. This was the first time all of us would be together in one captive-audience meeting, the first time we would be face-to-face with the man who was responsible for Starbucks' campaign against our union. We were excited and slightly nervous. The group chat pinged with partners getting ready for the meeting, posing with their fists up. Our unofficial uniform consisted of Starbucks Workers United T-shirts under leather jackets. Worried that security would be tight and make filming difficult, Richard had gone to the spy-supply shop in Cheektowaga, bought three pens with hidden cameras, and handed them out to a few partners.

Will Westlake called me. "Did anyone print a copy of the Fair Election Principles?"

"I didn't. Do you need me to go to the office?"

"I can do it!" He hurried to the Tri-Main office to get it ready and passed it to Casey, who was heading to the meeting.

Meanwhile, James and Gianna were staking signs into the ground around the hotel: STARBUCKS CUSTOMER FOR A STARBUCKS UNION. These featured the Starbucks siren with her fist raised high. The duo had gotten the signs into most of the medians and were putting them along the street in front of the hotel when the hotel maintenance man interrupted them.

"They're taking the signs down!" Gianna posted in the group chat.

I saw the man coming into the hotel with an armful of signs and hurried over. "Those are our signs! You have to give them back!"

"They're on my property, they're not yours anymore!"

As he tried to go into the storage closet, I blocked the door and tried to get the signs.

"I'll have you arrested!"

Kellen called softly, "Jaz, come on!"

It occurred to me that I should make sure I could still go to the meeting, so I turned around, still registering my insistence that he could not take the signs.

Partners were coming in now, too. We joined the line filtering past the sign-in tables. A row of stern support managers guarded the room, ticking partners off a list of everyone in the district. But—although Starbucks allowed us to enter our chosen names in the system and then used them for everything like punching in and out, scheduling, and other functions—the list contained our deadnames.

Marsh King, the severe seventeen-year district manager who told partners proudly that she had trained Rossann, glared at me.

"Jaz Brisack," I said.

"You mean [deadname]?"

"No, it's Jaz."

"That's not what it says here, it says [deadname]."

"That's wrong. It's in the system as Jaz, too. And you shouldn't be deadnaming partners."

Finally, she ticked it off and let me by.

The same thing had happened to Kellen, too. We passed through the doors into the ballroom, a little shaken.

MK, the district manager, bounced over to us. "How are you? Good to see you!" she chirped.

"Not great," I said. "We just got deadnamed out there."

"Oh! Let me go see about that!"

She hurried away and we heard nothing further from her all night.

"You can't really blame her," Kellen said. "She has two brain cells, and one of them is on a hippity-hoppity vacation."

Meanwhile, Maya had scored souvenir-size bags of Pike Place roast—"from the original store," a support manager had said worshipfully. I declined. Our coworker Bri took one and then, making eye contact with a "support" district manager, walked over to the trash can and threw it away. It was clear: Starbucks did not know how to throw a party. There was not enough food, and no one really wanted the drip Pike in silver decanters around the room.

Most of the room was filled by a circle of chairs, arranged in quadrants with a large open circle in the middle. Kellen and I sat a few rows back from the front, next to our coworkers Shariah and Maya. Gianna and James were up front, but most partners were grouped by store. Casey sat with the Williamsville Place crew; the Depew partners were off to the side. Support managers were sprinkled throughout, with more—clad in green aprons—standing around the outside of the ring.

The meeting began with Deanna speaking about how much Starbucks had meant to her: how the company, and Howard, had enabled her to go to college, to buy a car, to get health care. Starbucks was a company that took care of people. All of that had been due to the goodness of one man—a man who was here with us tonight.

And Howard Schultz stepped into the middle of the circle. I held up my phone and began recording. Kellen looked at me, slightly shocked. But none of the support managers tried to stop me.

Howard was less imposing than I had expected. Slightly stooped, he wore a too-tight gray sweater that pulled open at the bottom. He paced around the center of the room as he began talking about how he wanted to educate us about Starbucks. How half of Starbucks baristas had been with the company for under a year, how we didn't understand the company's heritage and tradition.

Three minutes in, the group chat pinged. I swiped away the notification, afraid it would interfere with my filming. But the notifications kept coming.

"I'm going to go a bit out of my comfort zone here," Gianna Reeve said, "but I'm going to ask Howard Schultz to sign the Fair Election Principles."

The chat buzzed with partners promising their support.

Howard was talking about his childhood, a carefully crafted telling of it. He told us he had grown up in the projects—a claim that previous investigative journalists had found didn't stand up to scrutiny or, at least, didn't tell the full story of where he grew up.[8]

Shariah had grown up in New York City. "I know that area," she whispered. "He's not really poor."

He talked about his father dropping out of high school, coming back from World War II sick and unable to transition back into civilian life, working blue-collar jobs, getting injured as a truck driver and losing his job and ability to provide for his family.

"He became the company that fucked his dad over?" Josh Pike said in the chat.

Howard continued on about what he described as the "shame and scars" of being poor and relying on charities to deliver food to his family.

Some of the partners in the room, including Cassie Fleischer, googled

Howard's net worth: $4.8 billion. Most of the Starbucks workers listening to the speech were poor. They were not ashamed—they were motivated to organize a union to change their financial situation.[9]

"I was going to build the kind of company that my father never got a chance to work for," Howard said.

"Summary of this speech: Howie's father needed a union," a worker posted in the group chat.

Howard went on, "A company that was steeped in respect and dignity for everyone who worked in the company regardless of whether they were educated or not, rich or poor, had gone to a good school or a bad school, gay, trans, Black, white, it didn't matter. The currency of trust inside the company was that we were here for one another."

We were, in fact, here for one another, although not in the way Howard Schultz wanted. Partners were looking around the room, catching the eyes of other partners, in silent recognition of this fact.

Then, Howard began talking about Starbucks' benefits. Health care, Bean Stock, the CUP Fund, which distributed donations (from partners, not from corporate) to others in need. "Now who forced us to do that? Who pushed us to do it? No one. We did it because we thought it was the right thing." Like everything else he had said, that wasn't really true, either: Starbucks had given those benefits in response to past unionization attempts. Without those previous efforts, Howard might have found his desire to do something for his father somewhat less of a clarion call.

"In the last two years it became obvious to me that the access to opportunity; the issues around equity; the issues around equality; the issues around neighborhoods around the country that are disadvantaged and are being left; the crisis of capitalism—that we had to try to do something for our people that perhaps they couldn't do on their own."

"Starbucks is the crisis of capitalism ffs," Arjae messaged in the chat.

"And that became the college achievement plan," Howard continued. "Again: the first company in America to offer free college tuition for every single employee who wants it. Free." He stretched out his arms. "Who forced us to do it? Who pushed us to do it? No one. Why did we do it? Because I wanted to do something that was so significantly different than the abuse that my father had in being the kind of person that was not respected and dignified and did not have any value. My father never owned a house. He had twenty credit cards. . . ."

Howard talked about being six years old and going to hear JFK speak with his mother. Kennedy had talked about the American dream. "It just imprinted me. I know what it meant to walk in those shoes because I was in those shoes. This poor kid from Brooklyn. The shame, the vulnerability, the scars, hiding in the shadows of being poor. Starbucks has been built to overcome that as best we can. We can't solve every problem, but what we can do is build a different kind of company. And we have."

He talked about how he still went into the office every day. How he led management leadership meetings. How he led board of directors' meetings. "For forty years—this is truth—there's two empty chairs in that room. And everyone has known that those two empty chairs is not some metaphor. It's real." He circled back through the American dream, the "lack of civility among our politicians in Washington," his faith in the American people and in Starbucks, and "the projects of Brooklyn."

Then, he pivoted. "Many years ago, I took a trip to Israel."

"Free Palestine," a worker posted.

Howard talked about meeting a rabbi—"He's not just any rabbi," Howard clarified, "he's like a cardinal in the Vatican. He's a big deal."

This rabbi told Howard a story. "He says to me that when people in Germany and in Poland were sent to the concentration camps, they were thrown into railcars, and sometimes the journey was eight hours, ten hours, fifteen hours. No light, no water, no food. And when they arrived at the camps, the railcars were slammed open, and you could hear that metal door just"—he slammed his fist into the palm of his other hand—"against the cold weather. Men were separated from women, and women were separated from children. And one person for every six was given a blanket. One blanket for every six people. And the person who got the blanket had to decide what to do with this blanket that I have for myself. And not everyone, but most people—most people—shared their blanket with five other people. And the rabbi says to me, 'Take your blanket, and go share it with five other people.' And so much of that story is threaded into what we have tried to do at Starbucks, is share our blanket."

The group chat had exploded.

"Omg is he about to share his money?"

"I need to know how Starbucks and the Holocaust can even be brought up in the same conversation, I was expecting a train wreck but WOW."

"Not Rossann wiping a tear."

Howard was wrapping up with a story about the rabbi telling him how he (the rabbi) was not worthy to touch the Wailing Wall, while pushing him (Howard) into the wall.

"And I go back to our core purpose, our reason for being," Howard finally said. "To build the company that creates the fragile balance between profit and doing the right thing. I hope what you've heard is a historical perspective of the company over a fifty-year period doing the right thing. Thank you very much."

Amid the applause, Gianna stood up. "My name is Gianna Reeve."

"Thank you, Gianna!" came a cry from the audience.

"I am an organizing member of Starbucks Workers United. I am a barista."

Howard hurried out of the room.

"You know how much this means to me and you know how much I love my partners."

From the four segments of the circle, the corporate executives had ringed around Gianna: Rossann, Denise, Allyson, and Deanna.

"And I resonate with Howard and what he said, because he wants what's best for this company, and he knows where the future is going for our company, and the strength we have is our strength with each other. How many of us are wearing Workers United shirts right now?" They unzipped their jacket to show the shirt underneath.

"Gianna," said Rossann. "Gianna, this is not a rally."

"Please let partners speak," said Gianna. "Please let partners speak."

Deanna and Allyson nodded to Rossann, telling her to leave. She hurried away from the center, too.

Another worker, who had just returned to Starbucks within the past two months, interrupted to ask questions about whether the union was being transparent on Facebook.

Gianna regained the floor and held up the piece of paper in their hand. "These are Fair Election Principles that have not been signed yet. We request that they respect our right to organize. They respect our right to equal time. And I do not have equal time. So Howard Schultz, please, if you care. If you care about your partners in Buffalo, please sign the Fair Election Principles. Please. I have a pen." They held up a spy pen.

Denise Nelsen, wearing a $700 Canada Goose vest, tried to push Gianna back into her seat.

"Thank you, Gianna!" someone called out.

Allyson walked up to the middle of the circle and began thanking Howard in absentia. Meanwhile, in the group chat, support for Gianna was bubbling.

"The baddest bitch alive," said Lexi.

"Gianna working class hero!" chimed in Brian.

Afterward, Gianna was shaky and afraid they would get fired for speaking up. We all circled around them as soon as Allyson had wrapped up and tried to reassure them.

"That changed everything for Genesee," Lexi said. "Workers whose initial union support had waned over the course of the company's union-busting campaign were in the audience, she told me. "They saw exactly what corporate is like and how they silence us. And we are going to win now."

**THAT MEETING CHANGED EVERYTHING** for many of the partners in the room. Coworkers who had been hesitant to get involved asked for union cards and signed them on the spot. Cassie would later say that Howard's speech was one of the turning points for her deciding to support the union. Maya and Shariah joked about the American dream in the car as I drove them home. It was a giddy, exuberant night, a feeling that lasted for hours: Richard and I read Twitter commentary on Howard's speech until two in the morning, laughing until we cried. Casey spliced the audio from the spy pen with my film of Gianna confronting Howard and posted it.

Then, Starbucks posted the entire speech.

Howard didn't seem to understand what he had done—even as the *Jerusalem Post* ran headlines, tagged under "antisemitism," announcing his Holocaust comparison. His defense was that he had told that same story before, in business meetings and even in the book he had written while exploring a presidential run. Chapter 20—titled "Share Your Blanket"—detailed his adventures in Appalachia with J. D. Vance as well as his trip to Israel with Rabbi Finkel.[10]

Howard simply didn't have anyone around him who would push back, offer criticism, or advise him against taking certain actions or making certain statements. Instead, he had surrounded himself with yes-people, those who didn't threaten his ego.

And he paid the price with the public. The news coverage continued for several days. Colin Cochran did an interview with the *New York Times*.

"Felt like it wasn't a very appropriate analogy," he said, giving additional material to the Twitter commentators: "My man Colin with the understatement of the century."[11]

Two days later, we were back in our stores for the final captive-audience meetings of the campaign. Only, some of us weren't allowed in.

**MICHELLE AND I HAD** divvied up the captive-audience meetings throughout the campaign, going to different ones to ensure that we were able to share similar messages and push back against corporate's worst talking points. This time, Michelle needed to attend the earlier one, as her stage-manager schedule didn't allow her to go to late-evening meetings. Cassie, who had to open the next morning, had been scheduled for the later one, too, even though she was still hesitant about the union. We conjectured that the scheduling was based not just on actual union support but on friendships and relationships: The first meeting was primarily the new hires, anti-union workers, and high schoolers, while the second meeting was the pro-union workers and our friends.

I was on my way to the grocery store when Michelle called me. "I'm at my store," she said, crying. "They won't let me in."

Management wouldn't let her or Cassie go to the earlier meeting, saying they had to attend the one they had been scheduled to attend. They cited Covid concerns, even though some of our opening partners were already in the store.

I made a detour and drove to Elmwood, where Michelle was still in her car. “They need me in there,” she said emotionally. “They expect me to be able to protect them.”

We sat together in her car for a long time, until she had to leave for the theater. I decided to wait a few more minutes until people began trickling out of the meeting.

Josh Mendez was one of the first to emerge.

“How’d it go?” I asked.

“They said a lot of things,” he told me. “Like that people wouldn’t be able to transfer if we unionize or pick up shifts at other stores. But I think we’ve got this.”

“That’s not legal. They can’t take away anything we have now, including picking up shifts. How do you think other people were feeling?”

“A lot of people are scared. But it’s going to be okay.”

“How do you think this is going to go?”

“Oh, we’re going to win. I’m voting yes.”

Natalie had taped the meeting. In it, management began by talking about how they had been listening to partners. “There was a carpet here. There’s no carpet here now.”

Then, they told Maya she might not be able to transfer to a store near UCLA if Elmwood unionized.

“I’m not even eighteen,” Maya said. “I can’t even vote for president, but I’m voting for this. I just want to focus on graduating. It’s so stressful.”

Management continued by threatening the right to pick up shifts at other stores and talking about how the benefits Howard Schultz had outlined two nights before could be in peril.

They talked about the Canadian contract, telling workers that the partners at the one unionized store in Canada could not receive the new seniority pay and other increases because they were covered by a union contract.

When they paused for questions, Cortlin mentioned that he didn’t feel that Starbucks was listening to him.

“Of course we listen,” one of the execs said. “When George Floyd was killed, we listened.”

Two weeks later, Cortlin filed a complaint with Starbucks corporate about what she had said. The company panicked. They flew her back to Buffalo, where she sat down with Cortlin to apologize and promptly began crying.

"Now I have to deal with white women's tears on top of it," Cortlin said.

The later captive-audience meeting was much quicker. They had given up on persuading us, although their PowerPoint did include a helpfully marked "no" ballot and statements like "Vote 'yes' if you want to pay dues!"

Meanwhile, the meetings at Camp Road and Genesee could not have been more different from each other. At Camp, Will and Gianna were barred from entering the store because a support manager claimed there were not enough macaroons for them and thus they needed to attend the later session. At Genesee, partners heard about what was happening at the other stores and marched in surrounding Lexi, Caroline, and Danka, forcing corporate to meet with them as a group.

**THE NLRB WAS SET** to mail our ballots out at 5:00 p.m. on November 10.

Two days before, Starbucks requested a stay from the NLRB, arguing that their appeal of the store-by-store voting decision was so critical that the ballots shouldn't go out until after the Board held a hearing on the use of technology in centralizing operations, which, Starbucks argued, meant that sixty years of legal precedent no longer applied. The NLRB had ignored their request, meaning that our ballots would go out as scheduled.

At 3:00 a.m. on the tenth, I woke up to the sound of tinkling glass and the cats running from the front room toward the back of the house, away from the crashing sound. Exhausted, I started to turn over and go back to sleep when Richard, who was staying in my guest room, called out, "Jaz?"

Sleepily, I came into the living room. Even without my contact lenses in, it was impossible to miss what had happened. The floor was covered with pieces of glass. Halfway across the room, surrounded by glass shards, was a large rock.

"I heard the car driving off," Richard said.

My first thought was to clean up the mess. I donned gloves and began picking up the pieces of glass from the floor.

"No one can know about this," I said. "It will scare people too much."

"You have to call the cops," said Richard. I needed to get a police report to substantiate what had happened.

It took nearly an hour for the cops to arrive. When they did, they began quizzing me on whether I had any enemies.

"I saw all the union signs in your car," one of them said. "What's going on with that?"

I explained that we were trying to organize and that ballots were about to go out.

"Is anyone opposing the union?"

"There are a hundred or more corporate managers in town," I said.

When a detective called me a couple of weeks later, I was at a meeting with a coworker and couldn't talk about the incident in front of her. The police never followed up, but for months afterward I continued to find shards of glass in the carpet and in the shoes that had been close to the window.

I told Casey what had happened over coffee that morning. She was the one person I knew could keep it a secret while understanding how shaken I was. It would be months before the window could be repaired—supply-chain issues caused by the pandemic were still affecting shipping. It took even longer for me to feel comfortable going into my house alone, especially if it was after dark.

Months later, I told Michelle and Lexi what had happened. Both of them told me that they had been keeping similar things quiet for the same reason. Lexi talked about having been followed home and then getting out of her car and yelling at the pursuing SUV until it drove away. Michelle had noticed that her tires were getting low sooner than they should have been and took her car to a mechanic.

"Look," they told her after checking the car. "Someone tried to slash your tires. More often than not they don't actually do it, but they do a little damage."

They could scare us, but they couldn't stop us. We were building momentum: That same day, Cassie had asked Michelle to meet to talk through the union. Cassie came with pages of notes and questions. After a two-hour conversation, Cassie said that she was on board and would come to a union get-together.

---

**ONCE OUR BALLOTS WERE** out, we needed to ensure that everyone got them back in. Mail delays meant that some of our coworkers never got their ballots and had to request new ones from the Labor Board. Our lawyers were concerned that Starbucks would claim that our even asking coworkers if they had voted constituted election interference, which Starbucks could use to try to overturn our elections. We had wanted to hold voting parties to fill out our ballots together; the lawyers told us not to be anywhere near our coworkers as they checked the box. When we tried to have a party to celebrate dropping our ballots in the mailbox, only Michelle, Cassie, and I gathered at Spot Coffee. When I went by work one evening to encourage coworkers to vote and try to ensure people had been able to drop their ballots off, one anti-union coworker asked me in front of the support managers why I was coming in when I wasn't supposed to be there.

But there were beautiful moments, too. Stephen, who was on a leave of absence in Minnesota, came back to Buffalo to vote. We had a moving conversation in the car as they filled out their ballot, making a flourish of holding it up so that I couldn't see what they marked even as they talked about how much their yes vote meant to them. I drove one of the new hires to the NLRB to drop off their ballot. As we walked along snowy sidewalks, they told me about their hesitation about the union, but that they saw corporate on the one side and their coworkers on the other and that they would always support their coworkers over corporate.

As the vote drew closer, my anxiety intensified. By the morning of December 9, the day that the NLRB would open and count our ballots, I was nauseous and shaky. We had stayed up the night before writing the press releases for different eventualities. What if we won all three? What if we only won one? What if we won two and lost one? We couldn't bring ourselves to write the worst-case scenario.

I got dressed and donned Richard's old UNITE Southern Leadership Team bomber jacket. Always seeking the labor symbolism, I wanted to show the thread that ran from the textile mill organizing campaigns to Starbucks.

As the hour of the count drew closer, swarms of reporters filled the Tri-Main office. The French television crew who had been insisting that we create moments for them to film (we had tasked Brian with keeping them entertained) tried to snag the prime spot. Casey was tireless in managing the crowd.

We had the Zoom ballot count projected onto a draped screen (which was actually my bedsheet). Richard stage-managed our production, having all the workers stand in a line facing the screen and link arms. Michelle Eisen and I clutched each other's hands, then I drew two columns on the yellow pad I held in my other arm. Elmwood was the first store to be counted. It seemed to take Tom Miller from the NLRB an eternity to hold up each yellow outer envelope, announcing who had sent in the ballot and allowing for possible challenges. We cheered as each name of a committee member was announced. Then, he pulled out the inner envelopes holding the ballots. We watched in anguish as he painstakingly sliced through all of the little blue envelopes and extracted the ballots.

Then—finally—after Tom had droned through the required but mindless instructions—*a tie vote will be a loss, as the union has failed to reach a majority; if a ballot falls to the ground do not pick it up, as only the Board agent is allowed to touch the ballots*—it seemed that the worst-case scenario might indeed be playing out.

"Yes," he said, holding up a pink ballot.

"No." He held up another.

"No. No."

I leaned over to Michelle, whose eyes were wide. "What is happening?"

"No."

We looked at each other. Had the whole store lied to us?

"Yes." Finally. "Yes."

The balance began to shift.

When we had gotten the voter lists, Michelle and I had gone through Elmwood, rating everyone as accurately as possible. If everyone on the list voted, we would need nineteen yes votes to win. We thought we had twenty-four definite yes votes.

"There's our firewall," Mike Dolce, one of our lawyers, said, looking at the list.

Because twenty-seven of our coworkers had voted, we needed fourteen yes votes to win.

When we reached thirteen, we held our breath.

"No."

I felt my stomach tightening.

"Yes."

The row of partners leapt up in excitement. I was dizzy and numb and barely got off the ground. Casey was in the air, her hair flying up. Gary had jumped to nearly half his height. Cameras flashed all around us.

In the end, we got our nineteen. There were eight no votes—double what we had expected. Michelle and I looked at the list of those who had voted again and again. Who had voted no?

Richard laughed. "I was exactly the same in my factory. Everyone was saying, 'You won! You should be happy!' But I wanted to know who had lied to me."

Tom Miller was moving on to the next tally: Camp Road. As he raised each yellow envelope, showing who had voted, Will started to worry.

The day before, he had taken three ballots down to the NLRB office to slide them under the door to be counted. Now, they weren't there.

Half an hour and one frantic NLRB visit later, it became clear that the ballots were peacefully resting under the American Federation of Government Employees office door, which had the same number as the NLRB suite. Unfortunately, the NLRB would not wait for them to be retrieved. Even with the ballots, and even if the one person who had accidentally forgotten to check the yes box, sliding a blank ballot into the envelope instead, had filled it out correctly, Camp would still have lost by one vote.

Gianna started tearing up. I hugged them and tried to comfort them.

Casey, in her public relations role, came over. "You have to smile," she said sternly.

"Casey," I said just as sternly, "this is not the time."

"All of the media is watching!"

Later, we would laugh about this conversation and about the elements of our personalities it revealed. At the time, we had to rally to get ready for the Genesee count. That one was more complicated. Corporate had tried to stuff their ballot box by including on the voter list all of the Niagara Falls Boulevard partners who had worked at Genesee during their store's remodel. Pro-union partners from Walden and Anderson who had also worked at Genesee were left off the list.

The challenges were determinative, but we knew that the NLRB would eventually throw them out. The actual Genesee workers' votes reflected a clear majority: fifteen yes, nine no. It would take over a month for the NLRB to resolve the challenges, but we began printing off the press release announcing two union victories.

As soon as the vote counts concluded, the adrenaline that had gotten me through the past several months began to drain from my body. As we rushed to do interviews, update social media, get ready for the victory party, and try to find time to eat sandwiches, I began fading. By the time we had ushered the last reporters out of the room—even as Cassie and I had to run to a downstairs conference room for a radio interview, and Casey and Richard spoke to the BBC at midnight in the Tri-Main lobby—celebrating felt like an obligation: "I guess we should have a drink," said Cassie, and she made us both cups of cold brew with Baileys in it.

That night, as Richard and I held a sleepy but celebratory debrief, I sighed, "If it's this hard to win a union at Starbucks, how are we ever going to overthrow capitalism?"

Richard, elated, was not worried about hastening the wider revolution. "We did it. We proved it could be done! Not to mention, Rossann swept the floors for the last four months. Didn't work! And Howard will always be remembered as the guy who talked about the Holocaust to bust a union."

But Richard was realistic about how much work we had ahead of us; the campaign was only just beginning. "Tonight we celebrate, tomorrow it's back to work."

# CHAPTER FIVE

# Partners on Point

In October 2021, as we were busy battling corporate swarms and attending captive-audience meetings in Buffalo, Brittany Harrison was sitting at her desk in the back of the Power and Baseline Starbucks in Mesa, Arizona. She hadn't been able to get coverage for her shift, so while her store manager colleagues were all going to their district manager's house for a meeting to discuss the Fall Launch, Brittany had to join via Zoom. She cupped her hands around her lukewarm coffee markout and logged on.

Because she was in the store, her partners were around, coming through the back of house to grab a chai backup or a packet of dragon-fruit inclusions and occasionally stopping to check in with her. Brittany let her district manager know she was recording, in order to make sure she could go back and review anything she might miss.

Tricia Lowder, the district manager, was an evangelical Christian who gave interviews about how "atheists drink Dunkin' Donuts" and how she brought her religion to work at a company she said was "preaching" ideas that were "extreme left." When she gave holiday gifts to the store managers, she wrapped Brittany's in a different color, making Brittany feel singled out for being Jewish. But today, Tricia was focused on a different crusade.[1]

"I know this is supposed to be about the Fall Launch," she said, "but here's the situation in Buffalo."

To Starbucks partners in those days, *Buffalo* was synonymous with *union*. After all, corporate often avoided engaging directly with the union, or even acknowledging that the union was the impetus for their actions. *Buffalo* was their euphemism, their code word.

Brittany texted her old Starbucks partners in California: "This seems super shady, maybe they shouldn't be saying this. I'm recording it."

"Holy shit, Harrison. You've got to do something."

"I could get fired."

"I got a call this last week," Tricia was saying on Zoom. "And, um, they're collecting a set of—they're collecting levels of people across the organization that have a proven track record in partner category blah blah blah. So I got a call. And so I don't know when it's going to start, but for the next ninety days, I'm going to spend two weeks in Buffalo, and then come home for two weeks, and then two weeks in Buffalo and then come home for two weeks. And by the way, if you've ever been to Buffalo, New York, it's nothing like Manhattan. So, yeah. So, don't think that I'm gonna be, like, hanging out at Rockefeller Center."

The other managers on the call laughed.

Tricia continued: She was joining a task force that was going to Buffalo to try to instill in partners the Starbucks mission and values, to save the company from the union. The partners who wanted to organize would "suck the life out of you," she said. "They don't understand Starbucks. They don't understand the mission and values."

She added, "We can talk openly about this, no one's recording."

"Harrison's recording," someone pointed out.

"You need to *stop* recording," Tricia said, her voice changing.

After the meeting ended, Brittany's partners, including Michelle Hejduk, a shift supervisor who was one of the store's anchors, had questions. "How was the fall meeting? Anything we need to know?"

Brittany swallowed hard. Starbucks had always emphasized that managers could share information with their partners. She was proud of the way she led, with openness and transparency.

"I'm not sure if I can discuss this," she began. "We didn't talk about the Fall Launch, so we have to have another meeting."

"What did you talk about?"

"About the union thing going on in Buffalo."

"Oh! We have questions."

"I'm getting the vibe that we're not supposed to promote that, but let's talk through it."

Starbucks' line was that what was going on in Buffalo was unique, that it was an extraordinary departure from the Starbucks experience, that there had been a breakdown in the leadership in Buffalo and the company was going to send people in to support the partners who were suffering in an unprecedented situation.

"But we've experienced those things, too," one of the shift supervisors said.

"I've also experienced that," said Brittany. "It's not unique to Buffalo."

That night, as she sat on the couch with her husband, Brittany felt a pit in her stomach. "I'm going to get fired, but it's the right thing to do."

She reached out to the Buffalo union over Instagram. Casey messaged her back and connected her with Richard as well. Brittany, who was only twenty-nine, shared more of her story: how she had worked in several stores in California before transferring to Arizona; how she had been diagnosed with leukemia and was undergoing chemotherapy. She told us that she had previously been a Starbucks devotee, even attending a leadership summit in Chicago where every manager had been given a replica of the key to the Pike Place store. They had all held the keys aloft, signifying their unity.

"It's a cult," said Brittany.

Other partners on the Buffalo organizing committee had used that descriptor previously, but I had diligently kept it out of any of our media interviews, afraid that it would make the union look too opposed to the company culture, marginalizing the campaign. But when Brittany said it, as someone who had participated in those very activities, it felt different.

Brittany sent the tape of Tricia's Zoom meeting to us and to the *New York Times*. She asked the reporter, Noam Scheiber, to withhold her name. To try to preserve her anonymity, the story quoted a district manager talking about "saving" Buffalo from the union.[2]

I took the newspaper clipping into a captive-audience meeting in mid-October, the one where Starbucks showed us the PowerPoint about the Workers United constitution, and asked them about that quote.

Ana, one of the operations coaches, piped up as a "proud member of the Buffalo task force" to talk about how she was only trying to "save the partner experience." It had nothing to do with the union, she said.

Brittany's tape was the best antidote to corporate's gaslighting. Until this point, the corporate executives had been extraordinarily disciplined in maintaining the line that they were not in Buffalo because of the union, but because conditions there were so unusually awful. Tricia had blown that cover. Recognizing Brittany's power, Starbucks targeted her. Although neither she nor Tricia had been identified by name in the *New York Times*, it was easy for Starbucks to identify the source. They started calling Brittany, asking if she was the whistleblower. They retaliated in other ways, too, withholding support from her and denying her request to work fewer days. Then, partners at her store started coming down with bronchitis. Brittany caught it, too. Unable to get other managers to help cover her store, Brittany struggled to work on the floor as her health deteriorated. Eventually, Tricia got what she wanted: Brittany's two weeks' notice.

Starbucks responded by firing Brittany, rather than allowing her to work out the two weeks. They sent her a notice that her health care was terminated effective immediately, too. Management threw out the decorations and items she had bought to make the back room a nicer space for her partners and discarded her personal collection of Starbucks cups.

We found out that Brittany was fired when she called Richard and he put her on speakerphone. Immediately, we set up a GoFundMe page, which raised over $30,000 in days. The public was outraged.

Brittany had every excuse not to take the risk of blowing the whistle on Starbucks' union busting. Her health was at stake, as well as the insurance she needed for chemotherapy. Starbucks' retaliation against her struck at her most vulnerable point.

Watching what Brittany was going through, her partners realized they had two choices: quit or organize. On November 16, she hosted a game night at her house. There, her partners started signing union cards.

"It's happening!" Brittany texted Richard, along with a photo of the workers around her kitchen table.

Quickly, the workers formed an organizing committee, signed their cards, and wrote a letter to then-CEO Kevin Johnson. On November 18, with assistance from our Buffalo lawyers, they filed their petition with the NLRB and we posted their letter on Twitter.

"We are aware of the anti-union campaign that you and Rossann plus other managers are waging in Buffalo," the organizing committee had written. "We are not intimidated but we are outraged. We know you refused to even acknowledge the large number of partners from stores in Buffalo who signed the initial letter asking you to sign on to the Fair Election Principles. Kevin, as one partner to another we hope you will reconsider your position on not signing and begin to return Starbucks to the principled company we believe in."

**MESA WAS THE FIRST** store outside of Buffalo to file for a union election. I hadn't known whether anyone would even want to organize a Starbucks elsewhere until we had won our elections and negotiated a strong contract. But interest was high among Starbucks partners across the country from the beginning. In Tallahassee, in Boston, in Texas, in California, in North Carolina, workers were watching what was happening and were reaching out.

We began to get on Zoom calls with them. Richard and I were the only staff working on the campaign at that time, and I was still clocking in four days a week at the Elmwood store. We joked that he was the "third party" Starbucks talked about, that Starbucks Workers United was hundreds of Starbucks partners plus Richard. He would immediately respond to new leads, emailing them his Zoom link and asking if they could hop on right then. If they could, he would turn the computer around and pull whoever was in the office at the time into the conversation. Casey and I would be working on a press release one minute and then be sprawled on the floor talking to someone on the other side of the country the next. We talked to a worker in Spokane at the beginning of September.

"The heavy lifting is done," they told us. "I've wanted to do this, and I've been thinking about it for a few months, and I was like, I don't even know where to start. And then I saw a retweet of your article, and I was like, I don't have to start it, because y'all already did. And I can't thank y'all enough."

The messages continued to pour in all through the fall. In Knoxville, Tennessee, Maggie Carter's partners were also coming to her, asking for more information about what organizing meant. The decisive moment that made her reach out happened after Starbucks unexpectedly announced a second, unplanned raise within weeks of giving the first, scheduled one. In states like Tennessee, this meant an increase of several dollars an hour.

"Why are we getting another raise?" her partners asked.

"Because of the union," Maggie said.

A few days later, she DMed us on Facebook: "I love the work you're doing. I'm a barista here in Tennessee and I would LOVE to see unionization take place."

We gave her Richard's email and told her we would be more free in a few days, as we were in a final push toward the vote.

Maggie emailed Richard, who sent her his number. They talked for two hours, and Maggie began building an organizing committee, with his guidance and Casey's.

"Richard knew exactly what to say to me when I needed to hear it," Maggie said much later, perching cross-legged on her bed while Colson, her son, played *The Sims* nearby and their dog lounged at my feet. By that time, she had become one of the key partners on point and was about to join the union staff. "He brought out qualities in me I didn't know I had. And that's something I've tried to learn as an organizer—how do you help people find that within themselves?"

Before Mesa, we worried that filing for stores outside of Buffalo would lessen our momentum and weaken our focus on winning the first elections. "We only have to win one" had become a bit of a mantra. Once we had demonstrated that the group of workers wanted a union, we could focus on rallying the labor movement's support and pressure to win the right to organize and a first contract. Sure, these were small bargaining units—twenty-five or thirty workers. But didn't they have the right to form a union? The whole labor movement would have to show that it would fight for them. As with Spot Coffee, we planned to boycott Starbucks in Buffalo to force them to end their union busting. But, unlike Spot, Starbucks had nine thousand nonunion stores across the country. Could we convince other unions to adopt stores and maintain picket lines to turn away customers if and when we called for a boycott?[3]

After Brittany was fired, we didn't have a choice about whether to file for an election in Mesa. We weren't going to tell the workers we wouldn't organize them, and we felt that Brittany's sacrifice made unionizing Power and Baseline a moral imperative. They filed for an election on November 18.

As we got closer to December, other stores across the country had increasing levels of support. We had agreed from the beginning that we wouldn't say no to workers who wanted to organize. By December 7, a couple of stores in Boston were ready to file. We asked them to wait a couple of days, as a matter of sequencing. If Elmwood won the election and other stores immediately joined the movement, that would demonstrate the energy and momentum of the campaign. The Boston stores filed for their elections on December 13, the Monday after our victory in Buffalo.

**AFTER WE WON ELMWOOD**, I got sick. The strain of trying to hold my store together had been intense, and the relief of winning gave way to an immune system collapse. I couldn't keep food down for nearly a week. As the holidays approached, I headed to Mississippi and North Carolina to spend a couple of weeks with my chosen family.

On Christmas Eve, I was on a blueberry farm in Mississippi, going for a ride standing in the back of an old pickup truck and playing Frisbee with my friends and their dogs, recovering from the exhaustion of the past few months. Richard and Casey, however, were on Zoom. Many calls and signed union cards later, Knoxville was ready to file.

A few days later, I headed to Jackson to spend time with my clinic-defense friends. After a long day of escorting patients, a few of us, including Derenda, the leader of the Pink House Defenders, went out to dinner. We talked about the Starbucks campaign, and I insisted the union would spread to Mississippi.

"But you know people see Buffalo and think, 'Well, that's the North, it's just not the same,'" Derenda said.

"That's true, but other Starbucks workers have already reached out. Seattle already filed, and Boston, and now Knoxville."

"Well, Seattle and Boston are the same as Buffalo down here, but Knoxville's different. That could change things."

On Christmas Day, Richard had four Zoom calls, including one with Maggie. In South Carolina, in Seattle, in Colorado, in Kansas, partners were reaching out. Different Buffalo partners were "on point" for different regions of the country. Colin Cochran worked with partners in North and South Carolina. Brian was working with Boston and Connecticut. Michelle Eisen was helping Michelle Hejduk in Mesa, Arizona, as well as a Hawaii store. Will was working with Oklahoma, Texas, New Jersey, Kansas, and elsewhere, as needed. James was talking to California stores. Natalie and Gianna and other partners were filling in where they could. I was on point for parts of the South and most of the New York stores, although Emily Vick, our union rep in Albany, stepped up and organized store after store while continuing to work with all of her existing shops. Other Buffalo partners were joining calls and providing support. Meanwhile, Casey was running the campaign.

"I don't think I ran the campaign," Casey said. "But I ran the email, which was inadvertently running the campaign."

Casey worked around the clock, still punching in five days a week at the Williamsville Place Starbucks while tirelessly responding to emails, logging on to Zoom calls, coordinating organizing in Florida and working with other stores across the country, and following up with the other partners on point to ensure no stores or leads were falling through the cracks. She drafted our press releases and, via Zoom, facilitated press conferences for partners around the country. In the beginning, most of these releases and conferences announced new stores' victories. The workers were elated and their words were genuine, authentic, and energizing.

Starbucks Workers United's engagement with the press was entirely run by workers, with Casey at the helm, not by fancy PR firms or communications "experts." Journalists talked to us about the difference they saw in our campaign compared with others. Sure, occasionally someone said the wrong thing. But our organizing committee calls always included a section on media training, emphasizing that people should speak from the heart and lead with optimism and positivity. That exuberant spirit carried over to social media, too, where workers ran all of the accounts, from TikTok to Twitter to Reddit. When people reached out, they knew they were getting real partners, who understood their struggles and who knew how to make memes. This created the trust needed to fuel the massive surge in organizing that took the campaign nationwide.

**I WAS ON THE** North Carolina coast with Eunice in early January 2022, as the Omicron variant of coronavirus was spreading through the country. It ravaged Starbucks stores, where the company had just taken away isolation pay for partners who had been exposed to Covid but weren't showing symptoms. My coworkers began calling me. Everyone at Elmwood had been exposed. Many of our partners were in isolation, leaving the remaining workers running themselves ragged with exhaustion and overwork. On January 3, I talked to Cassie, Angela, JP, Michelle, and other partners, who told me how dire the situation had gotten. That night, we emailed the company asking for urgent bargaining over the crisis and the modifications the company had made to our store's operating hours. I decided to head back up to Buffalo immediately.

The next day, I drove up in between Zoom bargaining sessions, pulling over in the mountains of West Virginia to log on. We asked Starbucks to allow us to close the store for five days—the same length of time as the newly modified CDC (Centers for Disease Control and Prevention) guidelines recommended—to allow partners to isolate and recover. Failing that, we asked for KN95 masks, Covid tests, and the right to refuse service to those who wouldn't comply with New York's mask mandate. Prior to the anti-union campaign, we had already been enforcing the mask mandate: I had personally told customers to put a mask on or leave, with the full support of our store manager. After the anti-union campaign began, corporate had a constant presence in our stores and no longer allowed us the autonomy to protect one another.

After caucusing, management denied all of our demands. They told us that the "layers of protection" they had in place were adequate. That KN95 masks weren't necessary. That our store had a high vaccination rate so isolation wasn't necessary and that they weren't even recommending testing to those who had been exposed. They told us that we were not allowed to refuse service to those who refused to mask, citing "de-escalation" and ignoring our concerns.[4]

I woke up early the next morning to a dead phone and six missed calls. Cassie and Michelle had been trying to reach me: They were organizing a walkout. One of our coworkers had had a medical emergency that morning, but because so many of our coworkers were out with Covid that no one could come in to cover their shift, they waited to go to the hospital. Finally, Michelle drove them and the latest support manager, Katherine, came in. Cortlin had called off, and Cassie called to tell me to call the store and offer to take the rest of his shift in order to join the walkout.

When I called the store, Katherine answered.

"Hi! I heard that y'all might need help this morning, and I can come in if you need me!"

"When could you come in until?"

"Eleven or noon, I think," I said.

"And you don't have any Covid symptoms?"

"None at all."

"Well, I'm not stupid enough to say no to help."

I threw on some work clothes, hurried to my car, and rushed to the store. When I got there, Michelle was on Bar 1. "She's had me here the whole morning," Michelle whispered. "I think she wants to keep an eye on me."

Katherine put me on register. Cassie had been running around on customer support all morning, furtively calling me in between fetching supplies from the back room. She had also gotten in touch with everyone else who was scheduled to work that morning. Kyli Hilaire, who had worked in our store until the previous August, when she transferred to one in Pittsburgh, where she was going to college, was back. I knew she would have joined the committee if she hadn't left, and now she was helping organize the walkout.

Nearly everyone was in favor of going on strike. We decided to time the walkout for just before one of our coworkers who didn't want to strike would arrive, so that she wouldn't be put on the spot. Just before 9:30 a.m., the rush of customers had slowed and snow had started falling. Michelle finished making the remaining drink orders before anyone else came into the café. As the last customer gathered his drinks, Michelle turned to the rest of us. "Now."

Alyssa put the oven tongs back in their holder; Josh set the coffee urn down; Kyli put the blender down by the sink. Along with Cassie, we headed to the back room to get our things. Because I was on register, I was the closest to the back room and the first in line walking off. For a moment, it crossed my mind, *What if no one else comes, too?* As I stepped off the floor, I looked behind me: Everyone was there, walking off together.

Katherine, who had been sitting at the manager's desk, began to panic. "What did I do?"

"You didn't do anything," said Michelle. "It's the company."

"Don't forget to clock out!" she began imploring us. "Don't forget to clock out!"

We walked out in a single column. It was one of the most empowering feelings. Denied our Covid isolation, we were taking it anyway.

One of our union reps brought us poster board to make picket signs. SAFETY FIRST. PROFIT SECOND, we wrote. ON STRIKE FOR COVID SAFETY.

It was bitterly cold, and we were not appropriately dressed. Mike Dolce arrived with a bag full of gardening gloves. "It was all they had at the 7-Eleven," he apologized. We ordered hot coffee from the coffee shop on the corner and took turns thawing in Michelle's car. Brian brought his speaker and Danka's father stopped by to give us a box of doughnuts. Kyli began doing social media for the strike. Many community supporters stopped by to walk the picket line with us or to drop off hand warmers or snacks.

We worried that our strike might hurt organizing among the new stores waiting for elections or starting unionization. Would Starbucks point to us and say that we had only just unionized and now we were already out on strike? Would this scare other partners?

Across the country, partners' response was overwhelmingly positive. On social media, people posted about how they wished they could have done the same thing at their stores. When Michelle Hejduk's new manager in Mesa tried telling her that the union was forcing partners out on strike, she called Michelle Eisen.

"At first, I was worried," Hejduk said, "but I figured they weren't telling me everything that was going on, and when I learned that it was a five-day strike and why y'all were doing it, I was like, 'Wait, we can do that?'"

Meanwhile, we continued to try to take Covid safety into our own hands, including by enforcing masking on our picket line. Starbucks stayed open during the strike, albeit with extremely limited hours. A few partners who were opposed to the union crossed the line, as did some of the newer partners who feared Starbucks' retaliation and were concerned about making rent. I drove to every hardware store in Buffalo that might have a few KN95 masks and then made deliveries across the city, including going into Elmwood to hand some to my nonstriking coworkers. At Camp Road and Walden and Anderson, even workers who didn't support the union were excited to get masks. I hoped that this showed people that our goal was simply to protect people and to empower people to protect one another.

We had set up a GoFundMe to try to raise enough to cover strike pay. The labor movement's support was unbelievable. We raised several thousand more than we needed and we put some of it into a solidarity fund to support workers at the Elmwood and Genesee stores when they were struggling to make rent, buy groceries, or quarantine from Covid when Starbucks wouldn't cover their lost wages.

One of our anti-union coworkers, who had crossed the picket line, came down with Covid a couple of days into our strike. She was in a precarious economic situation already and faced with possible eviction. I asked my fellow strikers how we felt about using some of the funds to help her.

They were overwhelmingly supportive of helping. Others within the broader movement were shocked: "You want to give some of the strike fund to a scab?" But I still believe it was the right thing to do. That individual worker never came around, transferring to a different store where she continued to campaign against the union. But other workers who had crossed the picket line in January would go on strike with us in the coming months. Blaming corporate and structures, not individual workers, is key to maintaining a strong union and strong morale. Moreover, extending help and kindness leaves pathways for workers to understand the union's guidance principles of solidarity and mutual aid.

Other stores were watching our strike, too, and deciding to try to take action to protect themselves and one another.

**IN JANUARY 2022,** I was cleaning my room when I got an email from someone named Nikki in Memphis who'd been trying to reach us. When I called her on the phone, she saw my Mississippi area code. It was the first time that had meant something to anyone on the campaign.

"Where have you been?" she asked. "The Taco Tuesday group is ready to go!"

The five coworkers who comprised the Taco Tuesday group had been meeting every week. They were closely bonded. Nikki, a shift supervisor, was already known for looking after her coworkers.

A couple of weeks before, Nikki had caught Covid at work and taken it home, where she gave it to her seven-year-old daughter. Nikki was livid about Starbucks' lack of safety protections.

As soon as we got off the phone, I called Richard to tell him what was going on.

"Can they all get on Zoom right now?" he asked. It was Martin Luther King Day. "It would be great if they could have their organizing committee meet tonight."

I called Nikki back.

"Let me see what I can do," she said.

An hour later, we were all on Zoom. In many ways, our intake calls followed a formula. Every day, Starbucks workers were reaching out to the campaign for assistance, for reassurance, for help, and to join a growing movement. They wanted to know, Would they be protected? How could they join? Did they need to sign something? Where would they get that? Did they need to pool their piggy banks to hire a lawyer? What would their store manager think? What should they tell coworkers who weren't sure what a union was?

We went over those standard questions, and more, with the Memphis workers. We talked to them about the steps of unionizing, explaining the jargon: what the NLRB was, how union cards worked (signing one meant RSVPing to vote yes), what an organizing committee was. We talked about what the company was likely to do, reciting corporate's talking points to inoculate them against management's threats. We did a quick media training, discussing best practices for talking with the press and staying on message.

Mostly, we emphasized the importance of moving quickly. The critical nature of speedy organizing campaigns could not be overstated. Forming an organizing committee and getting a majority of the store signed up on union cards within a day or two was the difference between winning and losing. Before management knew what was going on, there was plenty of wiggle room to plan and strategize. Once management found out, time was not on our side. And the company always found out before we thought it would. Sometimes, it was already too late: If management knew, they began scheduling "listening sessions," announcing store closures, holding one-on-one meetings, and targeting union leaders. Many potential campaigns faltered before they even got in touch with us: Sympathetic store managers in other parts of the country told us that Starbucks was moving aggressively where they found out about early union activity.

The Taco Tuesday group moved faster than any other store: That night, they turned into an organizing committee and took their campaign public. Partway through the call, Ginny Diamond joined. She typed out a draft of the workers' letter as they dictated, talking about Dr. King's legacy and how he had been killed while fighting for union rights in their city.[5]

"Please, in the memory of Dr. Martin Luther King, Jr., do not bring your so-called 'pro-partner' anti-union campaign to Memphis," they concluded.

But Starbucks did bring its union busting to Memphis.

The committee got a strong majority of cards signed by the following day and filed for an election the day after that. Shortly after going public, the workers did an interview at their store. The store was closing early for the day due to short-staffing, and the media arrived right at close. The camera crew filmed the interview inside the store.

In the days that followed, Starbucks corporate launched an investigation into every detail of that day. One worker had come into the store on her day off to sign a union card and had then helped show a coworker how to make a drink. A couple of the partners had taken their masks off once the customers had left the store. Corporate accused Nikki of letting the press into the store after close and claimed that violated safety protocols, even though the store had a policy that workers were not allowed to lock the doors until ten minutes after the official closing time. Corporate investigated another shift supervisor, Beto, for opening the safe to deposit money while another shift was technically the key holder, even though helping in that way was routine—and most of the shifts weren't trained on cash handling and hadn't been given unique codes to unlock the safe, forcing them to use one assigned to a former partner. Their former store manager, Amy, jumped to their defense, confirming that this had been the past practice and that no one had ever faced discipline for these actions.

On February 8, the Taco Tuesday–group-turned-organizing-committee became the Memphis Seven.[6]

I had made myself coffee and sat down at my computer. Then my phone rang. It was Nabretta, one of the committee leaders. "They're firing us."

Memphis had been hit with an ice storm the night before. The power was out at the Poplar and Highland store. Management had rigged up a generator to power a portable heater in the lobby of the closed store.

One by one, they were calling workers into the store and firing them. After their meetings, the partners were heading to Nikki's house for community and strategizing. By the time the firings ended, seven workers were all sitting in Nikki's living room, out of their jobs.

In retrospect, we should have called a national boycott of Starbucks right then. Across the country, Starbucks workers were making signs and taking photos with them: WE STAND WITH MEMPHIS. The public was overwhelmingly supportive, and the Memphis pickets—like those across the rest of the country—were well attended. Starbucks was vulnerable: The union campaign was dominating headlines, and our momentum was growing. We had always thought we would have to boycott Starbucks eventually to put enough pressure on the company to win the right to organize; this was an opportune moment to begin.

"This is a civil rights fight," said Richard. "A civil rights fight needs a boycott."

---

**THE REVEREND DR. WILLIAM** J. Barber II, a civil rights leader who had revived the Poor People's Campaign to advocate for racial and economic justice, was ready to endorse a boycott. Reverend Barber was a friend of Richard's, and we got on a Zoom call to tell him about what was going on, in Memphis, in Buffalo, and across the country. He agreed to lead a march in Memphis to call attention to what Starbucks had done and demand they reinstate the seven workers.

"But I also want to go to Buffalo," he said. "I want to see where it all started."

Reverend Barber ended up doing two events. The first one, in February, was a press conference at our union office in Buffalo. The second, in March, was a march to the store where the Memphis Seven were fired. Casey, Angel, Richard, and I flew down for the event. Maggie drove over from Knoxville.

"Starbucks calls these workers 'partners,' but they treat them like problems," Barber said. "We're here today to bear witness to these Memphis workers and say to them, 'You are not alone. You will not stand alone.'"[7]

However, we stopped short of asking him to call for a boycott, in large part because national leadership within Workers United was opposed to a boycott. They worried that it would be too difficult to pull off and that it would cost us support among workers. In Buffalo, we disagreed; at Spot Coffee, it had been the company's union busting, not the boycott, that cost us support. We only won the election and a first contract because the economic pressure of the boycott forced the company to change its behavior.

Richard and I argued about whether we needed to build an infrastructure capable of placing picket captains at thousands of stores before we called a boycott. He thought we had one chance at this, and that if we called a boycott but lacked the means to properly enforce it, it would be ineffective and only harden the company's anti-union stance. I thought that a slow start might still get significant results, especially if we left room for escalation. We both agreed that it was essential to get celebrities to take up the call, the sooner the better. If Taylor Swift called for a boycott or Ariana Grande posted a TikTok saying union busting was making her sad, we would win, we thought.

The other concern was time.

We needed to boycott the company to be able to win the right to organize and a fair contract, we thought. At the same time, workers were still clamoring to organize everywhere. While labor unions—from the air traffic controllers to the postal workers to the UAW—were offering to adopt stores and help us build the infrastructure Richard talked about, it would take the work of many Starbucks partners to keep the messaging, activity, legitimacy, and grassroots nature of the boycott true to the animating values of the campaign. Those partners were on Zoom, organizing other stores.

Richard wrote plan after plan for how we could pull this off, given all the obstacles. Some were blueprints to build the national infrastructure. Others outlined starting boycotts in certain geographic areas: in Buffalo or Seattle or Eugene, and then planning to expand to other critical markets. The plans would take tremendous resources, tremendous willpower, and a belief that winning the right to organize and unionizing workplace-by-workplace was the best way to build a fair and just society.

Staffers from Workers United opposed our plan for a boycott, telling partners across the country that not only was it not strategic, but that they believed (incorrectly) that it was illegal. They claimed that the union would face RICO charges if we called a boycott and that staff encouraging partners to boycott were exerting undue influence over workers and thus violating the NLRA, which was also untrue.

That didn't matter. Workers United's leadership wanted to centralize control, taking it away from the Buffalo partners. The same staffers held a series of conversations with key leaders across the country, telling them about salting. They made it sound like a manipulative and disingenuous activity. Some of us were even paid by the union, they said. Because we were union plants rather than real Starbucks partners, we lacked the credibility to lead the campaign.

The union's messaging was the same as Howard Schultz's. Starbucks corporate had put up flyers in stores about to vote on unionizing that talked about how I was paid by the union, seeking to undermine the entire campaign by attacking me. Early in the campaign, a Starbucks spokesperson had told a Buffalo reporter that I wasn't an independent operator—Richard Bensinger was the "puppet master" (the spokeperson's word) controlling the show. We joked that if anyone was the puppet master, it was actually me. But Starbucks, in that statement, revealed their true prejudices and beliefs: Workers, and even young organizers, couldn't actually want to organize or have the capability to pull off the feat—we had to be controlled by someone else, who was pulling our strings.

When Howard Schultz returned as CEO for a third time in April 2022, he immediately held a livestream that was touted as a "partner open forum," where he said that "companies are being assaulted by the threat of unionization." When a *Vice* reporter, Paul Blest, questioned Starbucks' PR team about the statement, they deflected by talking about a salt—me—rather than an assault. Howard accused the union of sending twenty salts into the Seattle Roastery when it organized, refusing to believe that his own partners could want a union without "outside organizations" stirring them up. (There were no salts in the Seattle Roastery.) In March of 2023, Howard appeared, under threat of subpoena, before the Senate Committee on Health, Education, Labor and Pensions to discuss the union campaign. A Republican senator brought up that I had been a salt and asked Howard to respond.[8]

"Well, if that is not a nefarious act, I don't know what is," he said.[9]

**THESE ATTACKS—AT TIMES** from the union as much as from Starbucks—often meant long and emotional conversations with workers around the country. Casey, who had built relationships and earned the trust of so many people, bore the greatest share of this burden, often holding back-to-back conversations for hours, including at union events when tensions bubbled to the surface.

But we were able to overcome these obstacles. When we talked about salting as it really was—not as the company or union bureaucrats portrayed it to further their own goals—workers overwhelmingly responded positively.

"I thought you were a vigilante," Kyli had told me, during the strike, when I asked what she thought about the fact that I had gotten the job to help organize. "I thought you were going to disappear after the election. But you didn't. You're still here."

After the strike, when Kyli went back to school and to her Pittsburgh store, she told us she didn't want to come back to Elmwood until she had organized her other store. They filed for an election right before she returned back for the summer; she and Michelle watched the victorious Zoom vote count in our store's back room during their shifts.

This was an illustration of the beauty of the campaign: Workers who learned how to organize were turning around, everywhere, and organizing others. We were often exhausted, sleep-deprived, and burned-out, but the optimism, joy, and courage of the workers we were helping was contagious.

In Seattle, the first store to organize—Broadway and Denny—held regular check-ins with Richard. Because of the time difference, they were often at midnight Buffalo time. I logged on to one of the calls on a day when I'd opened my store at 5:00 a.m., and I struggled to stay awake as we talked about the status of their store. Finally, I went video off to lie down. I woke up after the call had ended, the Zoom notification still on my screen.

I was embarrassed, but Rachel Ybarra, one of the Seattle partners, charitably thought that my falling asleep illustrated how grassroots and relatable the campaign really was. As a group, Starbucks partners were iconoclastic, wry, terminally online, and perpetually exhausted. For Rachel, that interaction underscored that the worker-organizers were dealing with the same struggles they were.

Some partners, like Sarah Pappin in Seattle and Quinn Craig in San Antonio, took matters into their own hands on a remarkably expedited time frame, becoming key leaders of the organizing campaigns in their regions.

Casey and I joined Quinn's intake call together. It was a fun discussion, ranging from the details of organizing to the leftist Texan identity politics of loving Albert Parsons. After the call, a couple of scheduling mix-ups meant that I missed some committee meetings. We had a couple more check-in calls, but soon Quinn was working mostly on their own, training and recruiting new committee members to help them. They began working with other Texas stores, too.

"On that first call, I could see how tired y'all were. I thought y'all were burned-out and had too much on your plates, so I thought, 'I can do this part.' So I did," they explained later.

Sarah Pappin had reached out in December, once the Broadway and Denny store filed for its union election.

"I'm an eight-year partner," she wrote. "I have been closely watching the unionization efforts going on in stores around the country and have started bringing that conversation into my store. As of right now, myself and two other partners are actively very interested in joining the growing list of unionizing stores. We are extremely dedicated to this cause, and we are willing to go the distance. We've been chatting with our other partners to get a vibe check and we believe that we can achieve a majority vote for unionization.

"We were planning on taking this process on slowly and quietly, however upon hearing the terrific news from the Broadway and Denny partners, I realized that things may start to move really quickly in Seattle."

Things did move quickly, and Sarah became a key coordinator in Seattle. She, and many other workers across the country, were stepping up into the role of "partners on point" even as they waited for election dates at their own stores. Across the country, the NLRB allowed Starbucks to litigate the unit determination hearings scores of times, delaying workers accessing their right to organize and giving the company weeks of additional time to union bust. Even worse, we couldn't file additional stores if we had pending petitions in a region without the NLRB consolidating the cases and delaying the earlier petitions from getting their election dates. Maintaining morale among waiting stores and identifying as many stores as possible that could file as a bloc when the window opened was critical.

In Knoxville, Starbucks' anti-union campaign had been intense. Management had held a captive-audience meeting that exposed most of the store to Covid. They had pulled partners into intense one-on-ones, flipping a key committee member and trying to pit people against one another. They demonized Maggie, accusing her of being aggressive and forcing people to sign union cards.

I asked her how she was holding up. Things were rough, she admitted. Terrifying, in fact. But she, like many other Starbucks workers, was tapping into a deep reservoir of resistance. She was a single mom trying to work her way through college. Growing up in the Republican-dominated South, she'd felt that it was impossible to change the political structures that had weakened every aspect of worker power.

"But what do I have to lose?"

Working through the pandemic put her health at risk every day. Meanwhile, she wasn't making enough to keep the lights on or to buy food. And she was used to pushing back.

"We're used to fighting for every right we have, as the LGBTQ-plus community. I have to think about whether I can hold my girlfriend's hand in public, but I do it anyway, most of the time. People hide their kids from me. I see that stuff. But that becomes a part of people who are marginalized in society—feeling comfortable in that fire, to fight."

Her fight was heroic, and she had also become a key partner on point, working with the Memphis Seven and with other local stores as she tried to hold her own together. But corporate was wielding every weapon it had to try to stop the union from winning. Things didn't look good for the election. The day before the vote count, Casey and I were talking on the phone.

"One of us should go," she said. "It's the first election in the South, and it's likely to be the first loss since Camp Road. But I'm just so tired."

"I'd love to go, actually," I offered. "Knoxville means a lot to me."

I booked my ticket and spent the rest of the mostly sleepless night trying to steel myself for losing. It wouldn't be the end, I rehearsed: There were other stores, including one in Alcoa, that were going to elections soon afterward. Even if Maggie's store lost, others would soon win and show that Starbucks workers could organize in the South after all. Most important, I couldn't cry—not in public, not in front of the workers. I focused on the importance of maintaining a stony exterior: I needed to be there for Maggie and the others, and I needed to emphasize in any media interviews that one loss wouldn't change the course of the union campaign.

The next morning, March 29, Maggie picked me up at the airport. We went to her store for coffee and said hi to her coworkers: Starbucks had a habit of scheduling pro-union workers during their stores' vote counts. Then, we went to a nearby union hall to watch the results.

The ancient projector didn't work, so we pulled up the Zoom call on our computers. As in Buffalo, the workers there stood in a row, watching, an anticipatory row of media lined up in front of us. Partners from the nearby, newly organizing stores Maggie had been working with were there, too, from Alcoa and from the Montvue store, which had an all-nonbinary organizing committee.

"They're incredible," Maggie whispered to me. "Whatever happens here, they're going to win."

Once the NLRB agent had finished opening the ballots, I did the math. We needed eight yes votes to win—there was one challenged ballot, but it belonged to the assistant manager, a lovely person who supported the union and wanted to fight to be included in it.

Then it began.

"No. Yes. No. . . ."

Six of the first seven ballots were no votes. Each one triggered a tightening in my stomach. Our chances of winning seemed to recede into the distance. Maggie was nervous, but her face was stoically set. *Don't cry*, I told myself sternly.

"Yes." The total stood at 2–6.

"Yes." 3–6.

I held my breath.

"Yes." 4–6.

"Yes." 5–6.

This was good, but I didn't want to get confident. There were many more uncounted ballots. If two of them were no votes, we had no chance of winning.

"Yes." 6–6.

I looked at the small stack of ballots remaining. This was good, but were there enough yeses left in the pile to pull this out?

"Yes." 7–6.

"Yes." 8–6.

We had won. Everyone jumped into the air, jubilant. Maggie and I cried from joy: My resolution not to cry had proven unnecessary. That night, we celebrated over cheese enchiladas with Colson and the courageous ASM from Maggie's store, who had risked her career to support the union.

Winning in the South was important. If we could do it there, anyone could do it. It only emphasized that this was not unique to Buffalo, to a region, to a particular group or subset of workers. Starbucks partners wanted to become partners. The momentum was still building.

**AT THAT TIME, VICTORIOUS** vote counts were regularly happening all over the country. These counts united Starbucks partners, who logged on to the Zoom livestreams to show solidarity, to support one another, and to share in the joy and optimism that each new win brought. Reporters often logged on to the calls. So did certain members of Starbucks corporate, along with a recurring cast of Littler lawyers and representatives from Edelman, Starbucks' PR firm. But on our side, there was a curious and adorable community of vote count attendees. Its most loyal member was a labor studies professor named John Logan.

While it had taken him a while to come around to the idea that Starbucks' union busting might really be unprecedented—after all, when had Richard *not* claimed that a particular company's anti-union campaign was the worst he had seen in his career?—John quickly became a fan as he saw the campaign spreading. He narrated the vote counts in a series of Facebook comments that made the gut-wrenching anxiety of watching the Board agent meticulously and deliberately open each envelope a little more bearable. John also wrote extensively about the campaign, exchanging long emails with Richard and one of our lawyers. He sent me his articles, but I—caught up in the hectic campaign—didn't respond for months. In the spring, I finally answered one of his questions, about Starbucks' shift from captive-audience meetings to one-on-ones, a subtle but significant development. We began talking on the phone, and I quickly realized that John had a deep understanding of labor and the campaign, a uniquely reassuring and humorous outlook on the movement, and a desire to help in any way possible. Over the coming year and a half, we would become inseparable.

In the meantime, the organizing continued to spread. Within the first

120 days after winning our union election at Elmwood, two hundred additional stores were in play, in various stages of launching their campaigns. Virginia quickly became a hotbed of union activity. Ginny Diamond had agreed to coordinate organizing efforts in the state. She understood the partner-on-point system and ensured that the organizing committees she was working with were in charge.

Meridian, a seventeen-year-old worker in Richmond, Virginia, typified what made Starbucks Workers United so special. When they began forming an organizing committee, they also convinced the other members of their high school drama club to apply for jobs at their store to help the effort, functionally salting their own workplace.

But the effects of Starbucks' union busting were beginning to emerge. The first Virginia store to go to an election was in Springfield, where the committee included a range of workers from a four-year partner who was a shift supervisor to a new partner who was a high school senior.

"When I turn eighteen, I'll be able to do this," the senior had said. "My coworkers will listen to me."

Unfortunately, Starbucks brought their containment strategy down hard on the Springfield partners. The district manager was in the store every day. Corporate slashed partners' hours. They had constant one-on-one meetings, threatening benefits. Howard Schultz told unionized stores that they wouldn't get the same benefits that he was giving nonunion stores.

The Springfield store lost, the first loss since Camp Road. The Workers United leadership lost their minds. Ginny called me after the vote count. She had five Richmond stores that were going to election shortly after.

"They told me to pull every petition," she said.

"That's insane!"

I agreed to try to find a Buffalo partner who could go down and help out. Brian Murray volunteered (and sent back field dispatches, mainly stunned statements about how many Popsicles Richard was eating nightly). But Ginny needn't have worried. With her quiet leadership and the workers' unconquerable spirit, the Richmond stores won easily—some of the tallies were even unanimous. A few weeks later, Richard and Ginny made a special trip down to Richmond to watch Meridian and their organizing committee perform in the school play.

Meridian was not the only person to utilize the tactic of "autonomous salting," or getting on the job and organizing without already being in touch with the union and coordinating around the process and target. Nick Wilson, an incoming freshman at the Cornell School of Industrial and Labor Relations (ILR), got hired at a Starbucks outside Chicago in order to help organize a store. When Starbucks learned his store was in the early stages of unionizing, they closed it down, but he remained as committed as ever to the cause. In Ithaca, he would meet someone who perhaps personified the platonic ideal of an autonomous salt: Stephanie Heslop.

Stephanie had already been active in the small but close-knit community of the Ithaca Left, organizing demonstrations, advancing the Working Families Party, and joining several organizations. But she had never been a member of a union. In September 2021, when she learned about the organizing efforts in Buffalo, Stephanie decided to apply to Starbucks.

A month later, another Ithaca partner, Evan Sunshine, reached out to the union. Brian Murray started messaging with him. The two stores in the city wanted to organize together, Evan said, and another one was set to open in the new year. But the proto–organizing committee was also worried about the quickly approaching end of the school semester, which would send college students home for a month and a half. If they filed before, they risked holding the election with most of the workers out of town.

They decided to wait. This made me nervous: Surely Starbucks would find out, and if it did, it would have more time to develop its union-busting strategy.

It turned out to be a brilliant decision. The new store—the Meadows location, the only drive-thru in Ithaca—set a record for the campaign, filing within a week of opening. All three stores filed on the same day for three separate elections.

Their organizing committee was unmatched. There was Hope Liepe, barely eighteen but already a leader in the workplace, who was also both a volunteer firefighter trained in emergency medical care and a wilderness-survival summer camp counselor. Brilliant and caring, Kolya Vitek was a natural on both a bullhorn and a skateboard: They were able to shore up their partners emotionally while holding the line fearlessly with management. Evan was an aspiring law student who researched every aspect of organizing and union busting and began crafting excellent bargaining proposals and wage formulas before his store had even gotten to an election. Benjamin South was a long-term partner who had worked with Bridget Shannon before she transferred to Elmwood; he only had a ninth-grade education and had faced many hardships, but he was one of the committee's sharpest strategists and an excellent spokesperson. And then there was Stephanie Heslop: tireless and loving, an excellent worker committed to ensuring Starbucks had no grounds to fire her, checking in with her coworkers and connecting the movement to other, broader struggles for justice.

I had just picked Casey up to head to Ithaca for the vote counts when my phone started ringing. It was an unknown number with a Washington State area code, so I declined the call. The person immediately called back.

"Hi," they said. "We just walked out on strike and we're not really sure what to do next."

"Hi," I said, trying to force my voice to sound reassuring, even as Casey, listening on speakerphone, looked startled. "That's totally fine, we can make it work! What you're going to need to do is sign union cards, which you can do with everyone there, and we'll get you connected with an organizer who can help."

They told us more about their situation and the terrible conditions that had made them decide to walk off. We told them about the vote counts we were heading to and the solidarity they were surrounded by and promised to get them the resources they needed.

For years, my favorite song was Paul Robeson's version of "Joe Hill." Its only minor defect, I thought, was the order of the words in one of the later verses: "From San Diego up to Maine, in every mine and mill, where workers strike and organize, it's there you'll find Joe Hill." I had joked with comrades about the need to ensure that workers organized first before hitting the picket line.[10]

Not so the Marysville, Washington, workers. Two months later, they won their union election, proving that union organizing didn't necessarily have to happen in the right order.

Meanwhile, the Ithaca elections were overwhelming victories. Alan Model, the Littler lawyer, had joined the count from his car. He looked increasingly glum over the course of our winning the three stores, each with only one no vote. "Did someone go around to all the stores and vote no?" we joked.

"Plausible deniability," said Brian. "Now management doesn't know who voted yes."

Back in Memphis, only one organizing committee member was left working at Poplar and Highland. Reaghan Hall had been out sick with Covid at the time of the press event in the store and had thus escaped Starbucks' firing spree. Tall and gothy, Reaghan projected confidence, poise, and optimism. After the firings, Starbucks planted a giant NOW HIRING banner outside the store and plastered advertisements on the windows. As the fired workers picketed outside, new faces came in, interviewed, got hired, put on their aprons, and clocked in.

Reaghan organized all of them. Management's presence made the store a tense environment, but Reaghan's funny and reassuring demeanor won the trust of her new coworkers. When the store finally held their vote count, the Memphis Seven had not yet been reinstated, meaning the company challenged their ballots. Because of Reaghan's tireless efforts, the workers had enough yes votes to win outright, without having to wait to litigate the challenges. The movement felt unstoppable.

Everywhere, more heroic and hilarious and brilliant and fierce leaders were stepping up, reaching out, and organizing. There were and are far too many to name everyone who contributed so greatly to the movement, people whose care and wit and humor and compassion and joy and determination led to the unionization of so many stores so quickly. There were people like Tyler Keeling and Josie Serrano, in Lakewood and Long Beach, California. Tyler was a force of nature: fiercely loving, attuned alike to the history of the struggle for queer rights and to the latest in meme culture, radical and gentle in equal measure. He was also hilarious, and his Twitter posts became a highlight of the campaign. Josie possessed an unmatched sense of design and humor, creating uniquely Gen Z flyers, memes, and videos that resonated with workers across the country, and earning the distinction of having the best fashion sense of anyone in Starbucks Workers United. When Brittany Harrison was working in California, Josie had been a partner in Brittany's store. When Josie had decided to organize their store—inspired partly by how outrageous Howard Schultz's Holocaust analogy had been—they reached out to Brittany as well as to the union for guidance.

The partner-on-point system was responsible for Starbucks Workers United's growth, success, and credibility. Most important, it was a self-replicating model. It was the Inside Organizer School on a one-on-one basis: We would join Zoom calls with workers and guide them through the organizing process, then they would turn around and start mentoring the next group. We were making "partners becoming partners" into a reality of its own, even if the company was still unwilling to recognize the partnership. Joining Starbucks Workers United meant joining a network, a support system, a friend group, connected by a shared desire to improve our jobs, hold the company to its stated values, and build genuine and authentic community with one another.[11]

The community that the partner-on-point system created was beautiful, warm, and motivated by care and solidarity. It was the best possible counter to Starbucks' portrayal of the union as a third party. It made the union accessible, genuine, communal, and familiar. And that feeling transcended Starbucks. Workers at Amazon, Chipotle, REI, Trader Joe's, and many other companies would tell us that they looked at our campaign and our successes and thought, *If they can do it, we can do it.*

# CHAPTER SIX

# How to Bust a Union

In 1936, workers at six Remington Rand typewriter factories, in upstate New York, Ohio, and Connecticut, went out on strike. In response, the company, led by its owner, James H. Rand Jr., assembled a team of professional union busters, who concocted a strategy to rout the union.[1]

Their plan included deliberately misrepresenting worker support based on voter turnout and cherry-picked data; closing some plants with strong union support and threatening to close others; temporarily closing others under the pretext of "renovating and re-arranging"; providing some workers with new benefits to try to prevent them from joining the strike; firing union leaders; labeling the union an "outside agitator"; and mobilizing the business community, the police, and anti-union workers to try to turn the community against the union.

When the NLRB found that the company had committed gross violations of labor law, Remington Rand refused to comply with the court order telling them to bargain with the union, instead appealing the decision into federal court and further delaying any measure of justice for the strikers. The company's scheme became known as the Mohawk Valley Formula, after the region where many of its factories were located.[2]

The passage of the NLRA the year before had legally established that organizing a union was supposed to be a matter of workers' choice. However, companies like Remington Rand took the view that they—not the workers—should decide whether their factories unionized. With the help of consultants and law firms, they devised a playbook for defeating union campaigns by creating a climate of fear. Other corporations quickly adopted the same tactics and the same disregard for attempts to enforce already-feeble labor laws.

Over the next few decades, the union-busting industry would transform from a landscape of hired detectives and paramilitary forces—Pinkertons, Baldwin-Felts detectives, Citizens' Alliances, American Legion posts, often operating with the full backing of the police or National Guard—to a scene dominated by law firms and consultants; from a literal battle, where striking workers put their lives on the line, to a psychological battle, where companies threatened workers with the loss of their jobs and livelihoods to try to intimidate them out of organizing. Companies continued to refine their anti-union playbook in campaigns at companies like Darlington Mills and J. P. Stevens through the 1950s and '60s.

This new wave of union busters included firms like Morgan Lewis, founded in the 1870s, and Bond, Schoeneck & King, the Syracuse firm that represented Remington Rand as it appealed the NLRB decision through the circuit courts, which had long histories of union avoidance—and continue that ignominious tradition, representing several companies in organizing drives I've been involved with in upstate New York. It also gave rise to new groups that sought to reverse the midcentury surge in unionization or to crush organizing in the South after manufacturers moved production in hopes of busting unions.[3]

By the 1970s, union-busting tactics centered around the practices of law firms like Littler Mendelson, which grew from a regional management firm into the largest anti-union practice in the nation, and Jackson Lewis, which wrote the 1979 book *Winning NLRB Elections* from the management point of view, and consultants like Charles Hughes, who ran a survey company that promised companies it could identify "union vulnerability" through its assessments of worker satisfaction and promised to "Make Unions Unnecessary"—the title of his book—by creating an atmosphere that would render unionizing nearly impossible.[4]

Marty Levitt—who proclaimed himself a converted union buster but frequently relapsed into union busting or made paid speeches to unions, depending on which side was more lucrative for him at the time—wrote a book in 1993 called *Confessions of a Union Buster*. Despite the unreliability of its narrator, the book lays out a number of tactics from the modern anti-union playbook, beginning with a company's attempt to expand the bargaining unit to include *all* workers rather than those in a single workplace and progressing through stories of threatening store managers' jobs if they supported the union, using sexism and racism to fight organizing drives, going to great lengths to turn out every no vote, using outsiders and surveys to suss out union sympathizers and troublemakers, and delaying elections by filing needless motions with the NLRB.[5]

These consulting firms still comprise a shadowy underworld of union busting. Legally, they're supposed to file reports on their "persuader activities," or interactions with nonunion workers. In practice, enforcement is lax: Many companies and consultants never disclose their records.

In Vermont, when we attempted to organize a local coffee shop in May 2023, the owner hired Sparta Solutions, a spin-off of a spin-off of one of the big union-busting consulting firms. Its website proclaimed that the agency was opposed to the media, environmental groups, and labor unions—not exactly a fit for the progressive town of Burlington. But, clumsy, awkward, and trite as their anti-union campaign may have been, it worked. They threatened workers' jobs, college summer leaves, and raises, firing one union leader and intimidating many more. The workers narrowly lost the election and are currently stuck waiting for the NLRB process to play out in order to have a chance at remedying the company's unfair labor practices.

Starbucks was the inheritor of these traditions. Despite its progressive reputation, the company would do anything to crush the union drive and discourage workers from organizing. When their initial "nice guy" tactics didn't work, they flipped a switch, creating an atmosphere of fear and intimidation that made it nearly impossible to maintain the campaign's early momentum.

Their playbook involved three main tactics: targeting individuals, targeting stores for closure, and targeting *all* workers in a sweeping form of collective punishment. Their communications recycled the same talking points that union busters had developed over the years, from the "outside agitators" characterization of union leaders to misrepresenting election margins, cherry-picking data, and even inventing quotes from the union. One of their leaflets featured tweets, allegedly from the Starbucks Workers United account, that we had never sent and which were dated into the future. (Our social media committee found the boring nature of the fake tweets more insulting than the impersonation.) Echoing Remington Rand's strike ballot letter, Starbucks' communiqués also tried to delegitimize the union by claiming that, even when it did win, it didn't represent a majority of the workers, citing the examples of a couple of stores where voter turnout was low or mail ballots hadn't made it back to the NLRB offices. With Littler Mendelson's help, Starbucks repurposed these age-old strategies for crushing workers' right to organize.[6]

**AT FIRST, IN THE** fall of 2021, Starbucks' attempts to bust our union weren't working. Somehow, and to the puzzlement of Howard Schultz and Rossann Williams, corporate's message—and the presence of hundreds of managers and execs—hadn't swayed enough workers to stop us from unionizing the first cafés. Captive-audience meetings had scared everyone and flipped a few votes, and threatening workers' benefits had picked off a few more. But Rossann sweeping the lobby, ops coaches moving the Frappuccino blenders around and removing carpets, and Howard telling us about sharing his blanket hadn't won them the election.

Workers were still organizing. In some cases, corporate's response was backfiring, like in the East Robinson store. Back in August 2021, as we were beginning to reach out to Starbucks workers we had identified as safe to talk to, I met with a worker from the East Robinson store at a café in Lockport, beside the Erie Canal. We mapped out her store, talking through who would support the union effort.

The worker—a sunny and enthusiastic eighteen-year-old freshman at the University at Buffalo—was new to Starbucks, but believed the company needed a union. Her analysis of her store revolved around one person: Vic, a five-year partner and popular shift supervisor, was the key to winning the union, and she would almost certainly be supportive of our effort.

Unfortunately, the worker I met with was too pushy in her approach to recruiting Vic to join the organizing committee. Eighteen missed calls and one cornering in the back room later, Vic was anti-union. I, however, knew none of this. A couple weeks later, three days before the first committee meeting, I was sitting with Richard, Cory, and Casey in the salt house, reading the BuffBux chat. Vic posted a message asking for anyone to come to East Robinson, which was down four partners. I borrowed Cory's work shoes and Casey's socks and ran to the store to clock in.

When I got there, Vic put me on bar and refused to talk about the meeting in any way. A couple other workers were similarly cold; only one person was open to talking about it. At no other store had I encountered an environment like this. Management had to have found out.

For the next few months, East Robinson became a black hole: The worker I'd first talked to was scheduled outside her availability, forcing her to quit. Another worker who had initially supported the union took off his pin and tried to stay quiet, as an ever-increasing swarm of support managers arrived at the store.

"Coming to this store after the others warms my heart," Rossann told Vic during one visit. "This store is my safe space."

Some of the new managers grilled Vic. *Who supported the union? Whom had she seen wearing a pin?* The managers let her listen in on their conversations and told her to enforce new rules, like not allowing rabble-rousers from unionizing stores to pick up shifts at Robbie.

"We don't want union people working here," the managers told Vic. "These union people are so annoying; thank god it's never gonna come here."

But East Robinson was not immune from the proverbial "sticks" of union busting. One manager started going after Vic for wearing light-wash jeans, claiming the pants violated dress code. Senior vice presidents and regional directors tried to come on the floor and pull partners off for one-on-one anti-union meetings during peak.

That one annoyed Vic. Despite her feelings about the union, she would body-block the managers, preventing them from pulling her frazzled and overworked partners off the floor. Or she would put executives and HR reps to work, making backups or filling cold-brew toddies—she was well aware that none of them knew how to make a single drink.

When the Omicron variant of Covid started and Starbucks didn't protect partners and tried to stop Vic and her coworkers from enforcing the mask mandate, she decided she had had enough. Toward evening on the first day of our Elmwood strike, a small and heavily bundled figure with double braids approached the picket line. It was Vic. "If I'm going to switch sides, I'm going to go all the way," she had decided.

She asked for a union pin. I took mine off my coat and handed it to her. I had repeated this move many times with different workers on different campaigns and in different stores. It worked every time (although Vic would later tease me when she saw me do it with others).

"I want to go back to my store and start telling my partners about the union," she said.

After the strike, we met at the Public Espresso near her house. I talked through the steps of organizing and gave her a stack of union cards.

When Vic took the cards into her store, partners were afraid to sign. The support managers were vigilant, keeping an eye out for anyone who took a card and sometimes pulling those partners into one-on-one meetings to try to dissuade them. We switched to electronic cards to allow for more privacy. We filed with barely 60 percent because I trusted Vic's instincts and leadership abilities and knew that delaying filing wouldn't work in our favor.

Workers at other stores that had faced intense union busting were also organizing in response to corporate's tactics. The Delaware and Chippewa store was across the street from the hotel where Rossann Williams and her corporate posse were encamped. The store's partners were the front line against the SWAT team. Every day, new corporate faces came in: surveilling partners, rearranging the store, holding management meetings, or ordering extra-dry cappuccinos. Some of the partners were friends with the workers at the unionized Spot Coffee location across the street. They began talking to them, and to us, about organizing the store.

**IN JANUARY 2022, RÓISÍN** asked us to join an emergency Zoom call. Key leaders were thinking about quitting; some already had. We didn't have a strong majority at Del-Chip, but the people who were still pro-union had already been through the full fire of Starbucks' union-busting campaign; we wouldn't lose them now.

"What do we have to lose?" we all agreed. "Let's file."

The last day of January 2022 was our first day of bargaining and the day ballots went out for the next three Starbucks union elections in Buffalo. Over a dozen stores across the country filed for election that day: the three Ithaca cafés, two in Rochester, one in California, one in Kansas, one in Missouri, five in Oregon, one in Washington State, one in Arizona, and Del-Chip in Buffalo. The organizing committee's letter spoke to what they had endured from corporate and the reasons they were organizing anyway: "to shift the balance of power away from corporate and in favor of partners acting democratically, in solidarity and in lockstep with each other's collective interests."

At the press conference announcing the filings, one of the workers, Mellenia, began, "I would like to thank Starbucks corporate for their presence in our store, without which I don't know if we would have organized." While that presence had been intimidating and stressful, it had also made workers even more determined to organize.

Seeing this response to their initial tactics, Starbucks corporate decided it was time to step up their anti-union campaign. The company had already been using lower-level management as ground soldiers in their union-busting campaign. But they underestimated the courage and conscience of several of those managers. David Almond had been forced out of his job managing the Transit Commons store when he refused to comply with the union-busting instructions he received from the new district manager, MK. David became a whistleblower, telling us what MK had ordered him to do: compile a dossier on pro-union partners and identify specific infractions that Starbucks could fire them over.[7]

Several months into the campaign, another whistleblower showed us an internal Starbucks PowerPoint that talked about the company's plan to fight the union.

"Our labor strategy was built from key industry benchmarks, while layering in our Starbucks partner-first principles," the presentation claimed. The industry benchmarks in question? Companies like FedEx and Walmart. From these models, Starbucks had sourced tactics that included creating "deployable teams (geography-based)," a "legal/labor relations hot-line," and a "suite of internal training programs, tailored to leadership and partner audiences." Under "Our Guiding Principles," corporate talked about the plan to "deepen our connection to our Mission & Values and each other."

The slideshow gave additional detail on their "Dedicated Labor Team," including its "Intelligence & Analytics" arm, tasked with anticipating new union hotbeds. (Not long after, Starbucks would hire a new "global intelligence" manager hailing from Pinkerton, the CIA, and the State Department.) This team tracked media and public opinion trends—as well as themes in the letters stores across the country had sent to corporate announcing their union campaigns—and outlined their PR and marketing goals, including internally, geared toward convincing the public and partners alike that partners already had a voice in the company.[8]

Most critically, the PowerPoint outlined Starbucks' tactical approach to "competing for our partners' hearts and minds vs. hoping we can give them enough reasons to consider maintaining a direct relationship with the company." It predicted that the union campaign was funded on an eight- or nine-month cycle and would peter out if we didn't get a contract quickly. "Workers United is a business competitor seeking to claim market share," the PowerPoint stated. Starbucks needed "to stop losing market share and prevent deeper market penetration." How did they intend to do this?

In one word: "containment." One slide talked about a 1949 forest fire in Montana: "The fire was advancing too quickly to use traditional approaches." Instead, the firefighters set fire to the grass in front of them on purpose. Burning the area themselves prevented the fire from spreading. Starbucks' plan was to slow and eventually stop the advancing of unionization by isolating areas with union activity from nonunion markets in an attempt to prevent the union from spreading outside its existing turf.

**BY FEBRUARY OF 2022,** we were already seeing the effects of this revised playbook. After Cassie Fleischer helped lead the Elmwood strike over Covid safety, Starbucks cut her hours, forcing her to take on another job. When she tried to reduce her availability, they fired her rather than accommodating her new schedule. Cassie's firing was the first in the nation outside of Memphis.

At the Depew store, Angel Krempa was a small but formidable force.

At times, they had been the only publicly pro-union worker at their store, but over the fall of 2021 they had slowly but surely built up majority support. They also typified a Starbucks barista, both in their personality—kind, caring, hospitable, always believing the best of others—and their looks—they had multiple piercings and affixed many pins to their apron, including one that said BEE KIND and the Hope for the Day Foundation pin they'd worn at every job they'd worked, which read HAVE HOPE: IT'S OKAY NOT TO BE OKAY.

They were out of dress code, corporate claimed. Even though the manager who hired Angel in February 2020, prior to pandemic masking mandates, had assured them that having several piercings wasn't a problem, the dress code technically only permitted one. Management began threatening to write Angel up and fire them if they refused to take out the others.

One of the store managers cornered them about their piercings: "Did you take them out?"

"I'm following the dress code," Angel said. They wore a mask at all times. They couldn't take it off even to eat a sandwich or take a sip of water, for fear management—or an anti-union coworker—would see the other piercings. During breaks, they hid in their car to eat.

Then management confronted them about the way they tied their apron, the suitability of the shoes they had worn for years, and their pins, including their pronoun pin and their Hope for the Day suicide prevention pin. Against Starbucks' own policies, management started scheduling Angel and another pro-union shift supervisor to "clopen"—close the store one night and then open it the next morning, leaving inadequate time between to take care of oneself. After months of harassment, the other pro-union worker told me they were forced to drop out of the Arizona State University program, take a mental health leave, and check themself into a hospital.

They were not the only worker Starbucks had put in that situation. For example, I met Kathryn Bergmann at the first organizing committee meeting. She was in a crowd of people at the evening session. She had a radiant smile and long curls, and her signature, like her personality, was outsize on the committee sign-in sheet: flowing and beautiful. When I spoke with Will and Gianna, they talked about how she effortlessly pulled support toward the union, a force of positivity.

Kathryn was about to start college in Rhode Island. Not long after the first committee meeting, she transferred to a store near her school. During her first couple of shifts there, Kathryn helped show her new coworkers better ways of doing things and identified cleanliness and health code issues, leading efforts to get the store up to standard. The store manager, who had noticed Kathryn wasn't in the system yet, told her she would get that sorted out and thanked her for helping improve the store.

A few days later, Kathryn's mom called: Her grandfather was very sick, and Kathryn needed to come home as soon as possible.

When management didn't get back to her, Kathryn told the shift supervisor in Rhode Island that she needed to go back to Buffalo. "Aren't you working?" the shift asked. Kathryn explained what was going on, and the shift supervisor said they understood.

That weekend, Kathryn got a call from a different shift supervisor: "Where are you?"

"I'm in Buffalo. It was supposed to be written down in the book. I told the person I was working with on Wednesday."

"Okay, don't worry about it."

That was when things changed. Kathryn had gone to Buffalo. *Buffalo*. Shorthand for "union." What store was she from? Was her name on the letter?

Kathryn felt management's tone shift in subsequent conversations with her. "You're not really a partner here," a higher-up told her. Where higher-ups had previously welcomed Kathryn's efforts to help improve the store, now she felt they were dismissive: "You are just a barista." A coworker in Rhode Island who had tried to console Kathryn during this period later described her as crying uncontrollably, fearing that she was being forced out of Starbucks and wouldn't be able to find another job that would accommodate her needs.

Kathryn decided to try to transfer to a different store in Rhode Island. Then, her mother fell ill. She needed to go back to Buffalo again. For the rest of the semester, Kathryn needed to alternate spending two weeks in Rhode Island for school and two weeks in Buffalo with her mother.

In Buffalo, she met with the new support managers at Camp Road. They told her that her previous manager had never submitted the paperwork for her to transfer to Rhode Island, meaning Camp Road was still her home store. However, when she proposed that she could either work during the two-week blocs she was in town or pick up available shifts during those periods, the managers told her she needed to talk to the new district manager, MK.

Kathryn was confused about why a district manager was involved—that hadn't been the case in the past—but agreed to the meeting. MK told her that because she had been gone for a few weeks she was behind on training and would need retraining to be a barista again. Kathryn wasn't allowed to work her proposed schedule. Instead, MK said, she could either quit or go on family and medical leave (FMLA).

Financially, Kathryn couldn't afford not to work. She worried that she wouldn't be able to find a job that offered as much flexibility as Starbucks always had, prior to their union-busting campaign. And Starbucks had a strict policy against working other jobs while on leave.

She remained in limbo for months. Management gave confusing nonanswers when she attempted to reach out. It was an anguishing situation. Richard spoke to her on long Zoom calls and tried to help her navigate the situation, including by filing charges with the NLRB. Kathryn also confided in Gianna about how sad and frustrated she was about what Starbucks was putting her through. They cried on the phone together. Starbucks knew that Kathryn had a history of mental illness.

In October of 2021 we expected Starbucks to try to keep her off the voter list, but she was on it, and she cast her ballot in the election. When her store lost, she posted in the group chat, "I think I'm going to be sick."

Over winter break, she began working at Camp Road again. But what Starbucks had done haunted her, and her love for the company had turned into heartbreak. That spring, she went on a mental health leave. In March 2022, she tragically died by suicide after battling depression.

**ALL THE CAMP ROAD** partners went to her funeral. Starbucks didn't even close the store for the entire day, forcing workers to go straight from the funeral to their shifts. Gianna didn't even have time to change out of her black dress. Starbucks did, however, send several corporate executives to the funeral, including MK, who sat in the row ahead of me, crying.

MK left the funeral and headed to the Depew store. A few days before, Angel Krempa's car had broken down. They had called to say they'd be a few minutes late, and they'd still opened the store. Starbucks had its excuse. MK went into the Depew store and fired Angel.

The NLRB found merit in most of the unfair labor practice charges we had filed in November of 2022, with a few exceptions. For example, the Board decided it was lawful for Starbucks to use its emergency text messaging system to send messages telling partners to vote no, or to announce Howard Schultz's appearance in Buffalo. They dismissed a few claims of surveillance, where Rossann and other corporate execs had watched partners outside stores or after captive-audience meetings. The Board said it was okay that Starbucks had segregated captive-audience meetings at the Depew store, with partners supporting the union attending different meetings from those who did not. The Board threw out a few additional charges because workers hadn't given affidavits. These were relatively minor.

But Kathryn Bergmann's charges never got a merit determination. Her death had occurred after she had given her affidavit but before she had been able to sign it. The NLRB insisted it couldn't consider an unsigned affidavit under any circumstances. We had to withdraw the charge, meaning the NLRB would not pursue an investigation of Starbucks' treatment of Kathryn.

In the days following Kathryn's death, one of the partners at Camp Road—not a union supporter—ordered a packet of pins from the American Foundation for Suicide Prevention and handed them out to coworkers. Everyone started wearing them.

Then, Tanner, the store manager, ordered partners to take off the pins, saying they weren't within the dress code.

In April, attempting to comply, Will stopped wearing his union pin and wore only the suicide prevention pin: Even the strictest interpretation of the dress code allowed one personal pin, although Starbucks had always allowed partners to wear more. That still didn't satisfy management.

They started sending Will home and cracked down on the other partners, too.

Alex, one of Will's coworkers, had worn two American flag pins throughout his time at Starbucks. He was anti-union and also anti-puppy, facts he shared in captive-audience meetings. Tanner asked Alex to take off the flag pins.

"Can you believe Starbucks is doing this?" Will asked, trying to establish common ground. "That's insane!"

"Yeah, I don't agree with it," said Alex sadly, "but they're my employer, and it's their right."

"But they've never enforced this before."

"But they have the right to, and if I want to work here, I have to follow what they want."

Starbucks often had themed days that explicitly flouted the dress code. On Pajama Day, a manager wearing pajamas made Will sign an acknowledgment of the dress code. But despite their own inconsistencies, management began sending Will home from his shifts every time he tried to clock in wearing the pin.

Across the country, the suicide awareness pin became a symbol of the union and its fight to protect partners. I wore one daily with no incident. Some workers wore several.

Back at Camp Road, Will continued to get called in to meetings with managers who told him all the reasons he couldn't wear the pin.

"That's not becoming to the Starbucks brand," one of them said. Another said the pin might bring customers' moods down.

Then, Will got a text from a manager in Syracuse asking if he would cover a shift. It was a wrong number—the manager meant to text someone closer. But Will agreed. He had already picked up a shift from me at Elmwood and worked a handful of shifts at the Williamsville store, covering for Casey, without incident. No one in Syracuse said anything about it, either. Only at Camp Road—where managers had dismantled the memorial to Kathryn that Gianna had created in the lobby with photos and flowers—was it an issue.

In October, Will mixed up the start time of one of his shifts. Finally, Starbucks had a means of firing him without directly addressing the pin. But they couldn't help themselves. Will's termination notice said that he had been fired for being late to work *and* for dress code violations, all of which related to the pin.

Suddenly, managers in other stores and other parts of the country began asking people to take off the suicide awareness pins. Some of the partners who complied—who did so because they knew their coworkers needed them in the stores—did so in tears. The cruelty of the anti-union campaign was unmasked.

**SHORTLY AFTER VIC FLIPPED** to being pro-union in January of 2022, Starbucks intensified their anti-union efforts at East Robinson. Support managers who had courted her and made her a union-busting co-conspirator were suddenly unfriendly. One of them spent most of the day the store filed for its union election crying at work. Vic brought bagels and doughnuts to work multiple times, trying to support her coworkers and make their shifts better. Managers would eat the doughnuts and then continue to union bust.

Conditions worsened at the store: Short-staffing was rampant and workers' complaints went unaddressed. "Can Robinson walk out?" Vic texted me one morning.

I was at work and didn't see it. Half an hour later: "Please?"

I finally saw it just before nine. "Hey sorry I just got off work," I texted back.

"Hello. Dying."

"Hi I'm sorry I'll head over now."

Vic told me that there had been five call-offs that morning. Half the staff left at noon, and the manager had already made someone work after throwing up, which was a health code violation. The manager forced Vic to clean up the vomit and keep running the shift.

Walkouts are exciting, especially when people who hadn't been union supporters reach the limits of their patience and join a strike. The East Robinson partners were elated to be able to take action after enduring the conditions in their store, and they were quickly joined by workers from around the city and community supporters, including Bradley, our dedicated Elmwood regular who attended all of our pickets and rallies, usually with his "strike dog," Jasper, at his side. Our walkouts may not have done a lot to hurt Starbucks' business, especially given the number of nonunion stores across the company, but they boosted morale and gave workers a feeling of control over their work lives—a feeling that most Starbucks workers were not used to.

I had called one of our lawyers from the lobby of the store as the workers prepared to walk out. We had talked through how to make sure everything was secured. But after the strike, management went after Vic. She should have locked the cash in the safe, they said, not just in the register, before walking out. Never mind that anti-union workers and support managers had left entire stores unlocked overnight without facing discipline.

In spite of management's union busting, East Robinson went from being Rossann's safe space in the fall of 2021 to a 7–4 union election win in June of the following year. Less than a week after the votes were tallied, management scheduled Vic to clopen and then fired her when she overslept and was twenty minutes late—a departure from pre–union campaign practice.

**IN BUFFALO, WE SPENT** the first month and a half after our election win at Elmwood pushing Starbucks to agree to bargaining dates. Under U.S. labor law, a company is not required to sign a first contract. The NLRA orders companies to bargain in good faith, but lacks the authority to punish those that don't. Thus, union busters often drag out bargaining in hopes of eventually decertifying, or convincing workers to vote out, the union. We finally got Starbucks to meet us at the virtual bargaining table on January 31, 2022.[9]

Leading up to the meeting, we had spent weeks working on our proposals and training our bargaining committee in extensive role-playing sessions. We polled our coworkers, cribbed some proposals from other union contracts, crowdsourced from friends in other unions, and even surveyed Starbucks workers across the country. Nearly all of the proposed contract language came from partners, talking through what we needed and trying to capture that in writing.

At one proposal-writing session, sitting cross-legged on the floor in my living room, leaning against the couch where Casey sat sipping her iced latte, I looked up from my computer, the surreality of the situation sinking in.

"We did it," I said to her. "I'm actually writing bargaining proposals that will go to *Starbucks*. We won. We are going to be bargaining and they are going to have to consider this."

I had gone from collapsing onto the floor after shifts, letting my cat, Frank, sit on my chest until I felt like enough of a person again to get back to work, to planning the campaign around the kitchen table with the first handful of salts, to writing health and safety language that Starbucks would have no choice but to read and consider, health and safety language that partners across the country could point to and say, "That's what we're fighting for."

The health and safety language we wrote would ensure that no partner ever again had to hide from an abusive customer in the back of house; that partners who needed accommodations would get them—and be protected if they refused unsafe assignments; that mental health would be taken as seriously as physical conditions. We were proposing just cause, meaning protections from unfair firings or disciplines. We were demanding once again that Starbucks sign the Fair Election Principles and stop their union busting. We were asking them to jointly establish a Labor Management Committee that would meet to discuss the issues affecting the store.

We were also proposing that they fill the symbolic empty chair on the Starbucks Board of Directors with a partner from our store. There are mandatory subjects of bargaining, meaning that legally the company has to talk about them, and permissive subjects of bargaining, meaning that it's up to the company whether to talk about them, but it will face no legal repercussions for refusing. The empty chair was permissive. Most corporate governance issues are permissive—workers cannot rely on the protections of the law to demand that kind of voice or stake in the company.[10]

Bargaining with Starbucks was by turns bizarre, absurd, and infuriating. To my surprise, rather than simply refusing to talk about the chair proposal, management decided to engage.

"There is no empty chair," said Alan Model.

"I think there is an empty chair," I said. "Howard has talked about it in his speeches."

"It's a metaphor," Alan deadpanned, implying that we didn't understand basic figures of speech. "Besides, we're negotiating for one store in Buffalo. Why would we put one Buffalo partner on the board? That wouldn't be fair to the rest of the country. Who is it going to be? Michelle Eisen?"

We went back and forth about this at different points in various sessions, for both the Elmwood and Genesee stores. I tried to make an information request about the existence of the chair, which Alan did not get back to me about. The debate continued.

**Alan:** The board meeting isn't about what we are discussing in this meeting.

**Jaz:** Why does the empty seat exist if baristas are not considered worthy to sit in that chair?

**Alan:** It's not actually on the board, but symbolic.

**Lexi:** At some of those meetings things that affect hourly partners do come up, I don't see why it's threatening.

**Alan:** Boards of directors don't make those decisions.

**MK:** The markout situation came from partners, it wasn't approved by the board of directors. What do you hope to have influence on?

**Alan:** You've heard of metaphors, right? No one has commented on anyone's intellect, but . . .

**Arjae:** But the seat isn't a metaphor. There's articles and speeches saying it exists.

**Alan:** Metaphorically. It's not a real chair. Some of you may need to go back to high school English.

Frustrating as corporate's response to us was *in* bargaining, their response *outside* bargaining was worse. Management had eaten up nearly the entirety of our first-ever session on January 31 discussing their proposed ground rules. Some of the rules were, frankly, insulting: "Can we agree that if either party is asked to respond to media requests about bargaining, that any responses will be fact-based only?" We replied that we had always been fact-based with the media, but that Starbucks was not returning the favor. I asked whether Starbucks would agree to be fact-based in dealings with partners and refrain from using the contents of our bargaining sessions to try to bust the union. They refused.

Their proposed ground rules also included "Can we agree to first bargain and attempt to reach agreement on noneconomic terms prior to bargaining over economic terms?"—which we agreed to. Then, after our first session, we started hearing from workers in stores that had filed for union elections, who were concerned about the reports they were hearing about bargaining. Had we actually signed a contract that didn't include wage increases or other improvements? they asked us.

It turned out that Starbucks had taken our initial non-economic proposals, labeled them a contract, and started using them to try to convince partners that unionizing was futile. At our next session, we presented a selection of economic proposals, including credit card tipping, restoring the free food and drink benefits the company had provided during the pandemic, compensation for working short-staffed, fully paid health care, and cost of living increases.

The bargaining committee was an admirable group. Michelle was tough and fearless, pushing back against corporate's claims. Lexi was sweet and patient in bargaining sessions, resulting in a less hostile Alan. Cortlin spoke with a no-nonsense approach and humor that cut through the company's excuses. Bridget was thoughtful and analytical, composing instant replies to Starbucks' messages. Natalie was stalwart, explaining and re-explaining the concepts behind proposals she had helped craft. Jasmine Leli—a new hire at Genesee who hadn't seen the months of union busting leading up to the vote—provided a much-needed fresh perspective and levelheadedness; the company's behavior during bargaining forged her into a strong and tireless union activist. Arjae had found themself the target of Alan's acerbic comments during several exchanges, including a discussion about changing Starbucks' dress code.

Alan talked about how important the dress code was to Starbucks' image and continuity. He talked about how it would bother him to go into a Starbucks in a different part of the country and see the workers there wearing purple shirts: "It would hurt Starbucks' brand."

"I think that firing workers in Memphis, which is front-page news across the country, is doing more to hurt Starbucks' brand than me wearing a purple shirt would," said Arjae.

"I'm glad to see you're a marketing expert," said Alan.

But Arjae rose above Alan's acrimoniousness. When we returned from the next break, they attempted to break the ice by asking Alan and the Starbucks execs about their star signs.

And then there were the partners from around the country.

Zoom bargaining allowed us to include partners from each new store that won an election. Michelle from Mesa, Arizona, was an early attendee of our negotiations. So was Maggie. Partners from Seattle, from Rochester, from the other Buffalo stores, began trickling in. So did the Memphis Seven. One of our bargaining dates occurred shortly after they were fired. Nabretta, Nikki, and Kylie showed up and introduced themselves as members of the bargaining committee.

Littler was not happy. When the workers from other stores would speak about proposals, Alan would ask them what store they worked at. Then he would say that we were bargaining about the Genesee store, or the Elmwood store, telling workers from Memphis or Rochester that they didn't belong on our committee because they didn't work at the specific store we were discussing.

We emphasized that the union had the legal right to select our own bargaining committee, and also that the other partners understood the common experiences our proposals addressed.

Then, Alan decided to break yet another ground rule—one that both sides had signed off on. We had agreed that, given the realities of the pandemic, it made sense to bargain via Zoom. If we changed that later, it would be by mutual agreement.

"We're not interested in meeting by Zoom again," Alan said in April. "Any future meetings will be in person. We'll book a conference room. . . ."

The ground rules were clear. The Covid rates in Buffalo were still high. And our committee was so geographically spread out that bringing everyone to the table in person would be difficult.

At that time, I thought it made sense to stick to the Zoom bargaining demand and focus our energies on boycotting Starbucks instead. Richard was working on plans to send to the international union leadership for building the infrastructure needed—picket captains, union support, etc.—to pull off a national boycott. And Starbucks wasn't interested in bargaining in good faith: The few proposals they had made primarily consisted of the same threats they had made to us in captive-audience meetings, including cutting off our right to pick up shifts at other stores.

"Your store is an island because partners chose to go union," said MK. "And it's not even an island with other union stores because each store has a different contract, so they have different rules. You can't have partners working under different rules in the same store."

"Partners picking up shifts could follow the rules of that store," we said. "This doesn't have to be so complicated."

"But it is. Partners chose to unionize, and now we have to negotiate contracts for each store."

Of course, Starbucks showed no intention of actually negotiating contracts for each store, or of making good-faith proposals. In fact, both Howard Schultz and his spokesmen were constantly discouraging bargaining. In an interview at the *New York Times*' DealBook Summit, Howard spoke at length about how he was striving to improve Starbucks' culture with regard to its partners. "Could you ever see embracing the union as a part of that?" the interviewer asked. "No," Howard replied.[11]

At that time, Starbucks' main PR person tasked with answering union-related queries was Reggie Borges, a rather hapless individual who was upset that his date nights with his wife were suffering from constant interruptions from journalists calling for comments on Starbucks' latest union-busting actions. Dave Jamieson from *HuffPost* asked Reggie whether the union would be able to secure a good contract.

"Developing a contract that meets or exceeds what we already offer to our partners is going to be difficult for them to do," Reggie said. "These contracts don't start at the baseline of the benefits that our partners get. That is the full-stop rule. The contract negotiations start at zero."[12]

The article added that Reggie called back later, after publication, to try to modify his statement. Over the years, the courts had adjudicated what companies were and weren't supposed to say during union campaigns. In *Exxon Research Engineering Co v. NLRB*, they had ruled that it was fine to say, "Contract negotiations begin with a blank sheet of paper," but in *Delmas Conley v. NLRB*, they decided that it was not okay to say, "Contract negotiations start at zero." (To a nonunion worker, of course, this is a meaningless semantics issue: There is little difference between the psychological impact of the two statements.)[13]

In my opinion, it seemed that breaking the law was actually part of Starbucks' strategy. The NLRB was short-staffed and lacked the resources to investigate and prosecute the countless unfair labor practice charges we were filing. In some cases, the Board seemed to be dismissing charges not for lack of evidence but for lack of capacity to deal with them. Starbucks was updating the union-busting playbook, and one of their tactics appeared to be fighting the charges for as long as possible to slow down the mechanisms of enforcing the law.

So, Starbucks doubled down. From seniority pay to a relaxed dress code, they began implementing our bargaining proposals—but giving them only to the nonunion stores. The credit card tipping proposal in particular would soon become central to Starbucks' union-busting strategy, when they implemented credit card tipping at nonunion stores, withheld it from organized stores, and then told unionized partners that if they wanted to have access to the tipping—which averaged $5 an hour in additional income—they needed to decertify the union at their stores. All of this was illegal, federal judges would eventually declare. But Starbucks only responded by appealing their decisions and announcing more new benefits they wouldn't be giving to unionized stores.[14]

Starbucks' break-the-law-to-avoid-consequences-for-lawbreaking approach was apparent in their conduct during the first Buffalo trial, which took place over the summer of 2022. The NLRB prosecuted Starbucks for over two hundred violations of federal labor law the company had committed in the fall of 2021. Casey Moore and I both had to testify twice during the trial: first, about the facts of Starbucks' conduct, and second, about the chilling effect that their actions had had on organizing elsewhere.

To get an injunction in federal court against a company's union busting, a union has to prove that the organizing effort was harmed because the union busting made workers afraid or unwilling to support the union afterward. But providing this "chill evidence" has its risks. Naming workers who are afraid to be public outs them to a company that has already proven it will break the law and retaliate against union supporters. Refusing to name them can risk charges of contempt of court or perjury.[15]

Starbucks' cross-examination veered far from the matter at hand into an attempt at discovery of any detail of the union campaign management wanted to know. When I said that workers had been terrified by what Starbucks had done, my Littler opponent tried to pry names and confidential details out of me.

"Can you tell me who has expressly told you that they were terrified about the union activities?" Jackie, the Littler counsel, asked.

"I have concern for their safety if I name names."

"Sorry. You have to name them. If you're going to testify that there's terrified partners in the market, I'm entitled to know who they are."

The opening bars of Paul Robeson's "Joe Hill" began playing in my head. But even Paul had been able to invoke the Fifth Amendment to avoid naming names before the House Un-American Activities Committee. Not being on trial myself, I had no such protection here. After I left the room, the judge would sternly warn Starbucks that he believed they were violating the law by interrogating me about protected concerted activity and encouraged the union to file charges, which we later did. In the meantime, however, I was stuck. Because the chill evidence was part of the federal court case, not the NLRB case, the administrative judge didn't have the authority to rule on any of the lawyers' objections to the lines of questioning. There was no way to avoid answering.[16]

So, I filibustered instead, bringing up partners Starbucks had already fired. But Jackie did extract the name of one current partner: Allegra Anastasi.

Within a week, I got a call from Allegra. She was sobbing: Starbucks had fired her for being a couple of minutes late. How was she going to afford her medication? An eight-year partner, she had transferred to the Del-Chip store when she moved to Buffalo from Wisconsin. Outgoing and popular, she had been a key leader of the union at her store after overcoming her initial fear. Now, the exact thing I had reassured her wouldn't happen had happened.

This experience made us even more resolute in our determination not to give Starbucks any additional information they could use to retaliate against partners. As part of the federal court case, they attempted to subpoena every communication we had ever had with Starbucks workers, as well as every message we had ever sent to a journalist. We couldn't give this information to the company without exposing vulnerable workers and violating the freedom of the press. Casey, Richard, Michelle, and I made a pact that we would go to jail rather than turn over any of the information. Ultimately, the Trump-appointed federal judge dismissed our request for an injunction, meaning the case would continue to slog through the courts rather than securing emergency relief.

It was clear that the law was not coming to save us. Seeing this, Starbucks seemed to ramp up their union-busting efforts.

**A WEEK AFTER ALL** three Ithaca stores unionized on April 8, partners at the College Avenue Starbucks went on strike. They worked at the most profitable, busiest store in the market, just down the street from Cornell's campus. Their committee seemed unbreakable.

For the past seventeen years, the store had had problems with its grease trap, a plumbing device that filters out grease before it goes down the pipes. It often smelled and sometimes posed more serious problems.

Then, the day before Easter, the grease trap overflowed. Oil and maggots—dead and alive—oozed all over the floor in the back of house. Management tried to tell the workers to clean it themselves. They refused: This required professional cleaning and draining. So—in what Brian Murray and I jokingly called the Ithaca Easter Rising, after James Connolly's 1916 rebellion—the workers walked out on strike. It was a joyful and exuberant picket line, despite the rainy weather. Kolya Vitek performed skateboarding feats. Ben South led chants through the bullhorn. Stephanie Heslop, a stand-up comic, attended to morale. Workers from the other Ithaca stores came to lend their support, too.[17]

Two weeks later, on June 3, Starbucks announced that, rather than fix the grease trap, the company would close the store. The grease trap could have been fixed. They came up with additional flimsy excuses for why the closure was legitimate, such as that there wasn't enough space in the store to install another ice bin. No one was convinced. Ithaca was the first city in the country that had seen every Starbucks vote to unionize—and on the same day. It felt like Starbucks was trying to send a message.

It was a message that partners everywhere felt. In Seattle, we had gotten a lead from the Pike Place store, the first-ever Starbucks. Nearby stores were interested in organizing, too. Then, Starbucks conveniently announced that they were merging all of these stores into what they called a Heritage District and that current partners would have to reapply for their jobs. This seemed to us an act of retaliation, a last-ditch effort by Starbucks to try to win on the marketwide-unit question, and an attempt to insulate the iconic Pike Place store and make it harder to unionize.

Over the summer and fall of 2022, the company announced the closure of more stores across the country, including unionized stores in Chicago and Colorado Springs and stores that were attempting to organize, such as the ones in Syracuse, New York. Starbucks told the press that the closures were due to health and safety issues. Howard Schultz said that he hadn't known that Starbucks bathrooms were frequent sites of drug use and overdoses. But the actual effect of these closures on partners was different: We felt that, just as in Ithaca, if partners spoke out about health and safety issues, Starbucks would close our stores.[18]

Starbucks bided its time across the rest of the Ithaca stores, running a slow attrition campaign of constructive discharges and the occasional firing. Meanwhile, we litigated the College Avenue closing through the Labor Board trial process. Then, roughly a year after the Ithaca stores had first won their elections, on May 5, 2023, Starbucks dropped a bombshell. They were closing the Meadows and Commons stores, too.

The Ithaca community rallied around the workers. Students—including Nick Wilson, the former autonomous salt who had watched Starbucks close his store after he and his coworkers began organizing, and Danielle Donovan, a brilliant and caring labor student—occupied Day Hall, the university headquarters. Richard and Casey were there, along with Chris Sessions, a filmmaker who was working with Richard and Michael on their Starbucks documentary. Chris recorded the unfolding drama.

Once inside the hall, the students needed to make a decision. "What are our demands?"

A statement or some other form of censure wasn't enough, Richard advised them. Cornell had a large contract with Starbucks: The cafés around campus sold their products under a WE PROUDLY SERVE banner. If Starbucks was done with Ithaca, Ithaca should be done with Starbucks. The students succeeded in pressuring Cornell to cut the contract.

This, of course, was a boycott. It was also a tremendous PR blow to Starbucks. Students and young people were a key demographic within their customer base, a demographic that was proving that rather than caving to convenience and marketing it would hold the company accountable for its actions. This was a preview of the kind of pressure that, amplified, could force Starbucks to sign the Fair Election Principles and actually bargain a first contract.

**IN THE SPRING OF** 2023, Starbucks' Board of Directors assented to a shareholder proposal suggesting that they hire an independent auditor to assess their labor rights commitments. The consultant they hired—a former labor relations director for Sodexo and corporate lawyer—found "no evidence" that Starbucks had followed "an anti-union playbook." In his report, he also asserted that "all indications are that Workers United had prepared thoroughly for its organizing efforts" and "had careful top-down leadership."[19]

Neither of these statements could have been further from the truth. Starbucks' anti-union playbook was as old as the history of union busting. And had Workers United's top-down leadership prevailed, the campaign would never have happened.

Workers United was a small and decentralized union that had evolved out of the early garment workers' unions via a long history of mergers, breakups, and general drama. Its history still revolved around the Triangle Shirtwaist Factory fire and the 1976 J. P. Stevens textile mill campaign, the basis for the Hollywood movie *Norma Rae.* Since its affiliation with SEIU, it had ceased to be the vibrant, organizing-focused union it had been in its heyday. By the time we were preparing to launch the Starbucks campaign in the summer of 2021, the union's top leadership thought taking on Starbucks was far-fetched and wanted nothing to do with the campaign—until our plan actually worked.[20]

After we won, the leadership began demanding credit and control, especially as our organizing effort spread across the country. They tried to take as much of the campaign as possible away from the workers who were running it, demanding access to email, social media accounts, the writing of press releases, and the deciding of messaging strategy. We insisted that the partners who were running these accounts and committees were doing things well: Experts including Bernie Sanders' comms team had told us to keep doing what we were doing, and—critically—partners around the country knew that they were initiating a genuine partner connection when they reached out to the union.

At first, Workers United's top leadership couldn't keep up. Casey was indefatigable, able to run organizing circles around everyone else. She continued giving new organizing leads to partners, who followed up immediately. Workers United tried to centralize this process, drafting a letter they wanted to send to every worker reaching out, which included instructions to send over a spreadsheet with names, contact information, and details on every worker in the shop before the union would schedule an intake call. Not only did we prevent them from using that letter, but we responded immediately and personally. By the time the international union learned of the lead, the workers had built relationships with their partner on point and were signing cards and moving their store toward an election.

Toward the end of the spring, Workers United reorganized itself internally, promoting staff it deemed loyal to the institution rather than to the campaign or to Starbucks workers, and deliberately moving away from the partner-on-point system. Shortly after, the union leaders invited the parent union, SEIU, into the mix.

Richard had foreseen that this would happen and tried his best to keep the campaign in the hands of the workers in the face of an impending takeover. We didn't want the national unions coming into the campaign, but it was impossible to keep them out. And we did need more resources—which they never put toward the things that mattered. "My job is to keep as much of the campaign in the hands of the workers as possible, so that when SEIU does come in, the workers are already running things," Richard told me.

Workers United's internal culture and ego battles may have posed obstacles, but the conflict between Starbucks Workers United as a grassroots, worker-run campaign and SEIU as an institution was much deeper seated. SEIU's national leadership was opposed to workplace-by-workplace organizing in the private sector. They felt threatened by it. Their president, Mary Kay Henry, was trying to protect her legacy by promoting the narrative that organizing individual stores and going to NLRB elections didn't work. She wasn't alone in this; rather, she represented the viewpoint within the union that considered organizing too challenging and too slow to change society.[21]

When McDonald's workers had started organizing in 2012, SEIU had prevented them from filing for union elections at their workplaces, citing legal difficulties around franchising. To be sure, organizing McDonald's on a store-by-store basis would have been challenging. But it would have empowered workers and won key rights. Instead, the union turned their campaign into a pressure campaign designed to raise wages: the "Fight for $15 and a union." The actual union was an afterthought. The real goal was for SEIU's allies in the Democratic Party to pass legislative reforms, from minimum wage increases to scheduling requirements. SEIU believed in lobbying politicians to pass what they called "sectoral bargaining"—by which they meant a system of wage boards and other administrative bodies, created by the government, that placed union officials on an equal footing with the leadership of corporations.[22]

Unlike sectoral bargaining in Europe, which arose out of a strong labor movement, SEIU's watered-down definition of sectoral bargaining beseeched the state to make a weak labor movement strong by bestowing certain regulatory powers upon it. Whether actual workers got a voice on their jobs or not, whether the workplace became a democracy or remained a dictatorship, wasn't really important. As SEIU moved into the Starbucks campaign, their beliefs around this question became increasingly apparent.

Having formed a coalition, Workers United and SEIU leadership consolidated control of the campaign. They had made it clear that neither Casey nor I were allowed to be in charge, and they had slowly taken away Richard's responsibilities as well. They took the style of Richard's recommendations around "adopting a store" and building the infrastructure for a boycott, but not the substance, turning his plan for sustained leafleting at nine thousand stores into a day of action every few months at a few hundred stores. The leadership slowly transformed the campaign from a vibrant and blossoming movement into a top-down bureaucracy that assembled for periodic "drivers meetings," where consultants and top union officials congratulated one another on their success in streamlining the campaign.

The leadership also dragged us into constant and demoralizing battles over communications and messaging. We argued that Starbucks partners rather than international union staff should continue to run the email because it kept the campaign authentic and kept partner-to-partner connections intact. We resisted their demands to purchase Twitter advertisements or to post content that altered the image, goals, and substance of the campaign. We negotiated over who would be quoted in press releases and what they would say. Our argument was that Starbucks was taking any opportunity to third-party the union; having workers quoted rather than union leaders gave the campaign its authenticity and pushed back against that narrative.

In February of 2022, the president of Workers United insisted that she be quoted in the press release announcing the one hundredth Starbucks to file for a union election, saying, "I would welcome a conversation with Kevin Johnson anytime. Labor relations should be collaborative, not adversarial. There is no success without worker voices."[23]

In the Tri-Main office, we read this statement, aghast. We were at war with Starbucks: They had just fired the Memphis workers a week and a half before and were on the verge of firing Cassie Fleischer. This was not a time for collaboration with an adversary that wanted to kill our union. Moreover, Starbucks was telling partners in one-on-ones and captive-audience meetings everywhere that the union would come between workers and the company. If anyone was going to meet with Kevin Johnson or other Starbucks execs, it should be partners. There would be no success for the campaign itself without worker voices *in the room*, not just in theory.

Casey diplomatically sent back edits. The union's communications director responded that partners didn't understand the "nuanced politics" involved and that the quote would stay as it was.

When the press release went out with that quote unchanged, right-wing anti-union commentators, as well as Starbucks, seized on it. "SEIU Drops Its Front in Unionizing Starbucks," read a restaurant industry publication headline.[24]

Casey spent nearly two years running communications for the national campaign. When the international union brought in SEIU comms people who tried to take over and insist on new policies—for instance, that workers shouldn't be allowed to speak to reporters without a staffer present—she held her ground, preventing them from implementing many of their plans and ensuring that partners retained control of the press strategy and social media accounts. She also convinced the union to hire Josie Serrano from the Long Beach store as a graphic designer and social media person. Josie's effervescent humor and design sense captured the irreverent idealism of the campaign, an essence that they and Casey fought to convey despite the obstacles.

"Strike with Pride" in the summer of 2023 illustrated the ability of workers to outmaneuver their SEIU handlers. Starbucks workers were overwhelmingly queer and trans, in large part because Starbucks' health care covered gender-affirming care, which was rare in an industry that mostly didn't even offer health care. Starbucks had a history of marketing themselves as a progressive and pro-LGBTQ+ company.

Now, however, Starbucks started threatening workers' access to gender-affirming care coverage. In Oklahoma, managers sat trans workers, including Neha Cremin, a brilliant and fearless organizing committee member, down for one-on-one meetings.[25]

"I know you've used the trans health care benefits," her manager said. With a union, they said, you could gain, you could lose, or you could stay the same. But there was a possibility of losing benefits.[26]

In Kansas, the manager at the Overland Park store told Maddie Doran, a trans committee leader, that since a majority of Starbucks Workers United members were cisgender, they might trade away gender-affirming care benefits for something else. Then, management fired Maddie anyway, days before her scheduled facial-feminization surgery.[27]

As anti-trans hate swept the country, Starbucks began to crack down on the very displays of pride it had previously encouraged and marketed. At Elmwood, I watched my manager take down the pride flags and decorations that Bridget Shannon had bought with her own money and come in early to hang up, saying we weren't allowed to have them.

The SEIU comms people insisted this wasn't a story. They, along with the union's PR firm, Berlin Rosen, had spent the spring pitching stories about "sectoral bargaining" or pleas from the Workers United president for Starbucks to meet her at a national bargaining table. So, Casey and Josie took to Twitter, posting a long thread about what had been happening in stores across the country.

The international union had scheduled one of its national strike days for the next week. Some of their staff thought the campaign could be solved by just striking unionized stores. If all of the union stores went on strike often enough, that would bring the company to its knees—even though we represented only about 3 percent of Starbucks' corporate-owned stores within the United States.

With Casey's and Josie's help, Starbucks workers switched the messaging of that strike, making Starbucks' refusal to bargain over taking down pride decorations the unfair labor practice that workers walked out over. In the end, the media response was overwhelming and positive, helping expose the cruelty of Starbucks' union busting, and the strike was unifying and uplifting, possibly setting a record as the largest work stoppage over LGBTQ+ rights.[28]

Instead of embracing the creativity and courage of the workers, the national campaign leadership, from both Workers United and SEIU, continued to insist on control—an approach that undermined the essence of the campaign. While loyalty and presenting unified fronts are important to union campaigns, demonizing differences of opinion and asserting that there is one right answer and that anyone who questions the strategy or lack thereof is disloyal or undermining the campaign destroy the very values at the core of what union organizing is about.

---

**OUR BIGGEST DISAGREEMENTS WERE** over strategy. Many of us—including those of us who had put together the initial strategy for the campaign—believed that we wouldn't be able to win without a boycott. I believed that a coordinated social media campaign that enlisted celebrities to call on the public to stop going to Starbucks could have filled in gaps where we didn't have enough picket captains to enforce a boycott at all nine thousand stores.

But there were additional ways to put escalating pressure on Starbucks to respect the right to organize. Bargaining could have been one of these avenues: perhaps forcing Starbucks to meet us at three hundred separate bargaining tables across the country—wasting thousands of dollars on Littler lawyers' fees and travel for corporate execs—would have forced them to fold.

After it became clear that Starbucks wouldn't bargain with us if we insisted on a Zoom option, many partners began to ask why we hadn't reconsidered our insistence on the hybrid system, since Starbucks representatives were walking out in protest. During the election campaigns, we had told partners that they would get to sit across the table from corporate on an equal footing and bargain their own contract. Now, workers at some stores, including ones in Buffalo, complained to me that they hadn't had a single negotiating session. In Richmond, workers started pushing to hold bargaining sessions for their stores and to close the Zoom screen to stop Starbucks from walking out immediately. Del-Chip asked for the same thing. A few partners even quit because they had been holding out hope for bargaining and canceling the sessions meant that their reason for staying was gone.[29]

There were many reasons the international union didn't support bargaining at one hundred, two hundred, or three hundred stores simultaneously. Some of these reasons were logistical, while another was legal. Starbucks' refusal to bargain, along with the company's other unfair labor practices, would block workers from filing to decertify the union at any store, preventing the company from starting to unravel our hard-won organizing progress. The downside of this legal strategy was that it inadvertently contributed to the stagnation that led some workers—excluded from the new benefits Starbucks was giving nonunion stores—to see decertification as their best option.

Although watching Starbucks' bad-faith bargaining had been infuriating at times, it was also a radicalizing and illuminating experience, offering a rare window into Starbucks' corporate psychology. It was an internal organizing tool, allowing a way for new people to participate and exposing the company's union busting to workers who hadn't previously been involved in the campaign. For these reasons, holding more bargaining sessions could have helped prevent the decertification attempts that began brewing in part because of frustration over a lack of forward movement.

In a private conversation in early 2023 with another organizer and me on bargaining strategy, a top union official voiced this concern: "How can we control the partners if we have two hundred and fifty bargaining tables across the country?"

He couldn't comprehend that control wasn't the most important thing. There were ways of coordinating regionally or locally to prevent someone somewhere at one of the hundreds of unionized stores from tentatively agreeing to a bad proposal. But even if that had happened—would it have really been worse for the campaign than stifling workers' right to speak for themselves, which was resulting in burnout and disillusionment?

The organizing model of the campaign had dramatically changed, too. Starbucks workers still wanted to organize: New workers continued to reach out, organize their coworkers, and win elections—sometimes unanimously, despite everything Starbucks had put them through. But the union's approach was different.

Organizing had become staff dominated, and the international union had mostly refused to hire partners into positions that ranged from organizers to student-solidarity coordinators. The union was hiring from the Democratic Socialists of America, from other unions, from anywhere except the one group uniquely able to reach other Starbucks workers wanting to unionize. When the union did finally start bringing partners on—as interns or as staff—it viewed this as a patronage system of purchasing loyalty. When Starbucks partners refused to toe the line, the union told them to find and train their own replacements.

In part because of this, the international union's approach to organizing shifted away from building deep relationships and trust between workers, instead relying on a tactic staffers termed a "clean play," after Starbucks' late-night deep-cleaning sessions. During clean plays, the union brought dozens of partners to a city and took them to various stores to get leads and contact info from the workers.

Because so many Starbucks workers *did* want to unionize, many believed that they were—as the AFL-CIO president had said—"ripe for organizing." This phrasing was problematic: Starbucks workers may have wanted a union, but it took months of developing trust and relationships to build an organizing committee in Buffalo, and that committee had had to withstand some of the most intense union busting in modern U.S. labor history. We had not been "easy pickings." But the international union believed that if we just showed up at nonunion stores and told workers what was going on, everyone would immediately join.[30]

This was based in part on what we had done at Pavement Coffeehouse, where workers had successfully built a committee by visiting their coworkers at work and filling them in on the organizing effort. Unfortunately, the Starbucks clean plays weren't based on the same model.

I went to the one in Los Angeles. To be sure, there were good things about it. It fostered community by bringing workers together from across the country. Thanks to the insistence and struggle of workers like Tyler Keeling, partners were running the intake and follow-up on leads coming in: I watched Tyler train Kyle, a long-term San Francisco partner, on calling the workers whose numbers we had procured in the stores. They had a genuine rapport with the workers they contacted.

But the strategy was fundamentally flawed. For one thing, Starbucks knew we were there and targeted their union busting on a micro level. For another, all of the Starbucks partners were assigned SEIU chaperones who knew almost nothing about the Starbucks campaign and had no idea what roles we had played in the campaign. Nabretta from the Memphis Seven and I were paired together; our chaperones not only didn't know who we were but didn't ask us questions, instead lecturing us condescendingly about their grad school projects, staff positions, and organizing wisdom. After each store visit, they demanded to know: "What was the worker's issue? Did you ask them what their issue was?"

If we responded that the worker was busy, the answer was something like "Well, how did you try to push past that?" There was no comprehension of boundaries, of personal space, of not creeping workers out. The LA clean play generated a large number of leads, but only one or two of those leads turned into organizing campaigns.

**A SMART UNION BUSTER** doesn't fire workers for organizing. Instead, it simply makes their lives as miserable as possible, forcing them to quit because of the toll the retaliation has taken on their mental, physical, or emotional well-being. The legal term for this forcing out is *constructive discharge*. It's notoriously difficult to get the NLRB to find merit in constructive discharge cases. Firings have documentation and clear statements from management. Constructive discharges don't. Companies argue that they didn't *actually* retaliate: The worker in question left for totally unrelated reasons. Perhaps they had found another job or needed more time for school or had a health issue to take care of, or they were just overwhelmed or stressed or reacting to the tension the union had brought to the workplace. The underlying message to the affected worker is clear: *It's all in your head.*

My constructive discharges from Starbucks and from the Starbucks Workers United campaign ran on parallel lines.

At Elmwood, the union busting had intensified. After Cassie's firing in February of 2022 and Kellen's constructive discharge in April, both over their right to have the limited availabilities that Starbucks partners had enjoyed for decades, our manager, Patty, had had enough. She put in her notice, and Starbucks sent in a brusque new manager whose main role seemed to be to get as many of us to quit as possible. Whereas Patty had tried to work with us, her replacement scheduled us for the opposite of what we wanted. If we wanted fewer hours, we were scheduled to the max of our availability. If partners needed hours, theirs were slashed.

When I needed time off to attend my sister's wedding in May, management made it as difficult as possible, forcing me to take a leave of absence instead of simply putting in a time-off request. To spend more time on organizing other stores, and because I was now being scheduled for much longer shifts, I tried to reduce my availability to one or two days per week. Management denied all of my new availability requests.

On the union front, I was getting exhausted and burned-out from being forced to try to organize within a framework that I didn't believe could result in victory, while any efforts I made to influence the strategy were met with resistance or personal attacks. When I did media interviews, the national Starbucks campaign leadership either asked why I was in the spotlight at all or accused me of putting forward the wrong messaging or talking too openly about salting. When I talked about the need for a boycott, I was told I was undermining the campaign and that I would be fired by Workers United if I continued to speak about it publicly. When I started organizing nonunion workers at other companies, in addition to Starbucks partners, I was accused of not caring about the Starbucks campaign and not being committed to winning; union staffers told partners I had helped organize that I had abandoned the campaign and them. When I shared my thoughts on Starbucks campaign strategy with other partners, I was accused of participating in a campaign-within-a-campaign and undercutting union leadership.

I had been staying at Starbucks regardless of the personal cost so as to remain as involved with Starbucks Workers United as I could be and to keep my credibility with partners. But the situation within the store was growing increasingly untenable, and I was marginalized within the campaign that I was staying on for. Starbucks wouldn't accept my availability and wouldn't stop scheduling me for shifts that I couldn't work. When I called off from those shifts, management didn't even write me up for it, but they told my coworkers that it was my fault the store was short-staffed and tried to pit them against the union on that basis.

After a summer of this standoff, I couldn't do it anymore. In September 2022, I put in my two weeks' notice at Starbucks, informing them that I would fight it at the Labor Board but that I couldn't let them retaliate against my coworkers as well as me. On the labor side, I decided that it was time for me to start working on other campaigns, campaigns that our region of the union would retain more control over and thus more ability to ensure that workers had the local autonomy, union democracy, and voice in the workplace they deserved.

# CHAPTER SEVEN

# No Unorganizable Workplace

Back in May 2021, not long after the first salts had arrived in Buffalo and were still crashing at my house, Brian Murray and I headed to the swamp south of town for a walk along the boardwalks. The marsh was framed by crumbling factories and grain silos, whose functions had dwindled to serving as graffiti canvases and a brutalist, Soviet-art-evoking backdrop to Buffalo. The Skyway, unnecessarily gigantic, jutted into the Cheerios-scented air beside the General Mills cereal plant.

It was late at night, and we got lost on the way back. I turned too early, missing the Skyway and instead taking us over a bridge toward Canalside. As we drove through the darkness, past shuttered mills and hunched hangars of warehouses, suddenly, to the side, a brightly illuminated, red-and-white vision.

Tesla.

"I didn't know there was a Tesla plant here," Brian said.

I hadn't known, either. "That's our next target!" I was only partly joking.

"Damn, can you imagine? First Starbucks, then Tesla. This union is so fucking cool."

Almost a year later, in February of 2022, the swamp was frozen over. Outside the nature center, Kay Kennedy, Al Celli, and I buckled on rented snowshoes. They were the aesthetically pleasing, impractical kind—wooden with leather straps. I kept tripping over mine as I followed Kay and Al down the packed snowy paths.

Al, who had just left Spot Coffee, started telling us about their new job. They were working as a data analyst at Tesla, labeling clips of roads to train the AI for self-driving cars. I asked if they wanted to unionize Tesla.

"Don't talk to me about organizing for at least a year!" Al told me, with a certain sternness. "I'm not a salt here, and I want to get a foothold."

Four months later, I got a text from Gary Bonadonna. I read it on my break at Starbucks as I drank blonde ristretto shots of espresso in the back of house: "Al just reached out to me and wants to talk about organizing the Tesla plant in Buffalo. I told them that you could call them in a couple days. Would you do that?"

Later, I would tease Al for their timeline reversal. But at the time, I was only thinking of this possible campaign: How could we organize Tesla? That question was at the front of Al's mind. How could we get a list of workers or build a committee in a workplace so secretive that the names of the workers in the Autopilot department didn't appear on the employee portal and the doors of other departments had brown paper taped over the glass panes?

But we both knew it had to be organizable. Fundamentally, I believe that there are no unorganizable workplaces, only workplaces that haven't been organized yet. This doesn't mean that every workplace is organizable all of the time. Workers' willingness to take on the risk and struggle of unionizing depends on several factors. Sometimes, conditions are so untenable that the question becomes one of organizing a union or quitting the job. Sometimes, workers love their jobs and the company but believe in democracy and in the labor movement and thus are ready to organize. Sometimes, even a "cold shop"—a place with insufficient worker interest to launch a viable union campaign—can become hot overnight if management makes a critical blunder. Often, the difference between a hot and a cold shop is the degree to which workers can overcome the fear of retaliation from the company, which makes the fight for the right to organize the cornerstone of a successful union campaign. But—somehow, at some point, with the right leverage or the right circumstances—every company is organizable.

Richard thought we were at least a little crazy. Al and I agreed to check in weekly, but I was often overwhelmed from the Starbucks campaign and lagged in following up. The plant was probably at its hottest in the spring and summer of 2022, but my limited capacity and the difficulty of contacting other workers meant that we weren't able to take advantage of that heat.

Al was tireless. They updated me on everything, from their efforts to win the support of their conservative Texan coworker by making plans to go shooting with him, to their plan to get information from supervisors by posing as an aspiring manager, to discussions within the JEDI (Justice, Equity, Diversity & Inclusion) and LGBTQ at Tesla chats. In June 2022, when SpaceX fired nine workers in California for signing a letter to Elon Musk about workplace issues, Al told me about the anger and fear rippling through the workforce.[1]

They showed me a post in a chat on MatterMost, the company messaging platform, where a worker said, "Now it seems like we can't talk about anything."

There was only one way to capture the simmering outrage Tesla workers were feeling. If we could get a list of workers' names, we would be able to get addresses and run a blitz, contacting as many workers as possible over a weekend, through home visits, calls, texts, and social media messages, to try to quickly and secretly build an organizing committee.

We just needed to figure out how to get the list.

**IN NOVEMBER 2022, RICHARD,** Al, and I met in a Buffalo café as a light snow fell outside, catching the glow of the streetlights.

A couple weeks before, the city had been crippled by a snowstorm that resulted in government-issued driving bans across the county. Tesla delayed announcing their closure until the last minute, meaning workers—especially those who worked the production night shift—worried they would have to drive on unsafe roads. Instead of paying workers their regular wages, Tesla deducted the costs from workers' paid time off (PTO) and sick time.[2]

Workers took to the Autopilot department group chat to complain about these policies and their safety concerns. Someone created a custom reaction to respond to posts: a black square with the word UNION.

Then, management deleted the chat.

Workers were furious. Sara Costantino, one of the Autopilot analysts, told the press, "I want a voice with my company—we don't really have one. The voice we did have, they took away."[3]

Another worker created a Discord server to discuss unionizing. To preserve the secrecy of the campaign as much as possible, the workers were calling the union "the Onion" and their chat the "Fans of Funyuns." Someone added Al to the group.

They told me about the swirling conversations on the server, muddy and pulling in several directions. Some of the workers thought they should try to organize in a tech-specific union, while others wanted to draw up specific lists of demands.

Al said they would try to set up a Zoom call with the workers, Richard, and me. At work, they discussed union matters constantly but quietly, paving the way for the call to go smoothly by talking to their coworkers about the qualities they wanted to see in their union. Most important, they said, workers needed to be in charge. Local autonomy—the idea that workers would have control of their own campaigns and their own unions once they won—was the key. They wanted a participatory and dynamic union that wouldn't be caught up in bureaucracy and stifle their creativity. Because Workers United Upstate New York emphasized local autonomy, workers saw it as the perfect fit.

On December 1, sitting at a table in the DC airport, I logged on to the first Zoom call with the fledgling committee. I had spent much of the day writing a plan outlining the union campaign strategy to share with them. In it, I tried to convey what made us uniquely suited to organize Tesla workers, a brilliant and diverse group of people who valued their independence but needed support. The first paragraph borrowed the opening of the Project Germinal job posting and then explained how Workers United Upstate New York would give Tesla workers the freedom to create a union in their own image, backed by the strength and resources of the labor movement.

The remainder of the plan emphasized the importance of moving fast to build an organizing committee capable of running the campaign inside the plant. It previewed what Tesla might do to fight the union, predicting a "nice guy" strategy alongside typical anti-union fearmongering. It also set the goal of filing for a wall-to-wall unit—meaning everyone who worked within the plant, encompassing all departments—with a strong majority of workers on union cards. Richard and I had discussed this extensively as we worked on the plan. Our only contacts so far were in the Autopilot division. The plant was much bigger: its other main departments were production, where people worked twelve-hour days assembling solar panels and refurbishing batteries, and customer service. We did not know whether these departments were interested in unionizing, and we had next to no means of getting contacts there without outing the campaign. My logic was that, just as we had needed to set our sights on the entire Starbucks market, we needed to aim to organize the whole company and then, if necessary, adjust later, once we learned what was possible—the "We Only Want the Earth" organizing model.

Additionally—although not included in the plan—we had talked to Gary about what resources our region of Workers United could put into winning the right to organize. Gary had agreed to spend several hundred thousand dollars, if necessary, to take the campaign to Tesla stores and other public forums. If Tesla tried to bust the union, we would take the fight public.

The Zoom call was inspiring and joyful. The workers were an immediately impressive group, and they needed a union badly. Tesla monitored everything they did, tracking every keystroke and second of their time. Many workers spoke of being unable to take bathroom breaks because they were so intensely timed and watched. They talked about the need for more PTO, more sick time, more of a right to be a person. People applied to Tesla because they thought it was one of the best jobs available in Buffalo, and in some ways it was, although workers were still living paycheck to paycheck. But Tesla exploited that ruthlessly, using workers' fear of losing the job to control their every move and extract as much productivity as possible.

The workers were eager, talented, creative, and smart, and they understood the need for secrecy and urgency. Al spoke about their experiences with Workers United, and the consensus was that our focus on local autonomy and commitment to organizing were exactly in line with what Autopilot workers were seeking. We made plans to begin meeting weekly, in person at the Tri-Main office. Over the next weeks, the committee that emerged was small but committed, consistent in showing up and strategizing about how they could build support and bring in new committee members while keeping the campaign secret.

Al was central to our germinating campaign, but they were no longer alone. Will Hance was enthusiastic and insightful, a cheerful and wry bulwark of the committee. He brought a commonsense and grounded energy to our discussions, propelling things forward. Zak Stirling, who had a deep understanding of workplace dynamics as the only team lead on the committee, walked me through the details of the metrics Tesla expected workers to meet. His explanations of what messages would and would not appeal to the broader workforce were invaluable, and his courage and principled stance in taking an additional risk as a lead won him the admiration and respect of his colleagues. Alex Hy, a recent high school graduate who had gone straight into Autopilot, was joyful and creative, encouraging coworkers to get involved with a consistently relatable and uplifting attitude. She did the first television interview about the campaign, outside the plant the first night. She was as incredible as she was terrified: authentic, honest, and heartfelt. Arian Berek, kind and enthusiastic, was a member of Zak's team, along with Alex Hy, and felt encouraged to join the union campaign in part because Zak's support for the union made it easier for his team to be public.

The committee also included a former Autopilot worker who had moved to the plant side and who wrote the instruction manuals for production. In that role, they were able to move around the floor and talk with people. From them, I began to piece together key details about the plant. Keenan Lasch had a deadpan wit that could have earned him a career as a stand-up comedian; he was piercing and hilarious in dissecting the company's statements and actions. Sara Costantino's care for her coworkers was immediately evident, and her positivity and love made her a messaging genius. She volunteered to lead the press committee. Tzivyi Abosch, on medical leave after breaking her wrist in a skiing accident, was tireless in volunteering on weekdays when few were available and constantly checked in on others. Nick Piazza was steadfast, hilarious, and always willing to volunteer for leafleting, press, and any other campaign needs. Jason Connolly worked a second job downstairs at another business in Tri-Main; they would come upstairs to attend union meetings and gave eloquent voice to many workers' thoughts.

Zahra Lahrache, who was a top performer but living paycheck to paycheck, took charge of the social media committee, curating memes and posting announcements once the campaign was public. Jan Patrick was a brilliant artist who had grown up between several countries and consistently pointed out that things didn't have to be the way they were. They set up the Discord server that we used to communicate, streamlining and organizing things fastidiously. And they designed prototype union logos, including the Buffalo emblazoned with the Tesla *T* that became the motif of the campaign. Underneath, in small white lettering, the campaign slogan: TAKE THE WHEEL BUFFALO.[4]

Tesla Autopilot attracted an interesting group of workers. The job required sitting at a computer for eight hours a day, labeling video clips to train the AI for self-driving cars. Those who could perform this job often shared certain qualities. It attracted an assortment of gamers, anime fans, endearingly nerdy and neurodiverse individuals. Many were queer or trans and saw Elon Musk's transphobia as a critical reason to organize. Most were young, and many had worked in food service prior to joining Tesla. Several Starbucks workers, including some former committee members and card signers, now worked at Tesla. They had taken the job to get out of the service industry and because it paid a little more, although certainly not commensurate with Tesla's immense profits. Others were artists or graphic designers who hadn't been able to make a living and ended up working at Tesla to pay the bills. Most were creative, innovative thinkers, keenly aware of the inequities of society and dedicated to helping make a change. They were not only capable of running their own union, they were a force that could radically transform the workplace and thus society. Richard and I saw our roles as supporting and mentoring these workers; they would run the campaign.[5]

Meanwhile, Al worried that my near-complete lack of knowledge of both anime and video games and zeal for recounting obscure labor history facts would alienate Tesla workers, who possessed a great deal of knowledge about the former and didn't necessarily need lectures on the latter. They recommended videos for me to watch to try to remedy the situation. When I tried to reassure Al that I could talk about things other than labor history, they looked at me skeptically. "I don't know—can you?"

In January of 2023, we made progress on the steps needed to launch a campaign. Over take-out Japanese food one night, we mapped what we could of the workplace, workshopped the letter that would announce the campaign and the Q&A and other materials we would share with interested workers, developed our talking points, and researched potential pressure points that could help us win the right to organize.

Then, as Will Hance was showing us a coworker's post on MatterMost, he found a menu on the side of the screen. When he clicked on it, scores of screen names showed up. The list.

It was imperfect and incomplete, but it included hundreds of Autopilot workers. This meant we would be able to blitz Autopilot.

The Tesla workers painstakingly copied out the names onto big yellow posters that we stuck on the wall as we began to map out the workplace. There were about five hundred names, out of what we estimated to be seven hundred total workers within the department. A Cornell student volunteered for the unenviable task of combing voter records to find addresses for the names on the list. They did it efficiently and uncomplainingly, turning around a list containing a large number of accurate addresses.

I worked with the committee to create a time frame for the blitz. As we looked at the calendar, I got an idea. What if we went public with the union on Valentine's Day and made Valentine leaflets, complete with candy, to hand out at the plant that morning? As Lexi Rizzo had said, "We fight for what we love." This was the perfect opportunity to spread that message.

As we prepared for the blitz, I focused on recruiting organizers—staff, members able to take a couple of days off, friends from other unions—to come to Buffalo and help the organizing committee reach more people. An Inside Organizer School trainer agreed to come. Sukhi Toor, who had been the president of the giant TJX distribution-center local in Toronto before joining the union staff, a great and warmhearted leader, was willing to drive down and help out. Chris Sessions, the documentary filmmaker, flew in early to help house-call. Emily Vick came in from Albany. Workers from Starbucks and the newly unionized Lexington Co-op grocery store stepped up.

Vic Conklin went above and beyond. When we got the list of addresses, we had a limited amount of time to make house-calling packets for the volunteers. I found the sorting of the spreadsheet based on geography somewhat bewildering. But Casey—who was working full-time on Starbucks press while also tirelessly helping with the Tesla campaign—and Vic got to work, printing a giant map of Buffalo and grouping the addresses accordingly.

"This is why you should have sorority girls on all your union campaigns," Casey said triumphantly at three in the morning, when all the packets had been made, printed, and slid into the folders we would be giving house callers the next day. "We know how to run things."

The organizing committee decided not to go out on the doors, instead spending the blitz calling and texting their coworkers. While I thought initially that having some of them house calling might increase our credibility, it made sense to keep their outreach less public and more effective. On a good day, you might have five or so conversations on the doors. Often, workers aren't home or don't answer the door. Sometimes, you can go all day without meeting anyone. The committee's work of text banking, social media DMing, and phone calling proved invaluable, reaching a much larger number of people, identifying supporters and anti-union workers, and helping the house-calling team make the best use of their time.

Casey and Vic were the data command center, translating the submitted Google form responses from the texting team and the house-calling group into a synced spreadsheet and updating call packs accordingly. I wanted to be out on the doors to get a better sense of where the workers and thus the campaign were at. Richard, an expert house caller, got the most critical turf: South Buffalo, close by the plant. Conservative in many ways, South Buffalo also had a certain sense of deindustrialized solidarity. Richard was proud to have gotten this assignment.

"This is the one thing I'm good at," he said exuberantly. "I can make the perfect house call."

"You're good at lots and lots of things," I said. "But we need perfect house calls."

On Friday night, we began with a limited evening blitz, assigning everyone to closer-by turf. Not everything was smooth sailing; one of our canvassers accidentally gave a worker's parents the link to the Google form where we were reporting back our assessments, forcing Casey to take it down and send out a new link. Lots of people weren't home, causing some frustration.

Around 7:30 p.m., Gary messaged in the blitz group chat, "I got chased by a dog and tripped in the dark and face planted in a mud swamp. Changing my clothes at a McDonald's. I'm done for the night."

"ARE YOU SERIOUS?" Casey texted back.

I called Gary, choking back laughter. Some of it seeped through anyway, especially once he said he was okay. He told me about walking into the McDonald's to change. The worker had looked up from the counter and said, "Wow, man, you sure got fucked up." The union-made Hickey Freeman overcoat he had been wearing had fallen casualty to the mud, leaving him shivering in a red-white-and-blue Bills T-shirt.

While Gary didn't get to share in the feeling, at least not this time, few things are more uplifting than a good house call. There's something beautiful about knocking on a worker's door, talking to them about their job, explaining what a union is and how organizing one works, answering their questions, and seeing if they are interested in helping lead the effort. Getting to see someone's whole conception of their role in the workplace change—realizing they and their coworkers have power and can become equals with management—is a special and beautiful privilege.

Saturday was a perfect spring day: warmth in the air, bits of green poking through the frosty ground, sunlight filtering through the bare trees along rolling country roads. I was house calling in East Aurora, the artsy village southeast of Buffalo. When I got to my first door of the day, a big wooden cabin-like house, two people were just getting out of a car with their dogs. As the dogs ran up to me for pets, I talked to the people, who turned out to be the worker's parents. (The house-calling team joked that we should make Tesla Union Moms merch because so many of us were meeting pro-union moms on the doors.)

"I think this is great. They really need it," said the mother.

"Would you be able to give me your daughter's phone number?"

"Let me call her!"

When the worker picked up, her mother handed me the phone. The daughter was very interested in the union. She talked about the need for better PTO and sick-time policies and how the lack thereof was putting workers at risk, and she said she would try to attend the organizing committee meeting.

At another door, I was greeted by a somewhat gruff man. I explained what I was there for and asked for the worker I was looking for by name. The man told me he was not sure unions were a good thing. "But people should make up their own minds," he said. "Let me go see if they want to talk to you."

The worker in question appeared a couple of minutes later. They were wearing strawberry and mushroom earrings. That made me hopeful. The second-floor window was full of beautiful and thriving plants, and I decided they must be the gardener.

We talked about what a union could look like. They were interested but wanted a clearer picture. "I've never been part of a union before."

I gave them a copy of the Q&A, invited them to the meeting, then talked about houseplants. (Like cats, houseplants are a great indicator of union proclivities.)

Meanwhile, Will Westlake had gotten Gary's packet from the night before.

"That was the sweetest angel of a dog," Will messaged in the group chat. "And his owner is pro."

The dog's owner was a former Starbucks card signer who had gotten hired at Tesla at the beginning of the Starbucks campaign. That was a consistent pattern: Many pro-union baristas had wound up at Tesla. I spoke with a former Elmwood Starbucks barista who had been there just before I got hired and was pro-union but worried about Tesla's response. My coworker Kellen's brother would soon join the organizing effort, despite being a very new hire. Committee member Ivy Timmer had been a Workers United member at Spot Coffee; she talked about facing harassment at work and the union stepping up to ensure she was safe.

This overlap was part of what made Buffalo Autopilot the perfect place to take on Tesla, and our region of Workers United was ideally situated to do it. It was a different industry from Starbucks or Spot, but the campaign evolved naturally out of our geographic model of organizing workers at other industries and urging our members and former members to consider helping with campaigns at other workplaces and encouraging their friends to organize. Tesla workers had much in common with Starbucks partners: The resilience, courage, brilliance, ownership of their campaign, determination to make their company and their union the best it could possibly be, were all similar. Part of organizing a union, Richard had told me early on, is willing it into existence. No group of workers has ever willed a union into existence more than the Tesla workers. We were going to win because we had to.

**WE HELD A LARGE** committee meeting on Monday night, February 13, to give the committee time to talk to trusted coworkers at work during the day. Casey and I were working together in the office that afternoon, exhausted but exhilarated. Between the workers' outreach and our house calls, we had contacted hundreds of workers and gotten a large number of positive responses.

"We did it!" Casey said. "And I've never done a blitz before."

"Neither have I," I said.

Casey looked at me, surprised, and we high-fived.

That night, around twenty new workers joined the call. A few were afraid of retaliation, but nearly everyone joined the committee. We knew many more workers were interested in joining the committee who hadn't been able to make the meeting or were waiting to see what happened after the first round went public. We had a decision to make. Should we launch the campaign with a smaller committee and then build to a larger committee within the next two or three days, or should we wait a few more days, until we had the bigger committee? We chose the former. Management had caught wind of our blitz and sent out an email warning workers about speaking with us, meaning our window for secrecy had closed, and we wanted to show hesitant but supportive workers that the committee members would be protected. This mirrored our Starbucks strategy, where we had taken a smaller committee public and then quickly grown our numbers across the city.

I had given the scoop about Tesla to Josh Eidelson at Bloomberg, embargoing the story but putting him in touch with committee members. He told me that this campaign had caused more Tesla workers to speak to him on the record within a few weeks than other Tesla campaigns had in years.

The workers began their letter announcing the campaign with Elon's signature opening: "To Everybody." They wrote, "We believe that by having a union at Tesla, we will further the mission of sustainability and foster a progressive environment for us all. Unionizing will further accelerate the world's transition to sustainable energy, because it will give us a voice in our workplace and in the goals we set for ourselves to accomplish. Having greater sustainability in our own work lives and individual well-being will translate into greater ability to meet those goals, which is why we strongly believe that sustainability starts with us." The letter called on Musk to sign the Fair Election Principles and build a collaborative relationship with the union.[6]

We stayed up late in the office, stuffing red envelopes with valentine leaflets and Starburst candies, adding last-minute signatures to the letter, which got to twenty-five by the end of the night, and finally printing off a copy for Al Celli to present to management in person the next day. When I got home, after midnight, I set my alarm for three thirty in the morning: I would send the letter to Tesla, confirm to Josh that he could contact the company for comment, then hurry down to the plant for the leafleting.

It was a freezing-cold Valentine's morning. We huddled together in the Tim Hortons across the street from the plant for a few minutes, then staked out the different corners of the intersection, clutching our stacks of envelopes and activated-charcoal hand warmers.

The reception from the production workers was overwhelmingly positive. Some of the drivers honked their horns with excitement when they learned what was happening. "Where have you been?" one person asked. Another group of workers said, "Oh my god, we've waited for a union for so long!" and "Thank you, Jesus!"

"This car full of people rolled up after," Al posted in the committee chat. "They must have missed us or talked about it in the car. And a guy came out and was like, 'I need four, five of those,' and I look in the car and they were all cheering."

This mood would continue through the day. In the afternoon, I reached out to a new committee member in production who messaged back, "Look forward to hearing from you! Been waiting for this day for a while!"

An Autopilot worker texted me, "I don't really talk to anyone at work but today they passed out the flyers and the guy who sits next to me told me he was thinking of quitting because there wasn't a union."

"Oh wow," I wrote back. "Well, we can change that :)."

"Hopefully, I'd love a union here!"

Many of the workers joining the organizing committee had one primary goal: making friends. The office culture at Tesla was isolated and alienating: A large proportion of people wore headphones all day, including during lunches and breaks, and kept their heads down. Some of the workers barely knew any of their coworkers. The union was changing that already.

As the sun came up, the production shift change ended and the Autopilot committee began to arrive. They posed for a photo in front of the big Tesla sign at the plant entrance, grabbed bags of valentines, and headed into the plant to leaflet their coworkers as people came in.

Once the committee had gone into the plant, we couldn't do much until people started getting off work. Some of us went to Swan Street Diner to get breakfast and celebrate. Richard, Casey, Chris Sessions, and I shared a booth. As Richard ate a celebratory waffle, he talked about how impressed he was with the courage and joy of the workers: in fifty years, he'd never seen anything like it, he said.

"I'm so happy right now," I said. "We're doing it. We're going to win."

Everyone was ecstatic, sleep-deprived but giddy.

"This feels too good," said Casey. "Something is going to happen, I can tell."

**THE NATIONAL LEADERSHIP OF** the Starbucks campaign had been giving Casey the silent treatment for the previous week. They were unhappy with her participation in the Tesla campaign, even though they had already known that it was happening. We had included Tesla as a target in our yearly organizing report, mentioning that we had leads there. The national organizing director of Workers United had agreed that Sukhi should come to Buffalo to help. Both he and Workers United's president had wished Richard and Gary good luck as the blitz was beginning. But bigger and more sinister forces were at play.

The international unions—both Workers United and SEIU—had spent the previous year and a half seeking to minimize Buffalo's leadership and take control of the Starbucks campaign. At the last minute, some of the Starbucks campaign staffers decided to schedule another national informational picketing action on Valentine's Day. Even though Richard disagreed with this tactic, he insisted we participate, believing that it was best to act as one union when the international called for an action. Between the morning leafleting and the evening debriefs, he and most of the other organizers and blitz volunteers went to Starbucks locations around the city to leaflet. Additionally, Casey had pitched journalists on the action the entire week before, but they weren't interested in covering the story because they didn't see it as newsworthy or different from past demonstrations.

The president of Workers United texted Gary, accusing him of choosing to launch Tesla on that date to undermine the Starbucks campaign. The timing of the Tesla blitz and launch had been set weeks before the Starbucks action, but that didn't stop her. "We are getting no press coverage for today's actions," she wrote. "All Tesla. We have given Howard the gift of diversion. I really don't understand the timing of all this."

Moreover, the president of Workers United said we shouldn't be organizing Tesla because it was the Steelworkers' jurisdiction. Years before, the Steelworkers had leafleted the plant, with little worker interest. After Tesla fired four workers, the Steelworkers' campaign never materialized. Now, they wanted to take over the Autopilot campaign.[7]

For years, unions had met to claim "jurisdiction" of various companies, asserting that they alone among unions had the right to organize a particular industry. The United Food & Commercial Workers would organize grocery stores; the United Auto Workers would organize auto plants; the American Federation of Teachers would organize teachers. In practice, unions expanded outside their primary jurisdictions all the time:

The UFCW had campaigns at bookstores and cannabis dispensaries, the UAW represented grad students and museum workers, and the AFT organized nurses. Moreover, unions often declined to organize, for reasons ranging from limited staff capacity to the remote location of a workplace to the size of a workplace to the fact that workers at a nonunion company were making higher wages than those at comparable unionized companies, which the union feared would be an embarrassment.

In theory, the idea of building power across an industry by bringing everyone into the same union was appealing, a throwback to the concept of One Big Union. In practice, workers were better off identifying whichever union was actually committed to organizing, which varied by region. A local of UFCW in one part of the country was not the same as another local elsewhere, while one Workers United joint board might take an extremely different attitude from another. Moreover, in Buffalo, our organizing program emphasized a geographic model and relationships between workers across industries: Tesla workers had more in common with unionizing baristas than they had with workers at a manufacturing plant that had been unionized fifty years prior.

The international union claimed, further, that the AFL-CIO was upset that we were organizing Tesla because, according to them, our launch had set their "strategic campaign" to unionize Tesla back by two or three years.

"What's infinity plus another two or three years?" I asked. "They're not going to organize anything anyway."

Never mind that whatever had existed of the Steelworkers' campaign had taken place before Autopilot even came to Buffalo two years before. Never mind that their claim to the plant centered around the argument that, because the solar-panel-factory-turned-Tesla-plant had been built on the site of a closed steel mill, it was "Steelworker ground" and thus their territory. Never mind that they had had no active campaign in years, including when the plant was at its hottest over the summer—this plan was decided upon unilaterally by Workers United and SEIU, some of whose top staffers had formerly worked for the Steelworkers and who still had connections within the union. Never mind what the workers wanted—the unions never asked them.

Never mind that this played into Elon Musk's hands.

That same morning, I got a text from Al. "They're firing people. This is not a drill."

"What happened?" I asked.

"Idk people are getting let go and their stuff is being packed up."

As the union obsessed over who would control the campaign, Tesla began firing workers, just as SpaceX had done the previous year. Tesla management claimed this was a routine layoff. However, my previous union organizing experience indicated that this was no coincidence, but was a reaction to the launch of Tesla Workers United.

Al began sending me names and numbers of some of the fired workers. In the group chat, the committee scrambled to try to identify the rest and send me their names and phone numbers. The number of workers listed on the MatterMost chat dropped dramatically over the day.

I began calling the fired workers. They told me the same story, over and over: They had gone into work thinking everything was fine. Then, as they were labeling clips at their computers, management had tapped them on the shoulder and summoned them into a meeting with HR, which was occupying a conference room at the front of the office. While they were in that meeting, someone would box up the belongings on their desk. After the worker had been fired, the "boxer" would hand over the box and security would walk the worker out. The committee tried to track who had been fired and who was about to be: "Oh my god, there's a box coming this way" became a common refrain.

There was a pattern to the firings. With the exception of Arian, no one who signed the committee letter lost their jobs. However, they were forced to watch Tesla systematically fire their friends. Lizzie McKimmie, who had joined the committee during the blitz, was close with her work neighbors. She watched as managers tapped four of them on the shoulder and boxers came behind to pack up their things. Tesla didn't fire Al; they fired their best friend. Cleverly and deviously, Tesla tried to avoid obvious unfair labor practice charges by retaliating against the workers who were closest to the committee without touching the actual committee directly. Many of the workers who were fired were about to join the committee and had demonstrated their support by sending pro-union MatterMost messages or displaying the Valentine's Day leaflets on their desk.

Some of the workers were afraid that they would be blacklisted for union activity if they filed charges; others were dejected and terrified. I tried to talk through their concerns, reassure them that they were protected under labor law, and convince them to allow us to file charges on their behalf. By afternoon, our lawyer, Mike Dolce, had filed a charge listing all eighteen of the names we knew at the time.

Management claimed that the firings were performance-related, but the timeline didn't add up. A month before, the company had sent an email outlining the time frame for performance reviews, stating that managers would begin having conversations about performance and that reviews would become visible to employees in March.[8]

In the meetings, some workers asked to see their performance reviews. Management told them the reviews weren't finished yet. Some workers had never had a disciplinary issue before. Normally, Tesla put workers who weren't meeting the required metrics on performance improvement plans. If their performance improved during that time, they would be taken off the plan. Tesla had a policy against firing workers for performance unless they had two negative performance reviews in a row and had told workers that accruing six "occurrences"—a vague system that meant some workers received write-ups for taking bathroom breaks—would result in termination. Many of the workers who were fired stated in affidavits that they were not or had never been on a performance improvement plan and had few or no occurrences. Some also claimed that they had previously been told that Tesla considered them top performers or that they had received recent promotions.

Our Valentine's Day leafleting had been remarkably successful. The flyers we had passed out had links that went to the Q&A, to the organizing committee sign-up sheet, and to a union e-card. The committee more than doubled in size as new people signed up. A handful of workers in other states had seen the media and social media around the campaign and had signed up for the committee, as well. I started reaching out to some of the Buffalo production-side workers the night of the fourteenth, and many of them texted back immediately. But when I tried to follow up after the firings, fear had set in.

"Hi just wanted to check back in!" I messaged one worker.

"Yea no sorry I can't talk to u and I wanna unregister for it," he wrote back. "Watched the news [which had reported the firings] and yea no I'm not losing my job cuz u wanna talk about this sorry. I'll be damned if I lose my job so no."

This fear, while present, was less paralyzing in Autopilot. In fact, rather than scaring workers out of organizing, it showed many just how important unionizing actually was. In Autopilot, more people continued to join the committee and sign cards. They began talking openly about the union on MatterMost. Nearly a hundred people changed their profile picture to the union logo. Tesla's union busting was not enough to stifle the union effort.

**THAT NIGHT, THE PRESIDENT** of SEIU, Mary Kay Henry, summoned Gary to a meeting at her DC office. "TIME IS OF THE ESSENCE," she said, in all caps.

Gary told me he was worried that she would trustee our region of the union. Trusteeship—a hostile takeover that ousts current leaders in favor of handpicked replacements—exists within many unions and is usually used to address corruption within locals. But SEIU's constitution allowed its president to do it for just about any reason, and the union had a track record of taking over dissident locals they thought threatened national leadership. The mere threat of trusteeship was usually enough to quell any incipient uprisings within the union.

The next day, Tesla continued their firing spree: By nightfall, thirty-seven workers were out of a job.

"We were in a panic for two days straight," one of the workers, Nick, told me. The atmosphere in the plant was suffocating: Nick described watching managers tap his coworkers on the shoulder and ask them to go for a walk. On Wednesday, he'd asked his supervisor if he was in danger of being fired. The supervisor wouldn't answer. Nick was fired the next day.

Richard and I talked and he convinced me that I couldn't tell the workers what was going on within the union bureaucracy. Not yet. Not while we had to fight what Musk was still doing. Not while there was still some hope of keeping the campaign. I was in a panic, too, over what was going on at SEIU headquarters. My stomach was constricted and my heart rate elevated. But I had to keep calling the fired workers, keep taking their statements, keep updating the lawyers, keep coordinating with journalists to break the story about the firings and talking to the workers about our social media strategy around it.

I knew what was likely to happen if SEIU gave the campaign away. I'd seen Nissan workers lose a winnable fight due to corporate terrorism and the union's failure to hold the company accountable. Tesla was a hotter shop. We were going to win if we could just keep the campaign out of union infighting. "I'll be damned if they do that here," I texted Gary.

"Yeah, well, I'm gonna lose my job. And I have an organization, existing membership, and a family to worry about. Good luck with your new boss."

"Gary, we absolutely can't give up this campaign."

A few hours later, he texted us, "I am flying to DC tomorrow evening. Meeting tomorrow night at 7:30 p.m." This would be Gary's first meeting with Mary Kay, who had never so much as called him throughout the Starbucks campaign.

"Love how this will get us a meeting ASAP but they've been sitting on boycotting Starbucks for six months," Casey said.

Later that night, I told Gary that we had to fight for Tesla. If SEIU's top leadership could get away with taking this campaign away, it would embolden them to repeat this behavior during subsequent organizing campaigns. If they threatened to trustee us, I argued, we should go to the media and tell the world what they were trying to do.

"Easy to take that position when there's no threat or risk to you," Gary said. "Anything I say to you is gonna be perceived that I don't care about the workers as much as you do. Which isn't true. So I don't know what else to say. Except this path is being made for me. I'm not choosing it. I don't see how these other groups don't come in at all. I have good points, and the truth on our side, and the passion. So I'm going to do my best. Not sure what else to say."

"Gary, if it means putting my job on the line I'm willing to do it. 37 workers got fired today and they are the ones facing the threats and risk."

"I'm not willingly abandoning these 37 workers," Gary wrote back. "Maybe try to understand for a second that I want to be here and still represent this 6,000-person union. A lot of things weighing on me . . ."

By the next morning, Richard knew that the takeover was inevitable. I was still holding out hope. We had to keep control of the campaign. We owed it to the workers, to the labor movement.

On a phone call, Richard, Gary, and I agreed that we didn't care who got the dues money, we cared about organizing the workers. I thought that we were saying that we needed to stay in charge of the organizing campaign, but that another union might receive the dues or even represent the members once the workers won their union. Later, I realized that we hadn't all been saying the same thing.

A few hours afterward, Richard and I were working in the office while Chris Sessions, back in filmmaker mode, edited video at the table. Mike Dolce had called and told me the NLRB had cleared their docket for the next day and were sending every board agent into town to take affidavits: I needed to get all of the fired workers to come in for in-person affidavits, and I needed to give one myself. I began texting and calling people, trying to schedule as many as I could. The committee decided to schedule a press conference for Saturday, discussing the firings and the union campaign moving forward.

Meanwhile, ahead of Gary's meeting, Richard was texting the president of Workers United about the situation. He let me read his message, and I felt like I was going to be sick.

Richard was talking about the takeover as a fact, not a threat, and had shifted to discussing the best possibilities going forward. One of his recommendations was bringing in the UAW, because he still had a relationship with some of the people in the region. They were more aligned with the Autopilot sector and would likely be more collaborative and willing to let us run the campaign in concert with their organizers, he explained.

"You've agreed to give the campaign away?" I shouted.

"We're not going to be able to stop this," Richard said. "I'm trying to make this a little better."

"How could you do this?"

Of course, Richard wasn't doing this; he was trying to improve the situation. But I was in a rage—against the union leadership, against the structures that would allow something like this to happen. But those things were not in the room. Richard, unfortunately, was.

So I grabbed him, one hand on either side of his shirt collar, and shook him. "We can't let them do this. We have to keep the campaign. The workers are depending on it. Thirty-seven workers were fired. We owe it to them." I broke down sobbing.

Chris Sessions looked on in shock. He was still relatively new to the labor movement. Later, I would ask him what he had thought—especially as this had been almost his first impression. "I just thought you both had a lot of passion," he said diplomatically.

I asked Richard to go out into the hall. Once there, I grabbed his collar again, trying frantically to get him to look at me, to understand that we couldn't do this, that we had to keep the campaign by any means necessary, that we shouldn't go down without a fight.

"I have to make this call," said Richard heartbreakingly.

"I need to be on the call. I need to listen."

"You can listen."

"Can you put her on speakerphone? I need to hear both sides of this."

"I can't do that." He shook me off and went down the hallway.

I couldn't bear to listen to just his end, powerless to do anything. For part of the call, I was sick in the bathroom. For the rest, I paced anxiously, catching an occasional word.

"What happened?" I asked, when he finally came back into the office.

"I said they needed to get the UAW in, too, and she said that she would think about it, but I don't know if that's going to happen."

Mary Kay Henry had summoned Gary to DC as a power play. That night, the meeting took place in her office, with the president of Workers United joining over Zoom and saying almost nothing; Workers United and SEIU had become a united front.

Mary Kay laid down the law: The campaign now belonged to the Steelworkers, and neither the workers nor anyone involved in the campaign had any say in the matter. She never said the word *trusteeship*. She didn't have to. The implied threat was enough for her to get her way.

---

**TO BE ABLE TO** help the workers, I tried to bottle up the anguish of watching this unfold. I was still promising the fired workers that we would fight for them in every way we could, still telling new committee members getting involved that they would be in control of their union. I felt like a traitor, assuring people of the soundness of a foundation I knew was crumbling. There was too much to do to process emotions: I had more statements to take, more affidavits to schedule, more new committee members to follow up with. I was still having calls with workers who represented the best of the labor movement: insurgent, optimistic, strongly believing in solidarity and in uniting people around making things better for everyone.

I talked to one of our new committee members, a former military guy who drove an hour and a half each way to work and who was outraged by the way Tesla was treating him and his coworkers. Tesla was discriminating against some of his work friends because they were immigrants, he told me. He was also upset that Tesla wouldn't give people time off to vote unless they asked for the time weeks in advance. "This is a dictatorship," he said. Even after the firings, he was still signing other production workers up on cards. I asked if he wanted to help with comms and he agreed, but was worried about being a liability: "Once I get going, it's hard to get me to stop."

That was true of the campaign, too. The committee were taking cards into the plant for their coworkers to sign, and they were signing. I was still handing out stacks of Workers United cards. I couldn't tell the workers that they were signing up to join a union that was selling them out.

When I finally got ahold of Gary after his meeting, I was stern. Richard had told me he felt terrible. I felt terrible. The workers felt terrible. We hadn't been able to do anything about it. Gary should understand this devastation, I thought. I was heartbroken that he hadn't been able to protect the campaign, which had been his job: After all, he was the only labor leader who let us organize, as Richard always said.

"This is the worst thing that could have happened," I said to Gary. I told him that I'd always thought that no matter what, we would fight for what was right. This was a betrayal of everything I'd thought the labor movement stood for.

I thought Gary was crying. I wasn't, because I still wasn't allowing myself to feel things too fully. If I did, I wouldn't be able to compartmentalize enough to still be able to be there for the committee. I couldn't allow myself to break down, yet.

The next morning, I went to my appointment with the NLRB, taking all of the yellow pads on which I'd been taking statements from workers. It was a strong affidavit, setting the scene for what had happened, outlining how the company had used collective punishment and profiled social networks to determine whom to fire, highlighting the deviations from Tesla's normal procedures. That day, the Board agents took fourteen affidavits—a possible record for the region. They seemed to view this as a slam-dunk case, hinting that they were moving quickly toward a 10(j) injunction, which would reinstate everyone more quickly due to the irreparable harm done to the campaign.

As I left the lawyers' office, I saw an email from the SEIU staffer who was acting as a parole officer over what the union had termed the "transition" of the campaign, scheduling a meeting with the Steelworkers for the next morning. I sighed. Al Celli needed to be on the meeting. That meant I had to tell them.

Richard and I discussed whether that would put too great of a burden on them, but we eventually agreed that we would inevitably have to tell them, and that it was too important of a call to wait any longer.

So I called them.

It was excruciating to have to explain that so much of what I had told them about the union—everything I had believed—wasn't true. That there was no guarantee of local autonomy after all. That the union leadership could make this decision without talking to any worker.

They asked if we should go independent.

"I don't know," I said. "I think it makes sense to see what the Steelworkers will allow us to do and then decide from there. But if y'all want to do it, I'll do it with you."

The only reason I hadn't quit was that I wanted the workers to be able to make a decision. If they decided to go with the Steelworkers, and the Steelworkers would let me, I would continue helping them with the campaign. To his credit, Gary agreed that I could work full-time on Tesla if the Steelworkers agreed. But if the workers decided to form an independent union, I would go with them.

I emailed the SEIU staffer, copying Al into the email thread.

"Who is Al?" the staffer wrote back.

I was livid. I had known that the union leadership making these decisions knew nothing about the campaign, but this drove the point home.

"As stated in a previous email, Al is the key leader of the organizing committee," I wrote. "Without them, we would have no campaign at Tesla. They've also organized their workplace with our union before, as well as helping lead the union at Spot Coffee as a steward. They will be able to speak to what the organizing committee needs to hear from the Steelworkers in order for this to work."

The next morning, we logged on to the call. The SEIU official began to critique the campaign. She never asked a question; she was certain she had all the answers. We had gone public too quickly, she said, with too small of a committee. She blamed us for "getting workers fired."

Al began to explain our strategy: how there were a hundred more workers who had been waiting for the first round of workers to go public and were now eager to join, even despite the firings.

The SEIU staffer threw a fit, repeatedly interrupting Al to insist that the campaign had been incompetent. It got so bad that the Steelworkers leader stepped in to try to stop her.

Al gave voice to what the committee would need. They talked about how important local autonomy was to people; how they wanted assurances that nothing would change in regard to fundamental values. They tried to explain that, while this would confuse and upset people, there was still a way forward, but that the union needed to approach the workers carefully and gently and make the case to them.

"This isn't about the workers," the SEIU official said.

SEIU and the Steelworkers had tried to cancel the press conference later that day. They wanted to control the narrative, they insisted. What if someone asked about what union was involved? Eventually, Richard managed to convince them that, if they actually wanted to have a chance at winning over the committee, their first move should not be to cancel an event the workers wanted.

When I got to the office for the press conference, the workers were deciding on their talking points, writing bullet points on a giant flip chart that Tzivyi would turn, a manual teleprompter. They didn't need someone to tell them what to say: They understood perfectly how to balance projecting positivity and resilience while condemning corporate terrorism.

Al looked like a general: They stood in front, upright, wearing their leather jacket with one pin on each lapel. They emphasized that workers didn't need to be afraid, that this was their right, that they were protected. In fact, having a union was the only way to win rights like just-cause protections from unfair firings: Tesla's actions had only underscored the importance of organizing. Will Hance spoke of the need for accountability and for workers having a voice at work. Keenan Lasch talked about the frustration with micromanagement and Tesla workers' need to have greater freedom, including the ability to take bathroom breaks as needed without being disciplined or fired. Alex Kowalewski talked about the union's goals: collaboration between managers and workers; realistic time expectations that didn't require the sacrifice of quality and helped ensure greater safety. Alex Hy renewed the committee's request that Tesla sign the Fair Election Principles. Nick Piazza addressed the fired workers, urging them to get in touch with the union and avoid signing away their rights in Tesla's severance agreement. Sara Costantino moderated the Q&A, ensuring that different workers had a chance to answer. When Noam Scheiber from the *New York Times* pushed for greater detail about the job itself, Lizzie McKimmie—one of the newest committee members—stepped forward and, after mentioning that the NDA prevented her from discussing the exact details of the data she was labeling, eloquently explained keystroke tracking and its impact on bathroom breaks and other work issues, including workers who got in trouble for asking questions and thus falling behind on metrics or who pushed certain keys so many times that the system flagged them as trying to cheat the keystroke tracking system.

"I enjoy what I do," Lizzie said. "I've had opportunities to work elsewhere, and I don't want to because I really do enjoy being there. I've been there for almost two years, but the stress of knowing that you could be fired at any time is scary. And the process—sometimes people know ahead of time, some people don't, but for the most part, you're sitting there talking to your neighbor, a manager comes and says, 'Hey, can I talk to you for a sec,' they go into an office, people come around the corner with a box, put your stuff in the box, and they're never seen again."

"Are you worried that coming forward and talking to us today may result in a poor performance review for you?" one of the reporters followed up.

"Absolutely. I really did hold out for a very long time on joining, but when I saw how many people really are interested in this, I felt like that was the best option that I could do to help my fellow employees, because I lost quite a few friends, and watching the managers come and were like, 'Hey, oh my god, they just got tapped on the shoulder,' and then watching the people with boxes come and take it and leave, it was a stressful day. And I spoke with my supervisor, saying, just so you know, I didn't really meet my time because it was a scary day."

"And you're willing to take this risk?"

"I am, because I do want what is best for my fellow employees and my friends and the people that I've seen and spoken to and with for the past two years, and I love this job and I really want to make it better. And I want to know that at any time—I'm a single mother, I live by myself, in an apartment, very paycheck to paycheck. And the fear that at some point, I'm going to lose it, over something that I can't really control—that is scary. So, yeah, I am willing to lose it, but, yeah—I want what's best for everybody."[9]

Emphasizing that the agency was taking this seriously and that workers had protections, I gave the update on where the legal case stood with the NLRB. The Board was clearing agents' schedules and taking a record number of affidavits, and the press secretary of the NLRB had even sent out an email to her national mailing list, flagging that the case had been docketed and that the Buffalo region of the Board was investigating. This degree of urgency was unprecedented.

As we wrapped up the press conference and as people began doing individual interviews, I began quietly asking people to stick around afterward. We needed to tell the committee about the Steelworkers. A large group gathered in a circle, sitting on the floor.

I tried to put the most positive spin on this that I could. As the committee, they had the power, I told them. They needed to demand that the Steelworkers recognize their decision-making autonomy. If they wanted to go independent, I would go with them. It would be hard, maybe impossible, to get the resources we would need to win independently, but I would do everything possible to make it work. If they went with the Steelworkers, I would back them to the end, no matter what, I said, as long as the Steelworkers allowed me to work on the campaign.

"If they won't let you work on the campaign, we'll go independent," said Will, with Al's assent.

Richard chimed in repeatedly, encouraging the workers to communicate their needs to the Steelworkers and to try to unite the labor movement around winning at Tesla. "If you have both unions behind you, that's better," he said. He tried to say encouraging things about the Steelworkers.

"My only reason for not liking the steel people right now is that it very much feels like they're trying to take over something that they weren't involved in, that we've tried so hard to do ourselves, and now they just want credit," Sara said.

"Kind of like a narcissistic stepdad," said Alex.

"We already have one named Elon," Sara said.

"Could you just explain, again, *why* we can't stick with you? I just don't understand," said Lizzie.

"I'm— It's just—that—" I broke. I started crying.

"You have to tell them," said Al. Casey and Vic moved closer to me.

"So," I started, between sniffles, "the main thing about this union, and the reason that I wanted to work with Workers United Upstate New York, is that I thought this was a union that had full local autonomy, and that—we could have our beautiful little Buffalo organizing project, and because of the Starbucks campaign and some of these other campaigns, we've had to encounter the international of Workers United and the international of SEIU, and they're much more bureaucratic, they're much less worker-driven, they want control, and they think they know better than all of us. And I would do anything to keep this campaign exactly as it is, but I don't have a choice, but—"

"I think we want to know who we have to talk to," Lizzie cut in.

"What fucking asshole's office do I have to walk into and be like, 'You just made Jaz cry, I'm going to beat your fucking ass'?" said Sara, and the whole room started laughing. "I genuinely believe this is not acceptable, we chose you guys for a reason."

"I guess what I'm trying to say is, I don't want y'all to have to face the wrath of the labor movement and the wrath of Elon," I said.

"We will," said Sara.

"I know you will, I know," I said. "But y'all can make demands as an organizing committee of the Steelworkers."

Will broke in, "We're going to do everything we can to make sure that y'all are not going anywhere."

"They can't do anything without you," I said. "If y'all go independent, you'll have our full backing. But I would basically try to negotiate with the Steelworkers and get the best deal you can, and I will back you up any way I can. It doesn't matter what the name of the union is, as long as you can keep that local autonomy."

Lots of people were talking at once. Sara started making a list of demands. "I think getting y'all is what we really have to fight for," she said. "That's the only way we will accept this."

"Sometimes you have to play ball," Will was saying.

I looked around the circle. This was the most beautiful committee I had ever seen. The spirit, the resolve, the solidarity, were unmeasurable. The newer members of the committee, like Mazin and Lizzie, were just as resolute, just as fierce, as the others. "I'm sorry," I said, still teary.

"You don't need to be sorry—we're pissed for you, not at you!"

"I'm sorry that this campaign got pulled out from under you," I said. "The sad thing is that the labor movement has always been like this, but the reason that we all still keep trying is because things like this—like they can't take away your committee, they can't take away the solidarity that you have."

"Our real enemy isn't SEIU or the Steelworkers, it's Elon Musk," said Richard. "There have to be resources here—we should all be going up to the Tesla dealerships in Toronto, they have a huge store there, and doing a press conference, media, you all should be going to New York City soon. The Steelworkers have the resources, and you should ask them—and then if you go in there and you don't like it, you can do your own thing."

"It's not who's above us, it's who we are," said Mazin. "If you guys can be there with us, that's what we want."

Sara drew up a list of demands:

1. Jaz + Richard
2. Local Autonomy
3. Social Media Shitposting
4. Bomber Jackets
5. X ______________________

"If they're willing to do that, then that's okay," said Will. "But if they're not, then we're all in agreement, we go independent. But what, in your expert opinions—is it a snowball's chance in hell if we're to go independent of winning? What is your real opinion? I know everybody wants to be as idealistic as possible, what is your real experience? Going independent, do we win?"

"I think new, independent unions are the way of the future," said Richard. "However, I think it's always better to get a union to back you. But our school we started, the Inside Organizer School, helps people organize independent unions—I've been doing it—but there's no question it's always better to get a union to back you, if you can."

Al made a key point: "They think they already have it." The committee was going to have to show the union that it needed worker support, not just to think it was in control.

"One more thing," I added, "is that y'all need to be able to make some of the strategic decisions, and Richard and I will be fighting for that, too, but things like— I think the Steelworkers are going to be—a little bit of a learning curve on Autopilot, and on why we only need to win one, because if y'all end up needing to go for an election of Autopilot first and then file for production after that, then you just have to make sure that the committee is the one making that decision, not someone else."

"Here's a good lesson, teaching moment," said Richard, "is like your press conference today. That was the best press conference I've seen in my forty-eight years of organizing. But let me tell you something. When you were preparing, I think, 'Oh my god, no one knows what they're talking about.'"

Everyone started laughing.

"But let me finish—if you'd done it my way, it wouldn't have been as good. That was better—the whole idea of the paper teleprompter, everything was just perfect. And I couldn't have done that press conference, and neither could the Steelworkers. Local autonomy isn't just an ideology, a good principle, it's practically smart."

Will Hance summarized the importance of maintaining that independence. "If we want to get the workers in the factory, in Autopilot, to join the union, they also have to understand that they're going into something where they have a voice, because if they're just going into another voiceless corporation, essentially, it's not going to benefit them. Which is what they're scared of, it's like you're going into another corporation that just takes your money and doesn't give you a voice, and if we don't ensure that, I don't think the workers there are going to unionize."

**THE ORGANIZER THE STEELWORKERS** assigned to the campaign didn't have the authority to make certain promises, so the workers—and Richard and I—tried to give her the benefit of the doubt. But she forbade workers from speaking to the press because they hadn't undergone the Steelworkers' media training. She scrapped our tentative plans for a rally in front of the plant to demand justice for the fired workers. We proposed making a joint announcement that Workers United and the United Steelworkers had joined forces to win a union at Tesla. She insisted that we not discuss anything about the Steelworkers' involvement—or the campaign—publicly. It was March 2023 and she insisted that anyone who didn't come to meetings wasn't really on the committee and continued to speak derogatorily of the original campaign and launch. According to her, the workers needed to listen to her because she understood organizing and they didn't. "You're in the Tesla world and I'm in the organizing world," she told the committee.

By freezing the campaign and keeping any talk of Tesla out of the media, the pressure that had been mounting for the NLRB to move quickly, to get an injunction into federal court, to take any action at all, began to fade. They assigned a different, less diligent board agent to the case. The "investigation" slogged on for months. When Tesla fired two more workers in April, the Steelworkers organizer refused to file charges, saying she didn't think the workers had a case.

I tried to get her to reconsider. At a meeting, I made the point that on the Starbucks campaign, the NLRB had been finding merit to charges that they might have dismissed in the past, like constructive discharges and terminations under similar circumstances. This was Tesla: The Labor Board would likely take it more seriously. She refused, and then—after the meeting—called her higher-ups, who called SEIU's parole officer, who called Gary, who called me.

I told her that she could have just talked to me directly and set up a time for a call. When we did talk, she accused me of undermining her authority by disagreeing with her in front of the committee. I had only been expressing an opinion, I tried to explain. This was important to the workers, who had been reaching out to the fired workers, taking their statements, and trying to get them a measure of justice.

She tried to get me to promise I would never undermine her again. I tried to explain that my loyalty had to be to the committee and that I wasn't trying to undermine her but that I believed my job as an organizer was to advocate for the committee.

She began icing me out, even as she alienated the workers. Richard and I kept going to the weekly meetings, but we weren't allowed to take on responsibility. Meanwhile, the Steelworkers organizer, who was white, repeatedly called the one Black worker at a meeting—and no one else—"brother." She insisted that hypothetical would-be committee members who belonged to the Klan should be allowed to join the committee as long as they burned crosses on their own time and left their Klan behavior at the door. When workers confronted her about her racist remarks, she began talking about her Black child.

In May, the Steelworkers brought in another organizer, this time sending a recent graduate student whose area of expertise was Slavic poetry. She turned the committee meetings into weekly organizing-conversation role-plays. “Find out what my issue is,” she would say. “Will, find out what Mazin’s issue is. Mazin, find out what Sara’s issue is.” She told Al to stop wasting their time trying to get workers who didn’t agree with them on board, like Al’s conservative friend from Texas.

Over time, and despite that there was still tremendous interest within the plant, the committee, which had numbered about sixty when the Steelworkers took over the campaign, dropped down to five. Workers got tired and burned-out and stopped coming. Once it became entirely clear that the Steelworkers wouldn’t let me play a role in the campaign, I, too, stopped going to the meetings. Many workers quit, depressed that the union effort had faltered.

**IN EARLY MAY OF** 2023, three months after SEIU and the Steelworkers’ hostile takeover, I was driving home along the One-Ninety, past the industrial husks of silos, factories, and warehouses strewn across South Buffalo. To the right, I saw an LED sign: WELCOME TO BUFFALO, HOME TO THE COUNTRY’S MOST HYPOCRITICAL UNION. PAID FOR BY THE CENTER FOR UNION FACTS. WORKERSUNITEDFACTS.COM.[10]

The billboard and attack on the union were really about Starbucks, but its union-busting funder couldn’t resist going to Tesla, too. That morning, a truck covered in panels advertising the same website and the same attacks on the union had been parked outside the Tim Hortons across the street from the plant, the Tim Hortons where we had met with our committee, leafleted in the cold, and planned for interviews.

The Tesla workers were upset about the truck and wanted to pool money to buy a pro–Workers United billboard. On Twitter, they began responding to local news reports on the billboard by proposing an alternative design: WELCOME TO BUFFALO: THE HOME OF THE NEW LABOR MOVEMENT, BROUGHT TO YOU BY ACTUAL WORKERS.

Lizzie messaged me, after sending me a video of the billboard truck: "It's in Workers United's best interest to take us back, because that's what we want anyways." This was not the first time she had said this.

"I agree but sadly it's not possible," I replied.

"UGH."

"I'm sorry!!" I said. "Unions really suck sometimes (I could suggest better content for that billboard truck lol)."

"The Steelworkers killed this campaign."

"I know, but they had a lot of help killing it from SEIU."

"True. I'm all worked up and ready to fight someone lol."

"Hopefully we can get to the point where we can all fight Elon lol."

"Never gonna happen without Workers United tbh. There's gonna be a 12-step system to say one sentence."

"Lol I know but we have to try to maneuver within this because there's no way to go back to Workers United—the international union wouldn't let us."

"Well I don't like it lol."

"I know and I agree."

And yet, out of the despair, and the betrayal, and the grim reality of union bureaucracy and intrigue, the campaign was not dead.

When I talked to Chris Townsend shortly after the takeover, in February, he gently chastised me for not having read the union constitution. "They can trustee anyone at any time for anything," he said. "It's SEIU, that's what they do. At the UE,[11] we don't hold people prisoner. If a local wants to leave, they can. I used to go in when we were facing that situation and try to talk to them. Some of them, I kept in the union. A few left anyway. But we didn't hold hostages."

I told him I thought it had been a mistake not to go independent. He told me that I was mourning the dead: Campaigns don't recover from mass firings like that.

At the March session of the Inside Organizer School, though, eleven Tesla workers came. When they were all lined up in front of the stage, presenting about their campaign, Chris Townsend called me over.

"You were right about this one. It's not dead. How did you get so many people to come after something like that happened?"

But I hadn't gotten them to come. The campaign wasn't killable because the workers believed in the idea and the spirit and the solidarity and the hope of organizing. They had stood up to Tesla and its owner, the richest man on the planet. After that, SEIU and the Steelworkers certainly couldn't stop them. Al Celli and Will Hance remained tireless forces within Autopilot. Both personally sacrificed much of themselves to try to stick it out and build the union. Will's health was compromised by working in the giant Autopilot office, where everyone gave one another colds and sicknesses. Al worked through burnout and disillusionment, trying to hold everything and everyone together.

In August, the NLRB finally decided they were tired of dealing with the Tesla charge. Once the public pressure and spotlight were off them, they lost their motivation to act. Ultimately, even after an appeal to the General Counsel's office, the Labor Board declined to find merit in our charges, letting Tesla off the hook for firing nearly forty workers.

By September, the Steelworkers wanted out. At the last minute and without involving or asking the committee, they decided to house-call workers over a weekend. After a few visits, they decided that there was insufficient interest. "Do your thing," they told Al and the rest of the committee. They said they would return if there was sufficient interest.

Within two weeks, Al and the remaining committee members had more than quadrupled the committee, growing to twenty-two members by talking to coworkers in the office and holding meetings during lunch breaks. Within two months, they were at thirty-two and growing. The interest had never gone away. In November, Al texted me, "The conservative guy from Texas who I had those big plans to swing to be pro-union, joined the committee today."

Tesla is a case study in resilience and in the need for unions that will prioritize and defend the right to organize, no matter what obstacles they face. How many years do workers have to wait for unions to organize them? The Tesla workers deserved a union that would listen to them and give them the local autonomy and independence they needed along with the support and mentorship they wanted. They deserved a union that would have marshaled its forces not to fight internal battles or squabble with other unions, but to take on Elon Musk and corporate power unflinchingly. Union presidents should be like Al Celli, not like the bureaucrats in power.

Tesla will be union yet. Workers will continue organizing and continue building solidarity and community and will, inevitably, one day win. If the current unions aren't up to the challenge and the privilege, we will have to create new ones that are worthy of these workers.

CONCLUSION

# No Organizing Effort Is Ever Wasted

The road to Vermont is filled with cryptid references. Numerous Bigfoot statues adorn yards throughout the Adirondacks. A Loch Ness Monster–like creature named Champy supposedly resides beneath the surface of the sublime Lake Champlain. But the most unlikely creature of all resides in Burlington, Vermont: a company that didn't union bust.

In March of 2023, a month after the takeover of the Tesla campaign, I was in North Carolina with Eunice when I got a text from an organizer with the Vermont AFL-CIO, asking about shift managers' inclusion in bargaining units. We texted back and forth, and they told me it was about a Ben & Jerry's Scoop Shop, an ice cream parlor with about forty workers. I told them that I was interested and willing to help with that campaign if they needed a union to back them up.

A couple of weeks later, Vic from Starbucks Workers United and I drove the beautiful winding roads to Burlington to meet with the workers and the state AFL-CIO organizers.

"I haven't seen you this happy in a while," Vic said. "This is your rebound campaign."

We met the fledgling committee at the University of Vermont library. Beka Mendelson, the person who had launched the organizing effort, was a brilliant chemistry student whose wardrobe included sparkly "dress Crocs" and a range of overalls. Jess Schenk, another science student who also possessed great artistic talent, had drawn the union logo—an adaptation of Ben & Jerry's cows holding picket signs. Parker Kimberly, hilarious and sunny, had initially posted the Instagram comment about management's plan to take away tipping during Free Cone Day that had gotten coworkers talking about a union in the first place.

The "scoopers" of Ben & Jerry's, as the company called them, wanted a say in how the company ran. Pay was inadequate and inconsistent. Workers—especially shift managers—were often given increased responsibilities without receiving additional compensation. Church Street, the pedestrian-only street downtown lined with coffee shops, bookstores, gift shops, and restaurants, was at the epicenter of Burlington's severe opioid crisis. The workers were frontline responders. People had overdosed in the scoop shop before; in response, the company had closed the bathrooms to the public. Some people continued to use in the public seating area, and workers didn't have adequate training on health and safety issues. Beka talked about one of her coworkers bringing her a used needle found in the lobby's decorative VW van.[1]

"The Herd"—another Ben & Jerry's term for its workers, which Jess flipped on its head, depicting a cow with a picket sign reading LET'S BE HERD—were unanimously supportive of the union, which we named Scoopers United. Beka and the other committee members quickly signed up all forty of their coworkers on union cards. We sent a letter to the company, announcing our overwhelming support and asking them to sign the Fair Election Principles, and filed a petition for election with the NLRB.

The company was radio silent for eight days. Managers avoided direct conversations in the store. Then, on the ninth day, April 24, Beka and I got an email from the store manager. There was an attachment to the email: a signed copy of the Fair Election Principles. This was the first time a multinational corporation (in this case, Unilever) had signed them, and it made a marked contrast with Starbucks, which had declined to agree to the principles more than three hundred times, as each new store to organize renewed our original request. Most significant, it was the first time a company had signed the Fair Election Principles without being forced to by a public fight or a boycott.

"Scoopers United—who would have thought?" Bernie Sanders said at a celebratory press conference. His speech mirrored and borrowed from Richard's comments a few minutes before: A company couldn't claim to support racial justice, gender justice, environmental justice, if it didn't support economic justice and the right to organize.[2]

That evening at dinner, Richard was emotional: "Finally, someone signed the Fair Election Principles. Only took fifty years to get someone to do that. Bittersweet is what it is, I guess."

I flashed back to the night we'd won Elmwood, and how I'd been overwhelmed with how difficult it was to win even one store—how could we ever overthrow capitalism at this rate?

Yes, we should celebrate; yes, this was a model that could set an example of how a company should respond to unionization; yes, an incredible group of workers now had a voice in their workplace and a positive experience of organizing that they would carry into both their new local union and the rest of their lives and careers.

But why did this have to be so rare? Why was this cause for so much celebration—why wasn't it the bare minimum of how a company should respond? Why was there no labor law reform, no crackdown on union busting, that would make organizing as joyful and painless and straightforward for *all* workers as it was for the Scoopers?

Our happiness was also tempered by the fact that we still had to get a contract. For the next seven months, I drove back and forth to Burlington nearly every week. The seven hours of twisting roads became deeply familiar. So did the company's responses to our proposals, which weren't always positive. The workers had to fight for every bit of dignity that they won in the contract. Upper management liked to tell us that this was a group of college students, that they weren't buying expensive items, things like refrigerators, that everything from cost of living increases (which we didn't get) to paid time off (which we did win) weren't necessary for them.

But Ben & Jerry's management did want to reach a contract. They were partly motivated by a desire to maintain the narrative and image of a progressive company that included positive labor relations. And they acknowledged that the Scoopers' worker-led bargaining committee presented a refreshing contrast with the top-down negotiating styles other unions frequently adopted. Beka set a goal of bringing at least one new worker to bargaining each week, a strategy that worked incredibly well. Instead of becoming cliquish, the union remained energized and participatory. The new bargaining committee members returned to work with new insights and information to share with their coworkers, keeping negotiations a constant topic of conversation. Most critically, all workers felt that their voices and their perspectives were included in the developing contract.

I tried to speak as little as possible in bargaining, to give workers the space to exercise their voice. For the first time, I played the "good cop"—speaking gently, emphasizing that both sides wanted the same things, and trying to smooth troubled discussions where necessary.

My own views of class struggle had evolved. I joked with Casey and Vic that I had embarked on my "class collaborationist era." It was refreshing to deal with a company that genuinely wanted to reach a contract and work with, instead of against, the union. But wasn't there a risk to developing too friendly of a relationship with a company, a risk that threatened worker militancy and the class struggle? If the working class and the employing class had nothing in common, as the preamble to the IWW constitution had famously stated, wasn't it antithetical to work together?

In reality, the labor movement doesn't have the luxury of performative militance. We represent 6 percent of the private sector. Our job is to organize nonunion workers and raise that number. What could we accomplish if we represented 40, 50, or 80 percent instead? But to achieve that, we can't spend all of our time fighting the few companies willing to coexist with a union. It's important to remain focused on what has the potential to build the most power for the working class: organizing the unorganized and fighting the corporations that are the biggest threats to our ability to do so.

In the end, the Scoopers secured a strong first contract. They won pure just cause, meaning full protection against unjust firings or disciplines, and comprehensive and strong health and safety language—the right to refuse unsafe work, the right to have a sharps box in the store and better training, including on administering Narcan, the right to refuse service to customers who harassed or threatened workers. We won a wage scale that eliminated tipping, taking workers from a starting rate of $15 an hour and tips to $20.79 guaranteed. The workers had never had a paid holiday before; now, they had seven holidays at time and a half.

---

**OVER THE SUMMER OF** 2023, the leadership of Workers United and SEIU had come up with a series of increasingly bizarre conspiracy theories that served as their justification for formally ordering me to stop talking publicly about a Starbucks boycott or "presenting myself as a leader of the campaign." I had not been presenting myself as a leader of the current campaign—in fact, I had been talking about the campaign as it was and then saying that my personal view was that Starbucks wouldn't ever respect the right to organize without a boycott. But, to the union leadership, facts were not particularly important: They charged Richard and me with everything from holding (fictitious) secret meetings with former secretary of labor Robert Reich on Martha's Vineyard to plan out a Starbucks boycott to organizing Ben & Jerry's in order to use the press around securing a contract to promote our own views of the Starbucks bargaining strategy.

Not only was that ridiculous, it also didn't make sense on a fundamental level. There was no genuine comparison to be made about negotiating a contract at Ben & Jerry's versus trying to force Starbucks to bargain in good faith. Both companies presented themselves as progressive and social justice–oriented and were vulnerable to a shift in public opinion around their brand. That was pretty much where the overlap ended. Starbucks was determined to kill the union at all costs. Ben & Jerry's had busted unions decades before, but now it seemed to have read the room and recognized that a productive relationship with the union would fit better with its image. Using the successful contract bargaining at Ben & Jerry's to say that we should be bargaining store-by-store at Starbucks would have been like taking Henry Kissinger to traffic court for his war crimes. Without a boycott or means of forcing Starbucks to respect the right to organize, simply bargaining would not have transformed them into a Ben & Jerry's.[3]

What the Ben & Jerry's campaign and contract negotiations did provide, however, was a model of what labor relations *could* look like, one that was aligned with unionization as it was originally supposed to be under law. Rather than being a war of attrition between companies and unions, organizing and bargaining were intended to be a simple fact-finding process—*Do the workers want collective bargaining?*—and an efficient mechanism for facilitating bargaining a first contract. Hijacked by union busting, this process no longer exists absent the goodwill of an unusual company, which is why unions' approval ratings are above 70 percent but private sector union density remains at 6 percent.[4]

**IS THERE A "NEW** labor movement"?

We are often told that there is, and that we are it—that is, when Twitter leftists aren't telling us that we are not actually working class because the vanguard will be industrial, or something like that.

Often, the *new labor movement* has seemed to be shorthand for a demographic description—younger workers, queer, socialist, environmentalist, with a passion for their jobs, organizing retail jobs like at Starbucks, Trader Joe's, REI. Some reporters have gone even further, attributing spikes in new organizing to factors ranging from the pandemic to a worker-friendly labor market to the percentage of workers who voted for Bernie Sanders or possessed college degrees. Richard called the Starbucks campaign, along with several of the other campaigns that sprang up in its wake, "a generational uprising."[5]

What this movement is really characterized by, in my opinion, is something different. Many of the workers leading these campaigns and voting yes to join unions *are* young and *do* have left-wing beliefs. But the energy for organizing isn't limited to workers who fit that description. Across geography, generation, industry, and other categories, workers overwhelmingly want to organize. They aren't attracted to unions as institutions, but rather to the idea of organizing for a voice and power with their coworkers.

I've worked with manufacturing workers whose small talk before the first organizing committee meeting centered around their negative views of Bud Light's ad featuring a trans woman, Dylan Mulvaney.

"But look at what Bud Light did," I said. "As soon as the backlash started, they dropped her—they didn't try to defend her. They don't care about her—they just want to make a buck. And that's how all these companies act."

"That's the truth, for sure."

Unionizing has a unique power to move people, to stop the taught impulse to punch down and redirect that anger upward. I do not say this as a pure class reductionist. To be sure, these workers were clear about their own class interest and inherently aware that the company was exploiting them—even if they might have expressed it in different terms. At one point, I was a class reductionist, believing that organizing workers into unions would inherently resolve every issue—racism, sexism, transphobia, and homophobia, and tendencies toward fascism. That was naive. Unionizing may require acts of courage and even heroism, but it does not transform workers into saints. Moreover, the leadership of many unions are themselves guilty of discrimination, lack of inclusion, and political backwardness, and complicity with the institutions we claim to be fighting. Some unions even tout the "bipartisanship" of their members instead of providing political education or class analysis.

However, at their best, unions do bring people into proximity with one another. They do create genuine solidarity. They can help people unlearn prejudice and understand systems of oppression in new ways. Instead of boasting about our bipartisan appeal to conservative members, unions should welcome them and then try to help broaden their horizon and use their understanding of class to move them on other issues. Unionizing is the only way to unite people around class and build genuine community and solidarity between groups the ruling class seeks to pit against each other.

Organizing is not just about converting conservatives, of course. But without class liberation, other forms of liberation aren't possible. As we saw at Starbucks, support for LGBTQ+ rights without union rights equals pinkwashing. Oppressed groups cannot secure liberation without also winning economic liberation, and unionizing offers the only way to do that.

Unions remain the only place where workers can build institutional power outside of the state or capital. As such, the labor movement is the only avenue to liberation that *can* be truly free from co-optation. That's not to say that unions are incorruptible—our past and present history offers many examples to the contrary. But organizing allows workers the ability to take ownership and agency over the systems that try to strip people of their dignity, personhood, and self-determination.

---

**TO QUOTE THE LYRICS** of "The Internationale," the worldwide communist anthem (written by a French anarchist), "We want no condescending saviors." Of course, in the 150 years since the song was composed, there has been considerable development and expansion in the condescending-savior department. Some of these modern categories have evolved but little from their historical forebears. In the early 1800s, Robert Owen had extolled his factory town as a model benevolent dictatorship. He boasted of providing free schooling instead of child labor—although he did hire children aged ten or over, generously limiting them to working only ten-and-a-half-hour days. He opposed the corporal punishment common in most factories of the time, instead implementing a system of psychological control he called a "silent monitor"—a wooden block that hung beside each worker's station, each side painted a different color, that supervisors would rotate based on the worker's performance. In the town—where he owned the store and the houses—he magnanimously provided street-cleaning services and private garden plots to the workers. In some ways, Howard Schultz is an intellectual heir to Robert Owen—a capitalist thoroughly convinced of his generosity and demanding gratitude from "his" workers. Schultz claimed that he *gave* his partners college tuition, Bean Stock, health care, counseling services, out of the goodness of his heart. From his point of view, each union election was a referendum on whether he was a good person.[6]

Virtue-signaling bosses are only one subspecies of condescending savior. There are many others. Politicians are often forefront in their ranks, basking in organized labor's all-too-often-blind support and occasionally making the smallest of incremental changes through legislation. SEIU's form of sectoral bargaining is a close cousin of the electoral mindset: Instead of running for office themselves, union officials, academics, and other labor satellites lobby politicians to establish wage boards and other administrative bodies and then ensure their own appointments to these panels. Rather than giving workers a say in their workplaces or the legal right to bargain with their bosses over their jobs, this system elevates union elites without building true worker power.

On the most fundamental level, anything that claims to empower or speak for workers without actually enabling them to speak for themselves is suspect, even when well-intentioned. For example, converting businesses from traditional capitalist models to cooperatives is not a foolproof means of ensuring that workers have a voice on the job or even a stake in their economic futures. The vast majority of co-ops are not worker cooperatives to begin with—consumer co-ops are more common and provide no mechanism for workplace democracy, with a board of directors and general manager re-creating the tyranny of a CEO. From cooperative grocery stores to giant chains such as REI, consumer co-ops often attempt to bust unions just as regular corporations do. Even worker cooperatives do not always ensure worker power. Most do not grant workers automatic ownership status, and achieving such status frequently requires a large buy-in that many people living paycheck to paycheck simply cannot afford. Moreover, most worker cooperatives are nonunion, meaning that those who do not buy in as owners do not get to participate in governance, and many also engage in union busting when workers threaten that state of affairs.

On a more fundamental level, many unions become complacent about the status quo. Instead of rejecting the unjust structures of our society, union leaders often see the labor movement as a platform that allows them to participate in those structures—as speakers at corporate capital's favorite forums, as financial trustees of large pension funds, as appointees or courtiers among Democratic administrations, with social media feeds rife with White House selfies and fancy dinners. Although the working class has always been beset by these unfortunate attachés, they must never be allowed to define the movement.

At eighteen, I was also extremely optimistic about time frames. The revolution was around the corner, and the next union election might also send the capitalist system toppling into the dustbin of history. Of course, this was not the case. So what, then, is the point, exactly, if it is so incredibly difficult to win one election among thirty workers at a Starbucks? How does this ever become a big enough movement to actually overthrow the existing order?

A part of the answer, for me, is that every example—every victory, every milestone—helps other workers realize that, yes, this is possible. You can win rights and dignity at work, and the only way to do that is through establishing an independent and democratic organization with your coworkers. Each unionized workplace is a chip in the superstructure of the system we are trying to bring down because it is a call to others: If we can do it, you can do it!

On a more philosophical level, it is also the only way to provide the kind of political education and practical experience that can train people to assume control of the new society when we do win it. Georges Sorel, a French writer and Marxist scholar, laid out this idea in his 1898 essay "The Socialist Future of the Syndicates." He argues that unions are critical to ensuring workers' material well-being in the current society, increasing class consciousness, and developing what he calls "new juridical notions," or ways of seeing themselves in relation to the state. Karl Marx made a distinction between the proletariat being a "class in itself"—a class that existed in relation to the means of production—and a "class for itself"—a class that was organized for its own interests and fighting for self-determination. Sorel argues that the working class can become a "class for itself" by organizing unions, especially if those unions then take on other roles—from unemployment offices to social security administrators to safety inspectors—and encourage workers to look to the unions rather than the government for solutions to problems. Appropriating other functions of the state was possible, too: Some cooperative societies even recognized "free unions" of their members as equivalent to legal marriages![7]

Beyond the pedagogical importance of these actions, they were also practical, Sorel argued, enabling unions to build the infrastructure and culture capable of ultimately replacing capitalism. Syndicalism was a training school in governance, enabling the working class to practice these skills and prepare for its future role.

"What would happen," he asked, "if, after the social revolution, industry should be directed by groups who are today incapable of managing a cooperative?"[8]

This idea informed the Industrial Workers of the World's view of the role of unions. Their union preamble concludes, "By organizing industrially we are forming the structure of the new society within the shell of the old." This concept of unions remains critically important today. We are not, and never were, organizing only to bargain about wages, benefits, and working conditions. We are, and always have been, organizing to fundamentally transform society and to become more fully free, more fully realized, more fully human.[9]

**THIS IS WHY, EVEN** before winning a contract, unions like Starbucks Workers United have had an outsize ability to speak out about issues that matter and show that workers have the power to hold companies, as well as unions as institutions, accountable.

In October 2023, as Israel carpet-bombed Gaza, killing hundreds in retaliation for an attack by Hamas, I made a post from the Starbucks Workers United Twitter account. It showed an image of a Palestinian bulldozer breaking through the apartheid wall around Gaza, with a simple caption: "Solidarity with Palestine."

The international union lost its mind.

They forced another partner to take down the tweet within half an hour. They began calling Gary and yelling at him about his staff "supporting Hamas." Ben Shapiro's news site reported on the tweet in the most lurid language. Other right-wing news outlets began picking up the story. Rick Scott, the Florida Republican senator, called for a boycott of Starbucks until the company condemned its union for our stance. The Orthodox Jewish Chamber of Commerce—a small network of tiny businesses—joined calls for a boycott, asking those who had formerly boycotted Budweiser to turn their attention to Starbucks.[10]

Howard Schultz met with the head of the Orthodox Jewish Chamber of Commerce, who asked him to close all the unionized stores. Believe me, I'd like to! said Howard. He explained that that was illegal but that he would do it if he could to punish all of his unionized, Hamas-supporting baristas. Instead, he gave the Orthodox Jewish Chamber of Commerce a list, which he claimed included the addresses of all the unionized stores. If people were upset about the tweet, Howard said, they should direct their anger toward these stores. (The list also included some nonunion stores that happened to be down the street from unionized stores, but, of course, accuracy was less important than revenge.)[11]

Afterward, Starbucks sent out a text to partners using its emergency text messaging service, accusing the union of supporting terrorism and linking the company's statement, which relied upon the Ben Shapiro story. The company sued the union, alleging that our logo infringed on its copyright. Unionized workers told me that in response to their stores receiving hate calls and death threats, district managers told them to blame me, by name.[12]

But Starbucks partners were undaunted.

The international union—and others who were critical of the tweet—were upset that I had posted it unilaterally. But I hadn't thought that it would be controversial among Starbucks workers. We had taken stances about similarly "divisive" issues—such as trans rights and kicking police unions out of our labor federations—before because it was the right thing to do. This, it turned out, was no different. Starbucks workers stood against the unfolding genocide of Palestine and supported liberation for all people. And Starbucks customers responded, too, calling for a boycott of the company based on its pro-Israel stance and lawsuit against the union for supporting Palestine. The company's market share plummeted.[13]

Of the tweet, one partner told me, "We weren't upset that you posted the tweet, we were upset it was taken down."

On an external communications committee call, Neha Cremin from Oklahoma City volunteered to draft a statement that all Starbucks Workers United members could vote on. Another partner made a version of our logo with a keffiyeh pattern in the background. The final statement—which was much stronger than the original "Solidarity with Palestine!" message had been—condemned "the occupation, displacement, state violence, apartheid, and threats of genocide Palestinians face" and endorsed a longer and more comprehensive statement from Jewish Voice for Peace. Our members voted to endorse the statement by a margin of 97 percent.[14]

Two and a half years since the start of the campaign, Starbucks Workers United was still acting as a union for itself, not just a union in itself.

This ability to speak out about issues that mattered, and to act in solidarity not just with one another but with broader struggles for justice around the world, underscored what we had already won by unionizing. It also led to unexpected victories.

Starbucks' business dropped dramatically. Cafés in Indonesia and

Malaysia were empty. Turkey's train company cut its contract with Starbucks in response to the public outcry. In Morocco, business dropped so low that the franchise holder considered closing all of its stores. That same franchise holder laid off two thousand workers in the Middle East, citing the boycott. In the United States, Starbucks ran promotion after promotion designed to get customers to return, but sales numbers remained low through the winter.

Then, in February of 2024, Starbucks made a remarkable announcement: It was committing to a "foundational framework" to reach a contract and respect the right to organize. Many of the details were left vague or unspecified, but the underlying message was crystal clear: Starbucks needed good publicity. Their brand couldn't withstand the hits it was taking from their union busting and their support for Israel. Public pressure on the company had finally forced it to come to the table, just as we had predicted it would.

**EVEN IF STARBUCKS WORKERS** United never won a first contract, it would still have profoundly impacted the labor movement. That's not to dismiss the importance of winning a contract, our goal from the campaign's outset. We believed that discarding the contract element and focusing on addressing specific workplace issues or forming associational alt-unions would prevent workers from fundamentally changing power dynamics in their workplaces. A contract is the difference between at-will employment and true job protections; between the dictatorship of the workplace and democracy. Contracts are never perfect, but they are a necessary means of cementing victories and creating a foundation for future struggles to build on. A contract is also a landmark that other workers can point to and say, "If they can do it, we can do it."

In the fall of 2022, a labor journalist wrote a Twitter thread about Starbucks Workers United, saying that if we didn't succeed in getting a contract, that failure would discourage workers at other companies from organizing and set the labor movement back. In my opinion, the journalist's analysis missed something fundamental. Throughout history, most attempts to secure greater freedom, greater dignity, greater liberation, have been unsuccessful. Revolts among enslaved people usually ended in defeat, with enslavers using every barbaric and brutal means at their disposal, from torture to mass executions to gory public displays, to try to prevent future rebellions. Uprisings against oppression were usually unsuccessful, at least initially.

The Paris Commune fell after two months, and the state executed or deported its leaders. Patagonia Rebelde—a general strike among Argentine workers in the early 1920s—had ended with hundreds of workers killed by the cavalry's firing squads. The 1967 Naxalbari uprising in West Bengal, which spread throughout India, united agricultural workers and students against dictatorial landlords, but was met with draconian—and ongoing—suppression, including police killings of workers accused of harboring Maoist sympathies. The Easter Rising in Ireland lasted only six days, its leaders captured and shot by the British. (At the time of the Tesla campaign takeover, I couldn't help but wonder if the same union staffers who said that we were responsible for Tesla's firing nearly forty workers because we went public with too small of a committee would have also blamed James Connolly and his comrades for only having seven signatures on their Proclamation of the Irish Republic.)[15]

Expecting union campaigns to win is a recent phenomenon within labor history. Until the last century, unions were expected to lose—often even by the unions themselves. Faced with nearly unlimited corporate and state power; squaring off with police, paramilitaries, and federal troops; without the sanction of law and opposed by a press owned by the bosses; with workers living in company towns, subject to eviction and starvation if they resisted—was it any wonder that most efforts failed?

But these heroic efforts were not in vain. They inspired others, and sometimes they even won—occasionally forcing companies to respect the right to organize and recognize the union, often securing concessions that improved pay, conditions, or safety standards. Each subsequent effort built on what had happened before: every dime, every minute off the clock, every support pillar in a mine tunnel or safety guard on a machine, won with workers' blood.

Today, most unions refuse to file for an NLRB election with less than 70 percent of a workforce signed up on union cards. Unions that do take courageous risks in the hopes of organizing against the odds, like the RWDSU attempting to organize the Amazon warehouse in Bessemer, Alabama, are sometimes criticized by those prescient enough to realize that a union taking on Amazon might actually lose. Unions that take risks on behalf of workers and prioritize organizing the unorganized should be celebrated, never ridiculed. We filed for an election at Spot Coffee with 52 percent of the workers on cards and won by a 74 percent margin because we forced the company to stop their union-busting campaign. "Filing light"—without a strong majority on card—can save workers precious time that would otherwise give the company additional union-busting opportunities. This is not to say that everyone should go out and file for an election with 30 percent—but there are sometimes excellent reasons to try it; the Amazon Labor Union famously won in Staten Island after doing so. Losing an election is not the worst thing that could happen to a worker or an organizer—having a chance to win and not taking it is far worse.[16]

**LONG AFTER HER STORE** had won its election—after Starbucks had revealed the depths and cruelty of its union busting, as the bureaucratic tangles of union politics were threatening the independence and character of the campaign itself, and while it remained unclear when, how, and whether we would ever get a contract—I asked Maggie Carter if it had been worth it.

Her answer was immediate and unhesitating: Yes. "I'd do it again in this lifetime, the next, and the three after that. If not this, what? Go be abused somewhere else in the name of corporate greed?"

Maggie's words took me back to a conversation I'd had with Chris Townsend years before. I was telling him how I was still haunted by our loss at Nissan, how I felt like we'd let the workers and the movement down. At night, I would replay different scenarios in my head, trying to figure out what could have been different, what could have wrested a win, whether we could have pulled off a boycott despite the opposition.

"Don't be too down about it, comrade," Chris had said. "No organizing effort is ever wasted. All of it matters, win or lose. You never know who might have understood the dictatorship of the workplace for the first time, who might emerge on the front line of another picket line or another organizing drive. It all goes someplace. Remember that: No organizing effort is ever wasted."

Chris gave William Z. Foster credit for that line, although I haven't been able to find it in any of his writings. But the message was incredibly helpful. It drew a thread between past and present efforts, making the struggle feel continuous rather than disconnected. It was a sort of apostolic succession of the labor movement, but without hierarchies or institutions. This was the central concept of *Germinal*, the Émile Zola novel that had provided our Starbucks salting program with its name. The work we are currently doing wouldn't be possible without past efforts, and our current efforts have the potential to help pave the way for future liberation beyond our current comprehension of what is possible. In spite of aggressive union busting and the occasional defeat, organizing attempts—just like those of Zola's miners—plant seeds that will germinate and, one day, overturn the earth.

# ACKNOWLEDGMENTS

Organizing campaigns—especially national uprisings like Starbucks Workers United—would be impossible without the dedication, work, courage, vision, and solidarity of an immense number of people. One of the greatest challenges of writing a book like this is the limitation of space and the inability to include all of the individuals and stories that make up a movement.

This book would not have been possible without the support and assistance of my editor, Alessandra Bastagli, and agent, Katie Kotchman. In some ways, this book has been in the making since 2019, when Alessandra first reached out to me about writing about the South and my own story. What exactly I wanted to say didn't become clear until much later, when Katie and Alessandra both got in touch again after we won our union election at the Elmwood Starbucks in Buffalo, NY. I am deeply grateful for their patience with me: Many of the events of this book, including the campaigns at Tesla and Ben & Jerry's, took place during the writing process. Working full-time as an organizer while trying to write meant that my progress was at times nonexistent and almost always haphazard, and Katie and Alessandra both helped me realize that while the work came first, writing about that work might help others find meaning and take up the struggle as well.

I might never have found my way into the labor movement without the mentorship of Joe Atkins, the incredible journalism professor at the University of Mississippi who taught me that union organizing wasn't just something you read about, it was something you *did*. I was extremely fortunate to be at the university at the same time as Kiese Laymon, who rekindled my love of writing and demonstrated what care looked like in the classroom; Tim Dolan, whose guidance, advice, and friendship have been invaluable; and JoAnn Edwards, my debate coach, who taught me so much about presentation, expression, and thinking on my feet.

This book would not exist without the mentorship of Richard Bensinger, who is perhaps the through-line of this story. Over the past decade, Richard has been my mentor, comrade, co-conspirator, and friend. Despite the many obstacles to organizing that he encountered—from vicious union busting to union bureaucracy—Richard has never lost his love of the fight and his passion for helping the underdog win. He is a teacher who leads by example and who invites all around him to participate in designing campaign strategy. His joy in the struggle is infectious, and is why I stayed in the labor movement during the crises of faith that made me question whether it was truly worth it.

I am deeply grateful to Eunice Benton, my adopted mother. Eunice's love, care, and mothering not only kept me on track but showed me, for the first time, what healthy family relationships looked like. An incredible community organizer, Eunice had started a group called the Wise Women of Oxford, which created a remarkable community for progressive women and became the only integrated social club of its kind, appearing for weekly lunches at restaurants around town. Through Eunice, I met so many remarkable, courageous, and caring people, including Pat Miller and Gail Stratton, who became chosen family as well. I would like to thank so many additional Wise Women: Barbara Phillips, Effie Burt, Anne Steel, Ruby Kelley, Elizabeth Payne, Milly West, Dorothy Abbott, Sue Fino, and the college-aged Wise Women, Ainsley Ash and Suad Patton-Bey.

At the Pink House, the last abortion clinic in Mississippi, I learned about the physicality and tangibility of the fight against fundamentalism and control. Engaging with protesters helped protect patients and challenged the right-wing narrative around abortion. Derenda Hancock, the leader of the Pink House Defenders, could flawlessly switch between comforting a patient, with her marvelously gentle voice and disarming smile, and fiercely staving off an anti-choice protester. Derenda, Kim Gibson, Dale Gibson, James Parker, and the rest of the Defenders provided me with community, with mentorship, with life-changing experiences, and with an example of resistance and solidarity in the face of tremendous opposition.

The sections of this book on Southern labor history, and my own exploration of the subject, owe much to veteran Mississippi organizer Ken Lawrence, whose pamphlet *The Roots of Class Struggle in the South* opened my eyes to the censored tradition of organizing in the region, and to my comrade and friend Michael McMurray, whose solidarity took him from Mississippi to El Salvador, Iraq, and Palestine and back again, and who taught me a great deal about the interconnectedness of the movement and the need to hold unions accountable, too.

I would like to thank Morris Mock, Travis Parks, and the other heroic members of the Nissan organizing committee: Ernest Whitfield, Robin and Calvin Moore, Pat and Lee Ruffin, Eric Hearn, Jeff Moore, Chip Wells, Rahmeel Nash, John Taylor, Michael Carter, and Nita Miller. I would also like to recognize the other organizers I worked with during the campaign: Sanchioni Butler, Colette Tippy, Rickman Jackson, and the rest of the team.

I want to recognize the amazing organizing committee members from some of the campaigns I've worked on that did not make it into this book: Sammy Bubadias and the Didlake strikers; the courageous bus drivers of the Vineyard Transit Authority; Karen Corish, Camille Sneddon, and the Rainforest Café workers; Lee Tomik, Emily Belle, Lucas Fredericks, and Annie Gordon from the Sciencenter; Maggie Lapinski and Jamie Baird from Gimme! Coffee; Jonathan Khoury, Mary Elliott, Ian Benz, Casey Asprooth-Jackson, Tiffany Heard, Brandy Cooper, and Elizabeth Beltran from the Rochester Police Accountability Board; Genevieve Rand and the other Citizen Action workers; and Hunter Schwartz, Maxwell Bollman, and the rest of the Lexington Co-op committee.

The Buffalo industrial and geographic union project that forms the heart of this book might never have happened without the dedication, vision, and perseverance of Cory Johnson, a Maryland food service worker who met Richard Bensinger, attended the first-ever Inside Organizer School, and decided to relocate to Rochester to become a salt. After successfully organizing the Rochester Spot Coffee, helping Buffalo workers follow suit, and participating in negotiating for their landmark first contract and in setting up the local, Cory joined me in getting a job at a nonunion Starbucks in Buffalo. Cory is proof of the impact that one individual can have in the movement and in the world. Likewise, I am grateful to Gary Bonadonna Jr. for his leadership and courage in allowing us to organize in an industry so many considered unorganizable and in committing resources to winning the right to organize. Gary helped us turn the vision of a Buffalo industrial union into a reality.

I am fortunate to have worked with the amazing and courageous members of the Spot Coffee organizing committee: Phoenix Cerny, Philip Kneitinger, Kay Kennedy, Lukas Weinstein, Dave Mangan, Zach Anderson, Danielle and Tess Alessandra, Danny Schleyer, Clayton Pitcher, Jen Mace, Byrne Kolega, Katie Coward, Ben Steele, Chris Chase, and Matthew Egner. Yana Kalmyka joined the campaign as my fellow organizer, and I was lucky to have her as a singularly brilliant, caring, funny, and thoughtful organizing partner.

I would like to recognize Benny Seiders, the courageous Starbucks partner who began trying to organize their store in 2019 and who was fired just as the pandemic began. Their experience underscored the importance of salting and building enough of a base to be able to launch quickly once we began having organizing conversations. Starbucks Workers United owes its existence to the volunteers who uprooted their lives and came to Buffalo in the spring of 2021 to become Starbucks baristas and help bring the campaign to life. Thank you to Cory Johnson, Zachary Field, Casey Moore, William Westlake, Brian Murray, Danny Schleyer, James Skretta, Colin Cochran, Bill O'Malley, and Olivier Weiss.

I was lucky to work at the Elmwood Starbucks alongside so many incredible people. I am grateful to Michelle Eisen, without whom we would never have won Elmwood, for her courage, leadership, poise, and friendship. I would like to thank Cassie Fleischer, who trained me as a barista and quickly became a dear friend. And I would like to recognize all of my incredible Elmwood coworkers: Kyli Hilaire, Jeremy "JP" Pascual, Angela Dudzic, Kellen Higgins, Em Hirsch, Stephen Bishop, Leyla Gentil, Brianna Marciniak, Maya Panos, Kat Ginsberg, Cortlin Harrison, Natalie Wittmeyer, August Code, Myke Gollwitzer, Courtney Stroeher, and Alyssa Warrior.

Across Buffalo, the campaign brought together an amazing group of leaders. My personal hero, Gianna Reeve, who courageously confronted Howard Schultz and turned the tables on Starbucks' union busting, a fun and wonderful friend. Victoria Conklin, an amazing and hilarious person with the best redemption arc in Starbucks Workers United history. Lexi Rizzo, whose optimism and vision inspired her store to unanimously sign cards to join the union and whose tireless efforts secured a victory in the face of extreme union busting. I would like to thank everyone who joined the Buffalo Starbucks Workers United organizing committee, with a special shout-out to Jasmine Leli, Rachel Cohen, Danny Rojas, Sam Amato, Angel Krempa, Katie Cook, Samantha Banaszak, Róisín Doherty, Josie Homer, Devyn Goldberg, Loretta Scherrer, Maram Albakri, Erin O'Hare, Danka Dragic, Caroline Lerczak, Minwoo Park, Michael Sanabria, Rhys Want, Roger Huang, Kathryn Bergmann, Lauren Calandra, Josh Pike, Marcus Hopkins, Lilimae Chrzanowski, Khari Waits, and Stephen Simonelli.

There are too many leaders across the country to name everyone, but I'd like to recognize the amazing contributions of Alex Yeager, Kelwyn Gleber, Brian Nuzzo, James Schenk, Michelle Hejduk, Naomi Martinez, Maggie Carter, Sarah Pappin, Kolya Vitek, Evan Sunshine, Stephanie Heslop, Alisha Humphrey, Neha Cremin, Quinn Carter, Tyler Keeling, Josie Serrano, Mila Wade, and the Memphis Seven: La'Kota McGlawn, Beto Sanchez, Nikki Taylor, Kylie Throckmorton, Tino Escobar, Emma Worrell, and Nabretta Hardin. Special thanks to Brittany Harrison for blowing the whistle on Starbucks' actions at great personal cost. I am honored to have worked with the folks at the Starbucks Support Center who organized within corporate HQ to genuinely support their partners, and particularly wish to thank Cyril Bouanna, a manager who put his own career on the line to fight for justice. I am also grateful to our legal team: Ira Katz, Ian Hayes, and Mike Dolce, for their work and support, and to Emily Vick for her incredible and tireless organizing in the Albany region and beyond. I would also like to thank Bradley Kane for his incredible support and impeccable picket line attendance.

The Tesla campaign brought together an incredible group of workers, led by Al Celli, the most dedicated, fearless, direct, and principled person I've ever met. It was the privilege of a lifetime to work with Al and their colleagues: Will Hance, Zak Stirling, Alex Hy, Keenan Lasch, Sara Costantino, Zahra Lahrache, Tzivyi Abosch, Nick Piazza, Jason Connolly, Arian Berek, Jan Patrick, and others who are not known to the company and shall remain anonymous.

The book's hopeful conclusion was, in part, made possible by the fantastic workers of the Ben & Jerry's organizing committee, including Beka Mendelsohn, who deferred grad school for a year to stay in Vermont and help organize; Jess Schenk; and Parker Kimberly.

I would like to thank Chris Sessions for his work documenting the campaigns featured in this book, for his courage in taking on difficult and thankless organizing projects, and for not judging my outburst during the Tesla takeover.

I would like to thank the organizers who created and sustain the Inside Organizer School: Richard Bensinger, Chris Townsend, Ginny Diamond, Joshua Armstead, John Murphy, Tanya Ferguson, Adam Obernauer, Jim Schmitz, Jim White, Gary Bonadonna, and others who have contributed greatly but prefer not to be named. Thank you to Casey Moore for becoming my co-conspirator in trying to get the school off the ground, and for being such an incredible union organizer, TikTok influencer on behalf of unions, and amazing friend. I am grateful to Atulya Dora-Laskey, who organized the first Chipotle restaurant in the country, for her friendship, insights, comradeship, and contributions to the school. I appreciate Sarah Beth Ryther from Trader Joe's United, Steve Buckley from REI, and many other worker-organizers who have come to the school as participants, teachers, presenters, and facilitators, and would like to thank newer members of the IOS collective, including Thenjiwe Phillips, Ra Criscitiello, Todd Crosby, Maricruz Ceceña, and Marcos Escobar. I appreciate the help of Bill Sokol, Roy Bahat, Siena Chiang, Andy Levin, Robert Reich, Sharon Block, Mark Dimondstein, Marshall Ganz, Erica Smiley, Sara Nelson, and others who are helping to make the Inside Organizer School an independent organization, and am thankful to Brenda Muñoz, Ken Jacobs, and the team at the Berkeley Labor Center for giving me time to work on the school and supporting me.

I would like to thank my best friend, Shruti Iyer, for not letting me drop out of grad school; for long phone calls and sage counsel; for teaching me to cook and raising my spice tolerance significantly; and for being a wonderful, wise, hilarious, and brilliant friend. I am deeply grateful to my superb sister, Katrianna Sarkar Duncan, who offered thoughts on the manuscript, clarified which of my labor nerd references needed additional explanation, and corroborated complicated childhood occurrences. I would be remiss to omit my three cats, Frank (Little), Bill (Haywood), and Lou (Lucy Parsons), pandemic acquisitions who have kept me more sane than I might otherwise have been, despite their lack of proper training on emotional support animal techniques. And, finally, this book would not have been possible without my partner, John Logan, who deserves some sort of medal for putting up with me. In addition to being a wonderful whale-watching buddy, adventure companion, and grounding presence, John is a brilliant scholar whose thoughts, insights, and historical perspectives are scattered throughout this book (thank you for sparking my obsession with the Mohawk Valley Formula and all things Remington Rand typewriter–related).

# NOTES

## INTRODUCTION: The Right to Organize

1. "Starbucks on Elmwood Avenue in Buffalo Becomes First U.S. Store to Vote to Unionize," WKBW 7 News Buffalo, December 9, 2021, https://www.wkbw.com/news/local-news/starbucks-on-elmwood-avenue-in-buffalo-becomes-first-u-s-store-to-vote-to-unionize; "Tackling the Problem of 'Captive Audience' Meetings: How States Are Stepping Up to Protect Workers' Rights and Freedoms," Economic Policy Institute, accessed August 2, 2024, https://www.epi.org/blog/captive-audience-meetings; and Allyson Peck, "Allyson M. Peck," LinkedIn, July 14, 2024, https://www.linkedin.com/in/allysonmpeck/.
2. "'Our Movement Is Growing': How Starbucks Workers in Buffalo Fought Company's Union Busting and Won," Democracy Now!, accessed August 5, 2024, https://www.democracynow.org/2021/12/14/how_starbucks_workers_unionized_jaz_brisack.
3. "Howard Schultz Hasn't Won His Anti-Union Fight at Starbucks," *Jacobin*, accessed August 5, 2024, https://jacobin.com/2022/11/howard-schultz-starbucks-anti-union-fight-workers-united-unions; and "Archive," Starbucks Corporation, n.d., https://archive.starbucks.com/record/our-original-store.
4. "The Law," National Labor Relations Board, accessed August 5, 2024, https://www.nlrb.gov/about-nlrb/rights-we-protect/the-law#:~:text=In%201935%2C%20Congress%20passed%20the,workers'%20full%20freedom%20of%20association.
5. "Ludlow Massacre Forges Mine Workers' Struggle," American Postal Workers Union, May 28, 2019, https://apwu.org/news/ludlow-massacre-forges-mine-workers%E2%80%99-struggle; and "The Colorado Coalfield War Archaeological Project, Digital Atlas—Strike," accessed August 5, 2024, https://www.du.edu/ludlow/strike_000.html.
6. "The Ludlow Massacre," *American Experience*, PBS, accessed August 5, 2024, https://www.pbs.org/wgbh/americanexperience/features/rockefellers-ludlow/.
7. Meena Kandasamy, *The Gypsy Goddess* (London: Atlantic Books, 2014); and Shalin Maria Lawrence, "Many Dalits, Including Me, Were Not Aware of the 1968 Keezhvenmani Massacre for a Long Time. Why?," *South First*, December 25, 2022, https://thesouthfirst.com/tamilnadu/keezhvenmani-massacre-in-1968-why-were-many-dalits-including-me-not-aware-of-it-for-a-long-time/.
8. Ray Eldon Hiebert, "Ivy Lee: 'Father of Modern Public Relations,'" *Princeton University Library Chronicle* 27, no. 2 (1966): 113–20, https://doi.org/10.2307/26409644.
9. "U.S. Court Orders Chiquita to Stand Trial for Colombians' Murder Claims," Earth-

Rights International, accessed August 5, 2024, http://earthrights.org/media_release/u-s-court-orders-chiquita-to-stand-trial-for-colombians-murder-claims/; David Bacon, "The Coca-Cola Killings," American Prospect, January 9, 2002, https://prospect.org/api/content/0e702d73-49ab-54cd-9f41-17e871d9a634/; "Human Rights Defender and Union Leader Shahidul Islam Killed in an Attack in Gazipur," July 6, 2023, Front Line Defenders, https://www.frontlinedefenders.org/en/case/human-rights-defender-and-union-leader-shahidul-islam-killed-attack-gazipur; "Philippines: Killings of Unionists Go Unchecked," Human Rights Watch, October 15, 2023, https://www.hrw.org/news/2023/10/16/philippines-killings-unionists-go-unchecked; and "Marikana Massacre, 16 August 2012," South African History Online," accessed August 5, 2024, https://www.sahistory.org.za/article/marikana-massacre-16-august-2012.

10. "*O'Connor v. McDonald's Restaurants* (1990)," Justia, accessed August 5, 2024, https://law.justia.com/cases/california/court-of-appeal/3d/220/25.html.
11. "2008," American Presidency Project, accessed August 5, 2024, https://www.presidency.ucsb.edu/statistics/elections/2008.
12. Robert G. Ingersoll, *Hell*, accessed August 5, 2024, https://www.gutenberg.org/files/37699/37699-h/37699-h.htm.
13. *Britannica*, s.v. "Scopes Trial," accessed July 3, 2024, https://www.britannica.com/event/Scopes-Trial.
14. "Statement to the Court, upon Being Convicted of Violating the Sedition Act," accessed August 5, 2024, https://www.marxists.org/archive/debs/works/1918/court.htm.
15. "To the Public," *Liberator*, 1831, https://www.pbs.org/wgbh/aia/part4/4h2928.html.
16. "AMF, Inc., 228 N.L.R.B. 1406," Casetext, accessed August 5, 2024, https://casetext.com/admin-law/amf-inc-9; "Our Unions and Allies," AFL-CIO, accessed August 5, 2024, https://aflcio.org/about-us/our-unions-and-allies; "Disorganized Labor," June 29, 1998, *Bloomberg*, https://www.bloomberg.com/news/articles/1998-06-28/disorganized-labor; and "Labor's Lost Chance," September 28, 1998, CNN, https://money.cnn.com/magazines/fortune/fortune_archive/1998/09/28/248748/index.htm.
17. "National Labor Relations Act," National Labor Relations Board, accessed August 5, 2024, https://www.nlrb.gov/guidance/key-reference-materials/national-labor-relations-act.
18. "What Is the Taft-Hartley Act?," *Investopedia*, accessed August 5, 2024, https://www.investopedia.com/terms/t/tafthartleyact.asp.
19. "The State of Labor Unions Is Strong," AFL-CIO, August 25, 2023, chrome-extension://efaidnbmnnnibpcajpcglclefindmkaj/https://aflcio.org/sites/default/files/2023-08/GBAO%20AFL-CIO%20Labor%20Day%20Poll%20Memo.pdf.

## CHAPTER ONE: Here's to the State of Mississippi

1. "Mississippi Autoworkers Mobilize," *Dissent Magazine*, accessed August 5, 2024, https://www.dissentmagazine.org/article/march-on-mississippi-autoworkers-mobilize-canton-nissan/; "Danny Glover Speaks Out on Behalf of Workers at Canton Nissan Plant," *Daily Mississippian*, accessed August 5, 2024, https://thedmarchives.com/danny-glover-nissan/; Anna Wolfe, "Nissan Workers Divided as UAW Tries to Plant Flag in the South," *Clarion Ledger*, August 3, 2017, https://www.usatoday.com/story/money/cars/2017/08/03/nissan-workers-divided-uaw-tries-plant

-flag-south/536036001/; and Alex Rozier, "Union Leaders Call in Reinforcements Ahead of Nissan Vote," *Mississippi Today*, August 3, 2017, https://mississippitoday.org/2017/08/03/union-leaders-call-in-reinforcements-ahead-of-nissan-vote.

2. "APWU Members Join UAW's 'March on Mississippi,'" American Postal Workers Union, May 28, 2019, https://apwu.org/news/apwu-members-join-uaw%E2%80%99s-%E2%80%98march-mississippi%E2%80%99; and Mike Elk, "Pro-Union Rally in Mississippi Unites Workers with Community: 'We Are Ready,'" *Guardian*, March 5, 2017, sec. US news, https://www.theguardian.com/us-news/2017/mar/05/union-rally-mississippi-nissan-bernie-sanders.
3. "Nissan Canton Prepares to Celebrate 10 Years of Manufacturing in Mississippi," Official U.S. Newsroom, December 18, 2012, http://usa.nissannews.com/en-US/releases/nissan-canton-prepares-to-celebrate-10-years-of-manufacturing-in-mississippi; Associated Press, "UAW Study Shows Mississippi Nissan Subsidies Top $1.3 Billion," *gulflive*, May 17, 2013, https://www.gulflive.com/mississippi-press-business/2013/05/uaw_study_says_mississippi_nis.html; Mike Elk, "Mississippi Nissan Workers Hope for Historic Win in 14-Year Fight to Unionize," *Guardian*, July 24, 2017, sec. US news, https://www.theguardian.com/us-news/2017/jul/24/mississippi-nissan-workers-union-bernie-sanders-civil-rights; Timothy J. Minchin, "Labor Rights Are Civil Rights: Inter-racial Unionism and the Struggle to Unionize Nissan in Canton, Mississippi," *Labor History* 59, no. 6 (2018): 720–45; Heather McGhee, *The Sum of Us* (New York: Random House, 2021); and Stephen J. Silvia, *The UAW's Southern Gamble: Organizing Workers at Foreign-Owned Vehicle Plants* (Ithaca: Cornell University Press, 2023).
4. Derrick Johnson and Lance Compa, "Choosing Rights: Nissan in Canton, Mississippi, and Workers' Freedom of Association under International Human Rights Standards," Cornell IRL School, n.d.; Silvia, *The UAW's Southern Gamble*; and Minchin, "Labor Rights Are Civil Rights."
5. "Canton Nissan Plant Fined for Safety Violations," *Jackson (MS) Clarion-Ledger*, July 21, 2016, https://www.clarionledger.com/story/business/2016/07/21/canton-nissan-plant-fines/87381784/; United Auto Workers, "Worker Safety at Nissan," internal report, July 2016; McGhee, *Sum of Us*; Minchin, "Labor Rights Are Civil Rights"; and Timothy J. Minchin, "'They Didn't Want to Be Union': Southern Transplants and the Growth of America's 'Other' Automakers," *Australasian Journal of American Studies* 36, no. 2 (2017): 35–66, https://www.jstor.org/stable/26532933.
6. Michael Taylor, "France Raises Nationalization Spectre for Renault, PSA," *Forbes*, March 20, 2020, https://www.forbes.com/sites/michaeltaylor/2020/03/20france-raises-nationalization-spectre-for-renault-psa/; "Renault and Nissan Get Green Light to Launch New Alliance," *Euronews*, August 11, 2023, https://www.euronews.com/business/2023/11/08/renault-and-nissan-get-green-light-to-launch-new-alliance#:~:text=Whereas%20Renault%20used%20to%20own%2043.4%%20of,companies%20now%20have%20a%20cross-shareholding%20of%2015%; "Union Bosses/NLRB Schedule Vote at Nissan for August 3–4," *Magnolia (MS) Tribune*, July 18, 2017, https://magnoliatribune.com/2017/07/17/union_bosses_nlrb_schedule_vote_at_nissan_for_august_3_4/; and Joe Richard, "Causes of the Union Defeat at Nissan," August 8, 2017, http://socialistworker.org/2017/08/08/causes-of-the-union-defeat-at-nissan.

7. W. E. B. Du Bois, *Black Reconstruction in America* (Oxford: Oxford University Press, 2007); and Herbert Aptheker, *American Negro Slave Revolts* (New York: Columbia University Press, 1944).
8. Calvin Schermerhorn, "The Thibodaux Massacre Left 60 African-Americans Dead and Spelled the End of Unionized Farm Labor in the South for Decades," *Smithsonian Magazine*, November 21, 2017, https://www.smithsonianmag.com/history/thibodaux-massacre-left-60-african-americans-dead-and-spelled-end-unionized-farm-labor-south-decades-180967289/; and Anonymous, "Red-Handed Murder: Negroes Wantonly Killed at Thibodaux, LA," November 26, 1887, https://www.historyisaweapon.com/defcon1/redhandedmurder.html.
9. "Support Nissan Workers, Thousands Converge on Canton to Support Union," NAACP Mississippi State Conference, n.d., http://naacpms.org/support-nissan-workers/.
10. "Generation Temp: Auto Workers March for Civil Rights Again," *Labor Notes* (blog), July 22, 2014, https://labornotes.org/blogs/2014/07/generation-temp-auto-workers-march-civil-rights-again; Elk, "Pro-Union Rally"; and James Raines, "From Freedom Summer to Mississippi Nissan Plant: 'We Got the Power,'" *People's World* (blog), June 30, 2014, https://www.peoplesworld.org/article/from-freedom-summer-to-mississippi-nissan-plant-we-got-the-power/.
11. "Undoing Racism: Intensive Workshop," Facebook, accessed August 6, 2024, https://www.facebook.com/events/642562599286133/.
12. "Generation Temp," *Labor Notes.*
13. "Senator Bernie Sanders: The March on Mississippi," UAW, YouTube, accessed August 6, 2024, https://www.youtube.com/watch?v=bcAgAogEdic; and "Senator Nina Turner: The March on Mississippi," UAW, YouTube, accessed August 6, 2024, https://www.youtube.com/watch?v=5rOhX8_I9UE.
14. "Why Did Nissan Workers Vote No?," *Labor Notes* (blog), August 11, 2017, https://labornotes.org/2017/08/why-did-nissan-workers-vote-no.
15. "Nissan Canton Prepares," Official U.S. Newsroom.
16. United Auto Workers, "Worker Safety at Nissan."
17. "Ex-Contract Workers at Nissan Plant Paid Less, Get Union Pitch," *Northwest Arkansas Democrat-Gazette*, July 26, 2017, https://www.nwaonline.com/news/2017/jul/26/ex-contract-workers-at-nissan-plant-pai/.
18. Minchin, "Labor Rights Are Civil Rights"; McGhee, *The Sum of Us*; Sarah Anderson, "Solidarity for Black Workers at Nissan," February 23, 2017, https://inequality.org/great-divide/stand-black-workers-nissan/; and Scott Tong, "In Mississippi, Labor Rights Can Also Be Civil Rights," November 14, 2018, NPR, https://www.marketplace.org/2018/11/14/mississippi-labor-rights-can-also-be-civil-rights/.
19. "Pessimism of the Intellect, Optimism of the Will," Centre for Optimism, accessed August 6, 2024, https://www.centreforoptimism.com/pessimism-of-the-intellect-optimism-of-the-will.
20. "Willa Cather: A Brief Biographical Sketch," Willa Cather Archive, accessed August 7, 2024, https://cather.unl.edu/life/shortbio#noten10m.
21. Priscilla Murolo, A. B. Chitty, and Joe Sacco, *From the Folks Who Brought You the Weekend: An Illustrated History of Labor in the United States*, rev. and updated (New York: New Press, 2018); and "Mississippi Radio Station Warns Nissan Workers They Will

'Go Back to Picking Cotton' If They Unionise," *Independent*, August 5, 2017, https://www.independent.co.uk/news/business/news/nissan-mississippi-radio-workers-picking-cotton-unionise-uaw-reject-vote-a7878236.html.

22. Erica Smiley and Sarita Guota, *The Future We Need: Organizing for a Better Democracy in the Twenty-First Century* (Ithaca: Cornell University Press, 2022); and McGhee, *The Sum of Us*.
23. James C. Cobb, "How the South Uses Its 'Anti-Union Arsenal' to Keep Workers from Organizing | Essay," *Zócalo Public Square* (blog), September 6, 2017, https://www.zocalopublicsquare.org/2017/09/06/south-uses-anti-union-arsenal-keep-workers-organizing/ideas/nexus/.
24. Philip Sheldon Foner, *The Industrial Workers of the World, 1905–1917* (New York: International Publishers, 1965).

## CHAPTER TWO: The Inside Organizer School

1. Special to *People's World*, "Today in Labor History: Striking and Saving Lives," *People's World* (blog), January 23, 2014, https://peoplesworld.org/article/today-in-labor-history-striking-and-saving-lives/; and "Rochester Labor Council History: Organizing," accessed August 7, 2024, https://rochesterlabor.org/rlc-history/organizing_era2.html.
2. Joan M. Jensen and Sue Davidson, *A Needle, a Bobbin, a Strike: Women Needleworkers in America* (Philadelphia: Temple University Press, 1985).
3. Joan M. Jensen, "The Great Uprising in Rochester," in *Needle, a Bobbin*, by Jensen and Davidson, https://temple.manifoldapp.org/read/a-needle-a-bobbin-a-strike-women-needleworkers-in-america/section/1e0dfed6-eeb0-4de6-8e27-537deb535f4c: Internet Archive, https://web.archive.org/web/20230603102408/; and Joseph Gollomb, "Sidney Hillman," *Atlantic*, July 1938, https://www.theatlantic.com/magazine/archive/1938/07/sidney-hillman/653662/.
4. "Howard Schultz and Starbucks' Long History of Fending Off Unions," *HuffPost*, February 1, 2019, https://www.huffpost.com/entry/howard-schultz-and-starbucks-long-history-of-fending-off-unions_n_5c535aa1e4b01d3c1f11b1f5.
5. "Organize the Unorganized, by William Z. Foster," Marxists Internet Achive, accessed August 7, 2024, https://www.marxists.org/archive/foster/1926/organize-unorganized/index.htm#:~:text=The%20organization%20of%20the%20unorganized,life%20of%20the%20existing%20organizations.
6. David Lavender, "How to Salt a Gold Mine," *American Heritage* 19, no. 3 (1968), https://www.americanheritage.com/how-salt-gold-mine; and Laura Geggel, "Does Salt Make Water Boil Faster?," Live Science, September 22, 2016, https://www.livescience.com/56214-does-salt-make-water-boil-faster.html.
7. Mark Van Streefkerk, "SPoT Coffee Workers Make Union History," *Barista Magazine Online*, April 9, 2020, https://www.baristamagazine.com/spot-coffee-workers-make-union-history/.
8. "Sen. Tim Kennedy Urges SPoT Coffee Boycott after Controversial Firings," *Buffalo News*, July 4, 2019, https://buffalonews.com/entertainment/dining/sen-tim-kennedy-urges-spot-coffee-boycott-after-controversial-firings/article_6fdfc90f-d917-5452-9f4a-8a2dfe483c4e.html.
9. "Buffalo Police Mingle with Residents for 'Coffee with a Cop,'" Coffee with a Cop,

December 12, 2019, https://coffeewithacop.com/media-news/buffalo-police-mingle-with-residents-for-coffee-with-a-cop/.
10. Ralph Chaplin, *Wobbly* (Whitefish, MT: Kessinger Publishing, 2010).
11. Émile Zola, *Germinal*, trans. Havelock Ellis (New York: Barnes & Noble Classics, 2005).

## CHAPTER THREE: Project Germinal

1. Howard Schultz, *Pour Your Heart into It* (New York: Hachette Books, 1999).
2. Jimmy Jordan, "Gimme! Coffee: Tale of a Union Unraveling," *Ithaca Voice*, August 20, 2022, http://ithacavoice.org/2022/08/gimme-coffee-tale-of-a-union-unraveling/.
3. Lee Saunders and Elissa McBride, *AFSCME Organizer Handbook* (AFSCME, n.d.).
4. James Connolly, *Songs of Freedom: The James Connolly Songbook* (Chicago: PM Press, 2013), http://archive.org/details/songsoffreedomja0000conn.
5. "Campaigns—Workers United NY NJ Regional Joint Board," January 15, 2021, https://workersunitednynj.org/campaigns/.
6. "Starbucks Principles for Upholding the Third Place: For Our Partners, Our Customers and Our Communities," *Starbucks Stories & News*, January 24, 2019, https://stories.starbucks.com/press/2019/starbucks-principles-for-upholding-the-third-place-for-our-partners-our-customers-and-our-communities/; and "Workforce Diversity at Starbucks," *Starbucks Stories & News*, February 20, 2024, https://stories.starbucks.com/stories/2024/workforce-diversity-at-starbucks/.

## CHAPTER FOUR: Corporate Terrorism

1. Michael Sainato, "Starbucks Workers in New York Are Organizing to Form First US Union," *Guardian*, August 28, 2021, sec. US news, https://www.theguardian.com/us-news/2021/aug/28/starbucks-workers-buffalo-ny-organizing-union-first-us.
2. "Starbucks Statement Regarding Our Partners and Union Representation," *Starbucks Stories & News*, August 7, 2006, https://stories.starbucks.com/press/2006/starbucks-statement-regarding-our-partners-and-union-representation/.
3. John Logan, "Representatives of Their Own Choosing?: Certification, Elections, and Employer Free Speech, 1935–1959," *Seattle University Law Review* 23, no. 3 (January 1, 2000): 549, https://digitalcommons.law.seattleu.edu/sulr/vol23/iss3/4.
4. Howard Schultz and Dori Jones Yang, *Pour Your Heart Into It: How Starbucks Built a Company One Cup at a Time* (New York: Hyperion, 1997); and Chris Colloton, "Starbucks Grand(e) Idea: Freshly Brewed Union-Busting," *University of Cincinnati Law Review*, December 21, 2022.
5. Greg Jaffe, "Howard Schultz's Fight to Stop a Starbucks Barista Uprising," *Washington Post*, October 8, 2022, https://www.washingtonpost.com/business/2022/10/08/starbucks-union-ceo-howard-schultz/.
6. Lauren Kaori Gurley, "'It's Almost Comical': Starbucks Is Blatantly Trying to Crush Its Union," *Vice*, September 8, 2021, https://www.vice.com/en/article/its-almost-comical-starbucks-is-blatantly-trying-to-crush-its-union/.
7. Justin Stabley, "Why Scrutiny of Starbucks' Alleged Union Violations Is Boiling Over Now," *PBS News*, March 29, 2023, https://www.pbs.org/newshour/economy/the-union-busting-practices-that-landed-starbucks-in-hot-water.
8. Marc Fisher, "Howard Schultz Says He Grew Up in a Poor, Rough Place. Those Who

Lived There Called It the 'Country Club of Projects,'" *Washington Post*, March 13, 2019, https://www.washingtonpost.com/politics/howard-schultz-says-he-grew-up-in-a-poor-rough-place-those-who-lived-there-called-it-the-country-club-of-projects/2019/03/13/4f26b800-39e9-11e9-a06c-3ec8ed509d15_story.html.

9. "Howard Schultz," *Forbes*, accessed August 8, 2024, https://www.forbes.com/profile/howard-schultz/.
10. "Former Starbucks CEO Howard Schultz Invokes Holocaust to Deter Union Vote," *Jerusalem Post*, November 10, 2021, https://www.jpost.com/diaspora/antisemitism/former-starbucks-ceo-howard-schultz-invokes-holocaust-to-deter-union-vote-684539; and Howard Schultz, *From the Ground Up* (New York: Random House, 2019).
11. Noam Scheiber, "Starbucks Seeks to Delay Union Election as Vote Nears," *New York Times*, November 9, 2021, sec. Business, https://www.nytimes.com/2021/11/08/business/starbucks-union-election.html.

## CHAPTER FIVE: Partners on Point

1. "Atheists Drink Dunkin' Donuts (Leadership Thoughts)," Tomorrow's Reflection, accessed August 8, 2024, https://tomorrowsreflection.com/atheists-drink-dunkin-donuts/.
2. Noam Scheiber, "As Starbucks Workers Seek a Union, Company Officials Converge on Stores," *New York Times*, October 18, 2021, sec. Business, https://www.nytimes.com/2021/10/18/business/economy/starbucks-union-buffalo.html.
3. Isaiah, "Will Starbucks' Union-Busting Stifle a Union Rebirth in the United States?," Century Foundation, August 31, 2023, https://tcf.org/content/commentary/will-starbucks-union-busting-stifle-a-union-rebirth-in-the-united-states/.
4. Emma Goldberg, "Starbucks Union Workers Near Buffalo Walk Out over COVID Concerns," *New York Times*, January 6, 2022, sec. Business, https://www.nytimes.com/2022/01/05/business/starbucks-union-walkout-covid.html.
5. "Memphis Sanitation Workers' Strike," Martin Luther King, Jr., Research and Education Institute, accessed August 8, 2024, https://kinginstitute.stanford.edu/memphis-sanitation-workers-strike.
6. Allison Morrow, "Starbucks Fires 7 Employees Involved in Memphis Union Effort," CNN, February 8, 2022, https://www.cnn.com/2022/02/08/economy/starbucks-fires-workers-memphis-union/index.html.
7. "Bishop Barber Joins Memphis 7 / We Shall Overcome Starbucks Union Busting," Repairers of the Breach, YouTube, 2022, https://www.youtube.com/watch?v=l1tKD55PYhc.
8. Danielle Wiener-Bronner, "Howard Schultz Returns to Starbucks as Interim CEO," CNN, March 16, 2022, https://www.cnn.com/2022/03/16/business/starbucks-ceo-howard-schultz/index.html; "Starbucks Founder and Interim CEO Howard Schultz Says Companies Are Being 'Assaulted' by 'Threat' of Unionization," *Nation's Restaurant News*, April 5, 2022, https://www.nrn.com/workforce/starbucks-founder-and-interim-ceo-howard-schultz-says-companies-are-being-assaulted-threat; Paul Blest, "Starbucks CEO Howard Schultz Says Companies Are Being 'Assaulted' by Unions," *Vice*, April 5, 2022, https://www.vice.com/en/article/starbucks-union-howard-schultz/; and Greg Jaffe, "Howard Schultz's Fight to Stop a Starbucks Barista Uprising," *Washing-*

*ton Post*, October 8, 2022, https://www.washingtonpost.com/business/2022/10/08/starbucks-union-ceo-howard-schultz/.

9. "Senate Hearing on Starbucks' Treatment of Union Organizing," C-SPAN, March 29, 2023, https://www.c-span.org/video/?526579-1/senate-hearing-starbucks-treatment-union-organizing.
10. Peter Gilbert, "Gilbert: Joe Hill," Vermont Public, November 17, 2015, https://www.vermontpublic.org/programs/2015-11-17/gilbert-joe-hill.
11. John Logan, "Starbucks Workers Have Won 100 Union Elections. Here Are the Lessons from 5 of Them," *Jacobin*, May 31, 2022, https://jacobin.com/2022/05/starbucks-workers-united-organizing-union-busting.

## CHAPTER SIX: How to Bust a Union

1. "Reminton Rand Strike," Working Class History, accessed August 8, 2024, https://stories.workingclasshistory.com/article/7919/remington-rand-strike.
2. "Remington Rand and the Battle for Public Mind," Greater New Haven Labor History Association, accessed August 8, 2024, https://www.laborhistory.org/Remington-Rand.
3. *Nat'l Labor Relations Bd. v. Remington Rand, Inc.*, 94 F.2d 862, Casetext, accessed August 8, 2024, https://casetext.com/case/national-labor-rel-bd-v-remington-rand-inc.
4. Jackson Lewis, *Winning NLRB Elections*, 4th ed. (CCH, 1997).
5. Martin Jay Levitt and Terry Conrow, *Confessions of a Union Buster* (New York: Crown, 1993).
6. Starbucks Workers United (@SBWorkersUnited), "Starbucks has new anti-union flyers," Twitter, April 13, 2022, 10:39 a.m., https://x.com/SBWorkersUnited/status/1514251970227355658.
7. Josh Eidelson, "Starbucks Ex-Manager Says He Was Told to Punish Pro-Union Employees," *Bloomberg*, October 11, 2022, https://www.bloomberg.com/news/articles/2022-10-11/starbucks-manager-says-he-was-told-to-punish-pro-union-employees-in-buffalo.
8. Staff, "Starbucks Hired Former CIA Agent in Middle of Union-Busting Campaign," *Morning Star*, August 3, 2022, https://morningstaronline.co.uk/article/w/starbucks-hired-former-cia-in-middle-union-busting-campaign.
9. Kristin Toussaint, "The First Starbucks Store Unionized Two Years Ago. Will 2024 Finally Be the Year Workers Get a Contract?," *Fast Company*, December 14, 2023, https://www.fastcompany.com/91125893/generative-ai-for-cybersecurity-is-it-right-for-your-organization.
10. Peter de Boor, "Understanding Mandatory and Permissive Subjects of Bargaining," *Senza Sordino* (blog), May 21, 2012, https://www.icsom.org/senzasordino/2012/05/understanding-mandatory-permissive-subjects-bargaining/.
11. Noam Scheiber and Julie Creswell, "Why Is Howard Schultz Taking This So Personally?," *New York Times*, December 11, 2022, sec. Business, https://www.nytimes.com/2022/12/11/business/howard-schultz-starbucks-union.html.
12. Dave Jamieson, "For the Starbucks Union Campaign, a Bruising Contract Fight Is Just Beginning," *HuffPost*, April 16, 2022, https://www.huffpost.com/entry/starbucks-union-campaign-contract-fight_n_6259c871e4b066ecde1350f0.
13. *Delmas Conley v. NLRB*, No. 07-1529 (6th Cir. 2008); and *Exxon Research Engineering Co. v. NLRB*, 89 F.3d 228 (5th Cir. 1996).

14. Steven Greenhouse, "Will Starbucks' Union-Busting Stifle a Union Rebirth in the US?," *Guardian*, August 28, 2023, sec. US news, https://www.theguardian.com/us-news/2023/aug/28/will-starbucks-union-busting-stifle-a-union-rebirth-in-the-us; and Chris Morris, "Starbucks Announces Pay and Benefits Increases—but Union Employees Won't Get All of the Perks," *Fast Company*, November 7, 2023, https://www.fastcompany.com/90979281/starbucks-pay-benefits-increases-non-union-employees.
15. Kate Rogers, "Starbucks Hit with Sweeping Labor Complaint Including over 200 Alleged Violations," CNBC, May 6, 2022, https://www.cnbc.com/2022/05/06/starbucks-accused-of-more-than-200-labor-violations-in-nlrb-complaint.html.
16. "You Are the Un-Americans, and You Ought to Be Ashamed of Yourselves," Marxists Internet Archive, accessed August 8, 2024, https://www.marxists.org/archive/robeson/1956/06/12.htm.
17. Rhea Jha, "Grease Trap Mishap Pushed Ithaca Starbucks Workers to Strike," My Twin Tiers, April 23, 2022, https://www.mytwintiers.com/news-cat/top-stories/grease-trap-mishap-forces-starbucks-workers-to-strike.
18. Stephen Gandel, "Starbucks's C.E.O. Howard Schultz: 'I Don't Know If We Can Keep Our Bathrooms Open,'" *New York Times*, June 9, 2022, sec. Business, https://www.nytimes.com/2022/06/09/business/dealbook/howard-schultz-starbucks-bathroom.html; Coral Murphy Marcos, "Starbucks Says It Will Close 16 Stores Out of Concern for Employee Safety," *Guardian,* July 13, 2022, https://www.theguardian.com/business/2022/jul/13/starbucks-close-16-us-stores-concern-employee-safety#:~:text=Starbucks%20will%20close%2016%20US,close%2C%20a%20Starbucks%20spokesperson%20confirmed; Fernando Alba, "Armory Square Starbucks in Syracuse to Close; Company Cites Safety Issues," Syracuse.com, October 19, 2022, https://www.syracuse.com/business/2022/10/armory-square-starbucks-in-syracuse-to-close-company-cites-safety-issues.html#:~:text=The%20West%20Jefferson%20Street%20store,decision%20to%20close%20the%20store.
19. *Abridged Report to Starbucks Board of Directors Concerning Starbucks' Adherence to Freedom of Association and Collective Bargaining Commitments in Its Global Human Rights Statement*, Thomas M. Mackall, LLC, October 13, 2023, chrome-extension://efaidnbmnnnibpcajpcglclefindmkaj/https://stories.starbucks.com/uploads/2023/12/Abridged-GHRS-Report.pdf.
20. "North Carolina Textile Workers Win Union Recognition from J. P. Stevens, 1976–1980, Global Nonviolent Action Database, accessed August 8, 2024, https://nvdatabase.swarthmore.edu/content/north-carolina-textile-workers-win-union-recognition-j-p-stevens-1976-1980; and "About the Workers United Retirees Association," Service Employees International Union (SEIU), accessed August 8, 2024, https://www.seiu.org/wuretirees-about.
21. Aneurin Canham-Clyne, "How the Biggest Private Sector Union Wants to Transform the Restaurant Workforce," *Restaurant Dive,* accessed August 8, 2024, https://www.restaurantdive.com/news/how-labor-union-seiu-wants-to-transform-the-restaurant-workforce/648986/.
22. Steven Greenhouse, "'The Success Is Inspirational': The Fight for $15 Movement 10 Years On," *Guardian*, November 23, 2022, sec. US news, https://www.theguardian.com/us-news/2022/nov/23/fight-for-15-movement-10-years-old.

23. Sharon Zhang, "Over 100 Starbucks Locations Have Filed for Unionization," *Truthout*, February 22, 2022, https://truthout.org/articles/over-100-starbucks-locations-have-filed-for-unionization/.
24. Peter Romeo, "SEIU Drops Its Front in Unionizing Starbucks," *Restaurant Business*, February 22, 2022, https://restaurantbusinessonline.com/workforce/seiu-drops-its-front-unionizing-starbucks.
25. Josh Eidelson, "Starbucks Threatens Trans Benefits in Anti-Union Push, Staff Say," *Bloomberg*, June 14, 2022, https://www.bloomberg.com/news/articles/2022-06-14/starbucks-threatens-trans-benefits-in-anti-union-push-staff-say; and Hannah France, "Trans Oklahoma Starbucks Workers Concerned about Changes to Gender-Affirming Care Coverage," KGOU, July 27, 2023, https://www.kgou.org/stateimpact-oklahoma/2023-07-27/trans-oklahoma-starbucks-workers-concerned-about-changes-to-gender-affirming-care-coverage.
26. Paul Blest, "Starbucks Is Threatening Trans Employees' Healthcare, Union Says," *Vice*, June 14, 2022, https://www.vice.com/en/article/starbucks-union-employee-gender-affirming-care/.
27. Zane McNeill, "Starbucks Holds Life-Saving Benefits over Trans Workers' Heads," *In These Times*, August 3, 2022, https://inthesetimes.com/article/starbucks-union-campaign-trans-health-care; and Bek Shackelford-Nwanganga, "National Labor Board Files Complaints against 2 Kansas City Area Starbucks for Union Busting," *Lawrence (KS) Times*, May 16, 2022, https://lawrencekstimes.com/2022/05/16/nlrb-complaints-starbucks/.
28. Hilary Russ and Caroline Valetkevitch, "Focus: Starbucks Strike over Pride Decor Follows LGBTQ Anger on Hours, Benefits," Reuters, June 26, 2023, sec. Society & Equity, https://www.reuters.com/sustainability/society-equity/starbucks-strike-over-pride-decor-follows-lgbtq-anger-hours-benefits-2023-06-26/.
29. Fionn Pooler, "The Ongoing Fight for a Union Contract at Starbucks," *The Pourover*, December 22, 2023, https://thepourover.substack.com/p/the-ongoing-fight-for-a-union-contract.
30. Jerry Zremski and Harold McNeil, "Starbucks Workers Launch Organizing Effort in Buffalo with National Backing," *Buffalo News*, August 31, 2021, https://buffalonews.com/news/local/starbucks-workers-launch-organizing-effort-in-buffalo-with-national-backing/article_9e784ee6-0a66-11ec-9da7-631e5f74e419.html.

## CHAPTER SEVEN: No Unorganizable Workplace

1. Noam Scheiber and Ryan Mac, "SpaceX Employees Say They Were Fired for Speaking Up about Elon Musk," *New York Times*, November 17, 2022, sec. Business, https://www.nytimes.com/2022/11/17/business/spacex-workers-elon-musk.html.
2. Derek Seidman, "Buffalo Community Shows Support to Fired Tesla Workers Seeking Union," *Truthout*, February 25, 2023, https://truthout.org/articles/buffalo-community-shows-support-to-fired-tesla-workers-seeking-union/.
3. Josh Eidelson, "Tesla Workers Launch Union Campaign in New York," *Bloomberg*, February 14, 2023, https://www.bloomberg.com/news/articles/2023-02-14/tesla-autopilot-workers-launch-union-campaign-in-buffalo-new-york-tsla.
4. Florin Amariei, "Tesla Claims It Fired Buffalo Employees Before They Began Pushing for a Union," autoevolution, February 17, 2023, https://www.autoevolution.com

/news/tesla-claims-it-fired-the-buffalo-employees-before-they-began-pushing-for-a-union-210472.html.

5. Bevan Hurley, "Elon Musk Likes Anti-Trans Tweet from Notorious Right Wing Account," Independent, December 27, 2022, https://www.independent.co.uk/news/world/americas/elon-musk-anti-trans-twitter-libs-of-tiktok-b2251975.html.
6. Lora Kolodny, "Tesla Internal Data Shows Company Has Slashed at Least 14% of Workforce This Year," NBC4 Washington, June 21, 2024, https://www.nbcwashington.com/news/business/money-report/tesla-has-downsized-by-at-least-14-this-year-after-elon-musk-said-layoffs-would-exceed-10/3646592/; and "Tesla Workers United—Buffalo Organizing Committee," Action Network, accessed August 8, 2024, https://actionnetwork.org/groups/tesla-buffalo-organizing-committee.
7. Matt Glynn, "Tesla Accused of Firing Pro-Union Workers at Buffalo Solar Plant," *Buffalo News*, June 24, 2019, https://buffalonews.com/business/local/tesla-accused-of-firing-pro-union-workers-at-buffalo-solar-plant/article_90e5c79a-adbc-5669-939a-276ab24385ad.html.
8. Annie Palmer and Lora Kolodny, "Tesla Denies Autopilot Workers' Allegations of Union-Busting, Retaliatory Firings," CNBC, February 16, 2023, https://www.cnbc.com/2023/02/16/tesla-fires-dozens-of-workers-over-union-campaign-complaint-alleges.html.
9. "Tesla Workers United Full Press Conference," News 4 Buffalo, August 8, 2024, https://www.wivb.com/video/tesla-workers-united-full-press-conference/8403526/.
10. Samantha Christmann, "Billboard Campaign Targets Workers United," *Buffalo News*, May 2, 2023, https://buffalonews.com/news/local/business/workers-united-starbucks-workers-united-billboard-center-for-union-facts/article_164bfeec-e826-11ed-bddc-f7ddd333764d.html.
11. United Electrical, Radio and Machine Workers of America, a small left-wing union known for its independence and democratic structure.

## CONCLUSION: No Organizing Effort Is Ever Wasted

1. German Lopez, "We Looked for a State That's Taken the Opioid Epidemic Seriously. We Found Vermont," *Vox*, October 30, 2017, https://www.vox.com/policy-and-politics/2017/10/30/16339672/opioid-epidemic-vermont-hub-spoke.
2. "Scoopers United Press Conference in Burlington," CCTV Center for Media and Democracy, April 28, 2023, https://www.cctv.org/watch-tv/programs/scoopers-united-press-conference-burlington.
3. Liza Featherstone, "'It's Business, Man!': Unions and 'Socially Responsible' Corporations," *Dissent*, Fall 1999, https://www.dissentmagazine.org/article/its-business-man-unions-and-socially-responsible-corporations/.
4. Justin McCarthy, "U.S. Approval of Labor Unions at Highest Point Since 1965," Gallup, August 30, 2022, https://news.gallup.com/poll/398303/approval-labor-unions-highest-point-1965.aspx.
5. Kate Rogers and Amelia Lucas, "A 'Gen U' of Young Starbucks Baristas Is Powering a Growing Push to Unionize," CNBC, January 28, 2022, https://www.cnbc.com/2022/01/28/young-starbucks-baristas-are-powering-a-growing-push-to-unionize.html.
6. *Encyclopaedia Britannica*, s.v. "L'Internationale," accessed August 8, 2024, https://www.britannica.com/topic/LInternationale; *Encyclopaedia Britannica*, s.v. "Robert

Owen," by Douglas F. Dowd, accessed August 8, 2024, https://www.britannica.com/biography/Robert-Owen; and "Silent Monitor," Scottish Maritime Museum, accessed August 8, 2024, https://www.scottishmaritimemuseum.org/3d_collections/silent-monitor/.

7. Georges Sorel, "The Socialist Future of the Syndicates," Libcom, accessed August 8, 2024, https://libcom.org/article/socialist-future-syndicates-georges-sorel; and Edward Andrew, "Class in Itself and Class against Capital: Karl Marx and His Classifiers," *Canadian Journal of Political Science / Revue canadienne de science politique* 16, no. 3 (1983): 577–84, https://www.jstor.org/stable/3227396.
8. Georges Sorel and John L. Stanley, *From Georges Sorel: Essays in Socialism and Philosophy*, 2nd ed. (New Brunswick, NJ: Transaction Books, 1987).
9. "Preamble—Industrial Workers of the World," IWW.org, accessed August 8, 2024, https://www.iww.org/preamble/.
10. *Jerusalem Post* Staff, "Jewish Orgs. Call to Boycott Starbucks over Union's Support of Hamas," *Jerusalem Post*, October 18, 2023, https://www.jpost.com/business-and-innovation/banking-and-finance/article-768968.
11. Baruch Green, "Starbucks' Founder Schultz Phones Chief of Jewish Chamber of Commerce to End Boycott," *VINnews*, October 19, 2023, https://vinnews.com/2023/10/19/read-after-boycott-starbucks-sends-letter-to-orthodox-jewish-chamber-of-commerce/; and Beth Harpaz, "Why Is Starbucks Being Targeted by Activists for Both Israel and Gaza?," *Forward*, December 20, 2023, https://forward.com/fast-forward/574222/starbucks-protests-israel-gaza-union-boycott/.
12. *COLlive* reporter, "Starbucks Sues 'Starbucks Workers United' for Anti-Israel Support," *COLlive*, October 19, 2023, https://collive.com/starbucks-sues-starbucks-workers-united-for-anti-israel-support/.
13. Jordan Liles, "Did Starbucks Lose $12B from Boycotts 'Due to Its Support for Israel'?," *Snopes*, December 8, 2023, https://www.snopes.com//news/2023/12/07/starbucks-12-billion-loss-due-to-israel/.
14. "Home," Jewish Voice for Peace, accessed August 8, 2024, https://www.jewishvoiceforpeace.org/2023/10/11/statement23-10-11/.
15. "Paris Commune of 1871: Causes, Bloody Week & Legacy," History, November 17, 2022, https://www.history.com/topics/european-history/paris-commune-1871: *Alchetron*, s.v. "Patagonia Rebelde," January 22, 2024, https://alchetron.com/Patagonia-Rebelde; "A Historical Introduction to Naxalism in India," European Foundation for South Asian Studies, accessed August 8, 2024, https://www.efsas.org/publications/study-papers/an-introduction-to-naxalism-in-india/; *Encyclopaedia Britannica*, s.v. "Easter Rising," accessed August 8, 2024, https://www.britannica.com/event/Easter-Rising; and National Library of Ireland, "SIGNATORIES of the Proclamation of the Irish Republic," Google Arts & Culture, accessed August 8, 2024, https://artsandculture.google.com/story/signatories-of-the-proclamation-of-the-irish-republic/LQVhkGjJhbnNJA.
16. "Spot Coffee Workers Vote in Favor of Joining a Union," WKBW 7 News Buffalo, August 20, 2019, https://www.wkbw.com/news/local-news/spot-coffee-workers-wait-to-find-out-if-they-will-unionize.

# INDEX

## D

## T

**U**

# ABOUT THE AUTHOR

Jaz Brisack is a union organizer and cofounder of the Inside Organizer School, which trains workers to unionize. After spending one year at Oxford as a Rhodes Scholar, they got a job as a barista at the Elmwood Starbucks in Buffalo, New York, becoming a founding member of Starbucks Workers United and helping organize the first unionized Starbucks in the United States. As the organizing director for Workers United Upstate New York & Vermont, they also worked with organizing committees at companies ranging from Ben & Jerry's to Tesla.